FRATERNAL CRITIQUE

 NEW STUDIES IN RELIGION

EDITED BY Kathryn Lofton AND John Lardas Modern

ALSO PUBLISHED IN THE SERIES

Promiscuous Grace: Imagining Beauty and Holiness with Saint Mary of Egypt
Sonia Velázquez

Slandering the Sacred: Blasphemy Law and Religious Affect in Colonial India
J. Barton Scott

Earthquakes and Gardens: Saint Hilarion's Cyprus
Virginia Burrus

Unbridled: Studying Religion in Performance
William Robert

Awkward Rituals: Sensations of Governance in Protestant America
Dana Logan

Sincerely Held: American Secularism and Its Believers
Charles McCrary

Profaning Paul
Cavan W. Concannon

Making a Mantra: Tantric Ritual and Renunciation on the Jain Path to Liberation
Ellen Gough

Neuromatic: Or, A Particular History of Religion and the Brain
John Lardas Modern

Kindred Spirits: Friendship and Resistance at the Edges of Modern Catholicism
Brenna Moore

The Privilege of Being Banal: Art, Secularism, and Catholicism in Paris
Elayne Oliphant

Ripples of the Universe: Spirituality in Sedona, Arizona
Susannah Crockford

FRATERNAL CRITIQUE

The Politics of Muslim Community in France

KIRSTEN WESSELHOEFT

The University of Chicago Press
Chicago and London

The University of Chicago Press, Chicago 60637
The University of Chicago Press, Ltd., London
© 2025 by The University of Chicago
All rights reserved. No part of this book may be used or reproduced in any manner whatsoever without written permission, except in the case of brief quotations in critical articles and reviews. For more information, contact the University of Chicago Press, 1427 E. 60th St., Chicago, IL 60637.
Published 2025

34 33 32 31 30 29 28 27 26 25   1 2 3 4 5

ISBN-13: 978-0-226-83826-7 (cloth)
ISBN-13: 978-0-226-83828-1 (paper)
ISBN-13: 978-0-226-83827-4 (e-book)
DOI: https://doi.org/10.7208/chicago/9780226838274.001.0001

Library of Congress Cataloging-in-Publication Data

Names: Wesselhoeft, Kirsten, author.
Title: Fraternal critique : the politics of Muslim community in France / Kirsten Wesselhoeft.
Other titles: Class 200, new studies in religion.
Description: Chicago : The University of Chicago Press, 2025. | Series: Class 200: new studies in religion | Includes bibliographical references and index.
Identifiers: LCCN 2024025383 | ISBN 9780226838267 (cloth) | ISBN 9780226838281 (paperback) | ISBN 9780226838274 (ebook)
Subjects: LCSH: Muslims—France—Social conditions—21st century. | Community development—France—Religious aspects—Islam. | Communalism—France—Religious aspects—Islam. | Muslims—Political activity—France—History—21st century. | Muslims—Government policy—France—History—21st century. | Secularism—France—History—21st century. | Public policy (Law)—France. | Segregation—France—Religious aspects—Islam. | Islamophobia—Political aspects—France.
Classification: LCC DC34.5.M87 W47 2025 | DDC 305.6/970944—dc23/eng/20240805
LC record available at https://lccn.loc.gov/2024025383

For Klaus, Stella, and Felix

Though you have struggled, wandered, traveled far,
It is yourselves you see and what you are.

FARID UD-DIN ATTAR, *Conference of the Birds*,
trans. Dick Davis

Don't they know
at my little mosque
that this is a poem
written in the mirror
by a lover?

MOHJA KAHF, "Little Mosque Poems," *Hagar Poems*

CONTENTS

Introduction: Engaged Muslims in a Changing France   1

PART I: FORMING A CONTESTED COMMUNITY

1. An Ethics of Discontent   35
2. The People of Knowledge   64
3. Sisterhood and Its Obligations   91

PART II: THE POLITICS OF MUSLIM SOLIDARITY

4. The Specter of Communalism   119
5. From Secularism to Public Order   144

Conclusion: Social Ethics and the Fragilization of the Collective   163

Acknowledgments   169
Notes   175
Bibliography   201
Index   213

INTRODUCTION

Engaged Muslims in a Changing France

Dounia[1] is a public relations professional in her late twenties, working at a large firm in downtown Paris and living alone in a small apartment in Ivry-sur-Seine, just outside the Paris city limits.[2] Dounia moved to the Paris region for university study from a small city in central France, where her parents, who both immigrated from Morocco as children with their families, own a restaurant. In addition to her demanding professional career, Dounia often spends forty hours a week on her volunteer work, with an organization that seeks to increase educational and professional opportunities for young people from the Parisian banlieues, or "outer cities." The organization is explicitly anchored by Islamic social values, emphasizing perseverance, patience, and the pursuit of excellence. Its programs are open to all, but the large majority of volunteers and students are Muslim. Dounia's volunteer work for this organization, which draws heavily on her professional capacities in marketing, strategic planning, event planning, and administration, leaves little time for more traditional religious formation. "It would be fantastic to be able to really understand the Qur'an in Arabic," she admitted. "But it seems almost egotistical to me to take the time to do that. Our little brothers and sisters, they are here *now*, you know? They are facing challenges that will determine their entire future. Here, we're putting our values into practice. We're making a difference beyond ourselves, for the whole community." The concrete impact of her work on the lives of young people whom she sees as "little brothers and sisters" makes Dounia's long days and nights worth it. "Investing in our youth is a *sadaqa jariya*—a work of charity that will outlast us. They are the community of the future."

Like Dounia, Hamza has big dreams for the French Muslim community. With his crisp haircut and well-cut blazer, Hamza fits right into his trendy neighborhood at the edge of eastern Paris. Working as a software engineer by day and brainstorming ideas for startups by night, Hamza sometimes dreams of moving to California or Berlin, where he sees exciting professional possibilities. But his vision for the future of his community keeps him based in Paris. Now in his early thirties, Hamza has passed through numerous Muslim organizations—civil rights organizations, classes in Islamic sciences, and humanitarian aid groups. But what he noticed across all of these experiences was the need for deeper intellectual exchange. "At so many Muslim events, there is a speaker, he talks, maybe there are a few quick questions, and then, *salam ʿalaykum*, it's over. And people don't have the possibility of really expressing themselves, of exchanging ideas. But there is such a deep thirst for that, you can feel it across our community." Hamza had observed a profound need for self-expression, exchange, and debate among young Muslims in France. In response, he gathered a group of people from across his years of volunteer engagement for a series of meetings to brainstorm new models for collective intellectual life. "We had engineers, sociologists, feminists, Salafis, we had a real cross section of the community." Out of this core group came numerous models for new types of social and intellectual spaces linked to Islam that would nurture the spirit of open exchange, cross-pollination, and self-expression. Years later, Hamza remains engaged in the demanding work of facilitating these projects, organizing a team of twenty volunteers to produce innovative events and workshops that reach hundreds of people every year. He combines freelance work with full-time dedication to community organizing. Financing the events remains his most vexing problem. "You know, we're not saving the lives of people in Syria. We're not in courtrooms, defending civil rights. So it's hard sometimes for people to see the urgency of what we are doing. But in our way we are working to change the world. Change the conversation. Incubate ideas and projects that will go far, far beyond what we can see right now. I believe in that."

Dounia and Hamza are part of a growing population of middle-class inheritors of colonial and postcolonial immigration to France.[3] They are motivated by their commitment to Islamic values to engage in social change work, both within and beyond the Muslim community. As educated professionals who feel accountable to their working-class backgrounds, as racialized minorities, and as socially engaged Muslims, Dounia and Hamza, and many others like them, are situated at multiple fault lines in contemporary French society. They are dedicated to mobilizing a range of resources—cultural, intellectual, and material—to address the urgent problems that they see facing "the Muslim community" and French society at large. In particular, they view social critique, rich intellectual culture, advanced education, and the pursuit of justice as central to their Islamic values and heritage. Like many of their peers, they are often deeply frustrated with French Muslim institutions and leadership. They seldom feel represented in public discourse on Islam or by the Muslim leaders who appear most frequently in mainstream media. But their frustration with many elements of their community does not alienate them from this community—far from it. On the contrary, they inhabit their critique as a practice of solidarity and cohesion.

Dounia and Hamza's trajectories of religious engagement exemplify a certain segment of the Islamic culture of twenty-first century France. Emergent religious intellectuals and social activists are offering original analyses of sacred texts and contemporary politics alike, and they are articulating novel plans for action. New community associations are forming constantly, on both the local and the national level, mobilizing members of a growing and diverse Muslim middle class to engage directly with the urgent social problems that weigh on them, from access to higher education to support for new parents, from structural racism and sexism to the climate crisis. Students at France's top universities are integrating their Islamic education with their professional training and creating new spaces for intellectual inquiry and ethical reflection. Religious entrepreneurs have developed a whole new field of spiritual development, including personal coaching and psychotherapy, art therapy, and consciousness-raising groups. Muslim artists, filmmakers, and entertainers are drawing on the fine arts as domains of social critique and religious imagination. Female organizers and scholars are shaping Muslim conversations around gender and sexuality in new ways. Political activists are mounting substantive challenges to the existing model on which the French state seeks to regulate Islam, are combating widespread Islamophobia, and are arguing for a conception of citizenship that resonates with many French Muslims. In short, over the course of the 2010s, an emergent generation of engaged Muslims developed a large and lively sphere of socialization, intellectual activity, and political engagement, invested in big philosophical questions and concrete social change. At the same time, as we will see in more detail in chapter 1, these "engaged Muslims" saw themselves as a somewhat embattled vanguard, not as representative of young Muslims generally. They would be the first to point out that it would be inaccurate to generalize from deeply committed (and generally educated and upwardly mobile) community activists to the Muslim population as a whole.[4]

Nonetheless, you would hardly know of the vibrant "engaged Muslim" landscape from the coverage of Islam in the French news media or popular intellectual output, or from recent state-led initiatives relating to Islam. Headlines still focus on the "problems" of the headscarf, halal food, and terrorism. Best-selling books, some written by respected journalists and scholars, others by novelists, many by demagogues, warn of the dangerous Muslim "communalism" of the suburbs of French cities and of the imminent "great replacement" of autochthonous white French by the descendants of immigrants, Muslims in particular.[5] Across Europe, racial and religious discrimination is rendered "respectable" or even "virtuous" through the rhetorical opposition of Islam to women's and LGBTQ rights,[6] while the state engages in an "institutional negation of race" that attempts to render this discrimination invisible.[7] Muslim social activist groups that might seem to challenge the terms of this opposition, including prominent Muslim feminists, are often dismissed in the media as dissimulating and hypocritical, masking a project of "conquest" under pretended liberal democratic values and duping the bourgeois left into a so-called Islamo-leftism. The once marginal far right, long anchored by anti-immigrant and white nationalist politics, has become a major and growing force in French and European political life. In media and political discourse, Islam remains inextricably bound up with the working-class banlieues of major French cities. France's manufactured "Muslim problem"[8] or "Muslim question"[9] is framed variously (and often simultaneously) as a problem of socioeconomic inequality and urban marginalization, a problem of liberal democratic values and gender and sexual equality, a problem of national security and foreign affairs, a problem of the French Way of Life, of which pork sausage and bikinis are portrayed as important pillars, or a problem of white nostalgia for empire. With rare exceptions, this arena of political discourse on Islam, whether coming from the right or the left, either completely ignores or willfully misrepresents the lively Muslim culture described above.

On the policy front, state regulation of Muslim practices has only intensified in the years since the 2004 ban on religious symbols in public schools, which primarily affected young girls who wore headscarves. Since 2004, French law has evolved to allow some private employers to discriminate on the basis of religious expression; the Ministry of Education has specified that girls' modest dress, such as long skirts, can be prohibited by school administrations; and police officers have forced women wearing head coverings to disrobe on public beaches. In the aftermath of the terror incidents of

2015 and 2016 in Paris and Nice, the French state embarked on a new series of initiatives to manage and surveil the practice of Islam. These initiatives range from the closure of mosques and expulsion of imams to the expansion of funding from the Ministry of the Interior for academic research on Islam in France. They include the promotion of state-approved theological perspectives through the Foundation of French Islam and the 2021 Charter of Principles for French Islam. In a different measure, the "anti-separatism law" of 2021 places new requirements on all community organizations, including the signing of a "Republican contract" committing them to a particular understanding of French values. Despite over a decade of evidence that state-driven efforts to manage Muslim life are instantly delegitimized among the Muslim community at large, and despite the simultaneous growth of large-scale grassroots efforts at Muslim community representation, French political elites persist in promoting the project of an "official Islam of France." Approved spokespeople such as Bordeaux imam Tareq Oubrou call French Muslims to live "discreetly," with the "prudent comportment of an animal in an unfamiliar territory, who minimizes his movements and reduces his visibility in order not to be exposed."[10] This attitude alienates many Muslims, including a significant number who share elements of Oubrou's liberal perspective, but do not see themselves as "animals in unfamiliar territory," nor do they wish to organize their ritual and moral lives in terms of an ever-receding standard of what might conceivably pose a "problem" for majoritarian French society.

The hypervisibility of certain representations of Islam in public discourse and policymaking renders invisible the eclectic and dynamic Muslim culture of contemporary France. The discourse on Islam in the French public sphere at once accuses Muslims of blind authoritarianism and demands their immediate consensus on Republican moral imperatives. This discourse presumes that Islam is incompatible with critical thought and open debate, which are understood to be uniquely fostered by the Enlightenment tradition. In contrast to all these presumptions, this book is about how the Muslim scene of greater Paris has been, in fact, characterized by active disagreement and complex arguments over how to live well and what kind of communities to build. At the same time, it is also about how this practice of building community has become the target of increasing public scrutiny and state regulation. *Communautarisme*, or "communalism," and the supposed danger it poses to "public order" are the primary watchwords in the political discourse on Islam.

ARGUMENT AS A FORM OF SOLIDARITY

Far from validating the anxieties of French state elites, however, French Muslim projects of community are forms of agonistic social critique with much potential for civil society more broadly. French Muslim thinkers and activists have developed a concept that some of my interlocutors glossed as "fraternal critique"—argument as a form of solidarity.[11] While the term itself was only sporadically deployed in the French Muslim scene, I found it to aptly encapsulate much of the discourse that I found there. Discontented with existing religious institutions and moral frameworks, beset by gendered and racialized media stigma and state surveillance, and facing urgent social problems, many young French Muslims are focused on the moral and material improvement of their community through grassroots social activism and renewed intellectual culture. Through their debates, they have developed an ethical framework and method that some of them call "fraternal critique" (*la critique fraternelle*). This term is used to highlight argument as a practice of solidarity and cohesion, and to hold that rather than fragmenting the Muslim community, social critique can be a way of refocusing on the collective as the primary subject of moral formation. These interventions have important consequences, not only for the study of religion but also for broader conversations about the place of critique and discord in our civic life. In a political climate where argument and dissent are often set in opposition to unity and efficacy, the method of fraternal critique makes a timely contribution. Like engaged French Muslims, many people today are looking for a community worth fighting over—and worth fighting for. Fraternal critique is an ethical method, a theoretical offering grounded in the specific experiences of French Muslims that—precisely because of and not despite this situatedness—has applicability outside of the context in which it emerged.

I understand fraternal critique to be akin to Chantal Mouffe's concept of "radical pluralism," demanding a "break with rationalism, individualism, and universalism."[12] It refuses the rationalist assumption that reasoned argument from shared premises will lead to consensus. Mouffe writes that "the belief that a final resolution of conflicts is eventually possible . . . far from providing the necessary horizon of the democratic project, is something that puts it at risk."[13] Fraternal critique as an ethical method is an invitation to build community through tension and disagreement, refusing the teleology of consensus for an agonistic solidarity.[14] Critique is not only made with "critical distance"; it is part and parcel of religious modes of reasoning, argument, and persuasion that rely on intimacy and kinship rather than the "god trick of seeing everything from nowhere," as Zareena Grewal aptly quotes Donna Haraway.[15] As such, fraternal critique belies the supposedly uncritical nature of Islam in much Western discourse.[16]

Fraternal critique is also a conceptual double entendre, invoking both the Islamic value of brotherhood and the classic Republican virtue of *fraternité*. Excluded from the national mythology of fraternité, French Muslims simultaneously reclaim this ethical value as their own and develop an assemblage of alternate ways of thinking about kinship and solidarity born out of this exclusion.[17] Importantly, these parallel Islamic and Republican resonances of fraternal critique are not about claiming a hybrid "French Muslim identity." While the French state and dominant cultural institutions focus on cultivating a cohesive "national identity," socially engaged French Muslims are more invested in traditions of ethical action and intellectual inquiry, of which fraternal critique is one prominent example. Many of my interlocutors understood their religious engagement in terms of what sociologist Abdelwahab Boudhiba termed the Islamic "message of fraternity, of justice, of effort, of liberation."[18] In his essay on fraternité, philosopher Edgar Morin called for the creation of "islands of living otherwise," describing these islands as "sites of fraternal resistance."[19] For socially engaged Muslims like Dounia and Hamza, fraternity is a form of resistance and a form of kinship that must be actively cultivated through expressions of solidarity, shared labor, intellectual engagement, and acts of love. As the expression "fraternal critique" indicates, debate and critique are understood to be among the activities that construct more robust ties of kinship.[20]

As a number of French Muslim thinkers have noted, fraternity is an Islamic value with a universal orientation, and strong resonances with the French humanist tradition.[21] As the often overlooked third element of the national motto, *Liberté, égalité, fraternité*, fraternité in the French tradition bridges concrete "human warmth"[22] and particular forms of collectivity with, in French philosopher Abdennour Bidar's terms, the call to "spiritualize our lives by entering into universal brotherhood!"[23] However, the French Muslim practice of "fraternal critique" holds Bidar's universalism at a critical arm's length, focusing on the cultivation of grounded communities and forms of relationship—akin to Morin's "islands of living otherwise"—that are in turn *resources* for (rather than obstacles to) the construction of broader collectivities, coalitions, and forms of solidarity. Rather than Bidar's spiritualized universalism, the culture of fraternal critique valorizes what Seydi Diamil Niane terms a "theocentric humanism"—an affective and unconditional love for humanity animated by a transcendent orientation toward the divine.[24]

While fraternité and brotherhood are distinctly masculine universals, women are prominent participants in the culture of fraternal critique. Simultaneously, women are also thinking about practices of sisterhood as a critical resource. In feminist contexts, "sisterhood," too, has been deployed as a universal with a very particular Western frame.[25] As we will see in detail in chapter 3, French Muslim women nourish sisterhood as a double critique—critique of intersecting forms of oppression—as well as a form of respite and care in the face of gendered Islamophobia. A version of sisterhood, glossed in some settings as *soeurénité*, becomes part of a broader assemblage of other ways of thinking about kinship and solidarity that emerge from the experience of being excluded from fraternité. Whether fraternal or "sororal," these forms of critique highlight the relationships between debate and care, disagreement and solidarity, as intertwined aspects of forging community.[26]

ARRANGEMENT OF THE BOOK

Fraternal Critique: The Politics of Muslim Community in France tells the story of the projects of community formation that shape the contemporary French Muslim scene, while also interrogating the political discourse of "communalism" that is used to justify increased state surveillance of Muslim collective life. This book presents a new generation of social actors across greater Paris, individuals who have been at the vanguard of Islamic intellectual culture and social ethics at the beginning of the twenty-first century. I show both how the aspiration to improve their community animates social movements among young French Muslims and how the fear of community is at the center of the state's policing of Muslim life.

Fraternal Critique comprises two complementary parts. In the first part, "Forming a Contested Community," we explore a lively culture of conversation across greater Paris that is nurtured at evening salons, in community organizations, in student groups at French universities, in civil rights organizations fighting Islamophobia and discrimination, at women's leisure days and feminist iftars, in decolonial protest movements, and in arts initiatives ranging from musical theater to photography to film. These conversations also, of course, take place in mosques, Islamic schools, and religious study circles, and, most of all, among friends, over long evenings or lazy Sunday brunches at trendy halal restaurants. In print, French Muslim political actors, spiritual leaders, artists, and students are developing a body of social commentary that extends these conversations and grounds them in Islamic and Republican traditions of critical thought. The three chapters of part I offer a window into the Paris-area scene of Muslim organizing and intellectual culture, showing how the moral project of shaping the Muslim community is being undertaken in a wide range of cultural and political settings.

In the second part of the book, "The Politics of Muslim Solidarity," we turn to the scrutiny and regulation of "Muslim community" by the French state and political elites, and the deployment of ideals of *French* moral community as a tool of governance. Part II marks a shift in method, from ethnography to analysis of law and policy, as well as a slight shift in time frame, from the early 2010s to the period following 2015, up through 2022. This second part of the book highlights the political conditions that have rendered projects of Muslim solidarity, such as those explored in part I, increasingly fragile. The specter of "communalism" is being used to justify unprecedented restrictions on civil liberties, often in the name of the defense of secularism. Anglophone observers often understand French secularism, or *laïcité*, to be a special philosophical framework underlying policies that regulate Muslim life.[27] The French state is usually understood as paradigmatically secular, with a politics of state neutrality toward religion. Theorists of secularism have long observed that far from this professed neutrality, secularism entails management of religious categories and forms of religious subjectivity. French policies related to secularism have shifted in important ways in the first decades of the twenty-first century, rendering the contradictions of secularism particularly clear. First, there has been what I call a "privatization of secularism," in which religious "neutrality" is increasingly applied to the private realm rather than the strict domain of the state. A key example was the infamous *Baby Loup* case, in which a private day care center was allowed to discriminate against employees wearing headscarves, at first because of its status as a "business of conviction."[28] The *Baby Loup* case, which I analyze in chapter 5, exemplified and accelerated the usage of secularist rhetoric to regulate expressions of Muslimness in the private sphere. Second, secularism is increasingly augmented through a new, "immaterial" conception of public order. For example, the 2016 Jouanno Report argued for a new "expansive understanding of public order" to go beyond secularism as a potential justification for more widespread restrictions on women's modest dress. This "expansive understanding" of immaterial public order enshrines a particular conceptualization of human dignity into policymaking, with a focus on gender parity. This immaterial conception of public order justifies the regulation of behavior or speech that, in the eyes of the state, threatens national values. Part II focuses on the ways that secularism in the historical and legal sense has been exceeded in twenty-first century French policy and political discourse, showing how the idea of "Muslim community" has become an object of increasing surveillance under the aegis of public order.

This two-part arrangement of the book arose out of multiple considerations. While I originally planned to write an exclusively ethnographic book, I increasingly realized that I could not do justice to the circumstances under which my interlocutors are operating without a deeper analysis of the political condition of Muslim community—and moral community more broadly—in post-2015 France. When I thought about what the people who shared their lives with me would want an anglophone readership to know, the political transformations of the post-2015 period were paramount. Thus, this second part of the book is a form of accountability. The two parts are also chronological: the main portion of my ethnographic research that forms the basis of part I ended in the final weeks of 2014, while the political dynamics I detail in part II extend from 2017 into the early 2020s. But most importantly, the ethnographic chapters precede and set the stage for the political analysis chapters in order to foreground the generative contributions of Muslim social actors, rather than foregrounding the oppressive political conditions in which they operate.

Accordingly, based on ethnographic research conducted with Islamic cultural, educational, and activist organizations across the Paris metropolitan area, and on close readings of laws and political reports, the two parts together address the following questions: What are the moral priorities of the current generation of French Muslim social actors? What ideals and aspirations do they have for Muslim life in France, and how do they articulate and implement these visions in a landscape where the very idea of the "Muslim community" as an object of cultivation is politically inflammatory? How do members of France's growing Muslim middle class, largely inheritors of postcolonial immigration who have pursued university educations and professional careers despite a legacy of social disenfranchisement and structural discrimination, frame their aspirations from a religious and ethical point of view? How do religiously engaged French Muslims draw on their eclectic cultural inheritances, including Islamic and Enlightenment sources, traditions, and patterns of reasoning, in order to envision the society they would like to live in, and to work toward the realization of those visions? On what terms does the state seek to regulate and manage Muslim collective life in the twenty-first century, and why is "communalism" framed as such a danger to the Republic? How has the political practice of secularism evolved in concert with Republican identity politics? Most broadly, this book asks why people remain deeply invested in communities that are marked by internal discord and feelings of exasperation and discouragement. Is it possible that these arguments and affective states actually hold moral communities together rather than splintering them?

By exploring these questions, this book brings into view the ways that young socially engaged Muslims are using their debates and disagreements to cultivate Muslim community as a primary ethical project. These debates and disagreements lie at the intersection of theology, ethics, and contemporary political life. They range from arguments over how to combine professional achievement with Islamic piety, how to relate the social experience of being racialized as Muslim to Islam as a spiritual tradition and moral community, if and how to engage in local and national politics, how to pursue gender-based activism while resisting the French feminist establishment, and, for some, whether it might not be better to leave France altogether. Through all of these conversations, internal discontent and disagreement are constituting, rather than fragmenting, the tissue of Muslim collective life in France.

DE-CENTERING THE OMNIPRESENT REPUBLIC

Across the sphere of engaged Muslim discourse and activism, social actors like Dounia and Hamza are developing ethical projects for the improvement of Muslim community that reject the terms of the tension between Islam and secularism. Engaged Muslims seek to counter the pervasive politicization of Islam without being drawn into the terms of that politicization. I was reminded of the difficulty of resisting the terms of the politicization of Islam by Widad, a high school teacher from the northern banlieue of Sarcelles in her late twenties, when I recounted to her my experience mailing a package.

It was a muggy, rainy late August day when I lugged a box full of books to a post office in Ménilmontant, in the twentieth arrondissement of Paris. I intended to send it by media mail, known in France as the "books and brochures rate," back to my apartment in Somerville, Massachusetts. With each research trip, I added to my growing library of texts that were nearly impossible to procure in the United States, sources that I would not even have been able to identify for the capable staff at my university library to track down. I eagerly collected the theological, devotional, and psychological texts that lined the narrow aisles of the Islamic bookstores of the rue Jean-Pierre Timbaud and the boulevard de Belleville, and the sundry self-published personal essays, collections of poetry, and social manifestos by young writers whom I encountered at conferences or through friends. I amassed copies of *Imane Magazine* and *Salam News*, both local Muslim periodicals that combined news and culture reporting with personal essays and practical life advice, and works of political commentary stocked by independent bookstores in the suburban neighborhoods of Pantin, Montreuil, and Saint-Denis. On this trip, I had also purchased a French-language Qur'an, the famous translation by the twentieth-century polymath Muhammad Hamidullah. Born in Hyderabad in 1908 and educated in Germany and France in the 1930s, Hamidullah spent most of his adult life in France. He pioneered the field of francophone Islamic sciences, writing many books in French over the course of the latter half of the twentieth century, destined for an audience hungry for traditional religious literature in the language that was accessible to them. While I was accustomed to switching between English and Arabic when reading scripture, I had realized that I needed to read the Qur'an in the version that most of my interlocutors were using.

I arrived at the post office with my cardboard box of books ajar and spattered with rain. I wasn't sure how heavy the box would turn out to be; it needed to be under five kilograms to qualify for the most advantageous "books and brochures" postage rate. After some time in line, I handed my box to the postal worker, a tall, thin white man with a flopping pompadour and wire-rimmed glasses. To my surprise, he opened the box and began sorting through its contents, piling them to one side of the scale.

"The weight is correct?" I asked, anxiously.

"The weight is not the issue, Mademoiselle. This package does not qualify for the special rate for books and brochures."

"Oh? Why not?" The postal officer straightened to his full height.

"Mademoiselle. The special rate applies to packages that contribute to the propagation of French culture in the world. These books do not meet that qualification. Every book must be written in French." I confessed to him, unwisely, that this criterion had taken me by surprise. Hastily, I filtered out two English-language novels that I had brought along for pleasure reading. Indeed, as I would later learn from a closer scrutiny of the postal service website, the books and brochures rate is "in the service of the influence [*rayonnement*] of French culture in the world. The books and brochures must be of an educational, scientific, or cultural nature, must not be advertisements, and must be written exclusively in French or in regional languages."[29]

"Okay, *voilà*. As you can see, the remaining books are all in French." The postal officer grimaced and gestured toward my pile of materials.

"These, Mademoiselle, do *not* contribute to the influence of French culture. The state has no interest in subsidizing materials like *these*." He took up the French-language Qur'an and flipped through it until he found, on an early page, the invocation "In the name of God, the Compassionate, the Caring" in an elaborate Arabic calligraphic motif. "There you go. The proof. *This* is not French culture." His mincingly articulated phrase—"*Ceci n'est pas de la culture française*"—immediately reminded me of René Magritte's surrealist icon, "The Treachery of Images," in which a realist depiction of a pipe is captioned, in the stylized cursive of a children's schoolbook, *Ceci n'est pas une pipe*. This is not a pipe. The paradoxes of Magritte's painting—that the image of a pipe is never, of course, itself a pipe, that words themselves are images, and that neither words nor images have any straightforward relationship to the objects they purport to represent, whose full reality is ungraspable the very moment it is flattened by representation and interpretation—seemed unexpectedly apt as a way to understand the grapheme of the *basmala* on the flyleaf of the French Qur'an. At the same time, it underscored the linguistic ideology of the "books and brochures rate" as interpreted by this particular foot soldier of the Republic—that French words (but as it turned out, not all French words) could serve as both symbol and effective agent of the radiating influence of "French culture," that ungraspable essence, throughout the world.

I took a breath. "How much would it be to send the package at the standard rate, then?"

"Seventy-four euros." My eyes widened.

"Thank you very much, sir. Good day." I piled my books and magazines back into the box, stepped out into the rain, pulled a roll of packing tape out of my jacket pocket, and taped the box up decisively. I walked it three-quarters of a mile to the next-closest post office, stood in a new line, and delivered it unceremoniously to a new postal worker. Nine euro fifty and several weeks later, the battered package arrived on my Somerville porch.

The incident at the Ménilmontant post office was a concrete instantiation of the way that French cultural nationalism is concretized in innumerable government policies that extend well beyond the domain of "secularism," and is framed in particular contrast to Arabness and to Islam, cultural concepts that both rely on and exceed the bodies of people who are racialized as Arab and as Muslim. The contents of my package—works of literature, political commentary, psychology, and one historic translation, all published in France—were manifestly products of "French culture." And yet, a policy articulated in terms of the "propagation of French culture" reifies a moral geography in which French culture can only spread outward from an essential, predetermined core.

I described this experience to Widad, who had been involved in Muslim student organizing and a Muslim women's cooperative, and was taking classes at a local institute of Islamic sciences. Widad laughed at my story and rolled her eyes.

> You see how embedded it is. It's not just the laws about the headscarf, which make the headlines. It's not primarily the radical provocateurs like [Marine] Le Pen. It's everyday, ordinary encounters like these. But, you know, the fact that some guy at the post office doesn't like the Qur'an, that really can't distract us. Even the polemic around the headscarf can't distract us. There is a lot of work to do.

Widad insisted on the necessity of making a clear space between one's own ethical commitments and priorities and the stigmatizing, exoticizing, or pressuring views of others. "Otherwise," she emphasized, "you are just *reacting*." Widad continued,

> Every so often there is something that crystallizes the exclusion that Muslims or racialized people face in France, and it awakens everyone's spirits, it wakes people up. But people wake up in different ways. Some wake up and say, okay, we can't remain defined by all this, so we have to do the work, we have an enormous amount of education to do within our community and beyond it, we have to change society. We have to make a new conversation. Others wake up and they say, no no, no thank you, I am going to stay in my garden. I will take care of everything here myself, and my children and I won't have to think about the politics outside, because my garden has nothing to do with that.

Widad admitted that she had sympathy for both positions, and sometimes felt torn between them. "But the problem is, when you want to construct your own fenced-off world, you're not speaking from reason, you're acting out of fear. And that's exactly what we must get out of. After all, we are Muslim. We have to be clear, we have to remain rational."

Widad's remarks encapsulate several of the intersecting approaches toward the French state that characterize much engaged Muslim discourse. On the one hand, there is an overwhelming fatigue with the incessant political attention to "Muslim issues," most notably the recurrent manufactured controversies over women's dress. This fatigue motivates some French Muslims to seek a domain of existence that escapes, as much as possible, what Ahmed Boubeker referred to as the "shell game of the gaze of French society."[30] This might be expressed through what Fareen Parvez describes as an "antipolitics" of retreat from French society in some circles, or through resolute distancing of oneself from broader Muslim contexts, or through transnational migration away from France.[31] Other French Muslims, by contrast, respond to the politicized frames of Islam, race, gender, and nation by developing a firm commitment to combating these politics through organized resistance and vocal critique. In this vein, new activist organizations have emerged that target specific issues, such as the ability of mothers to accompany their children's field trips while wearing head coverings. Still others focus on the development of new spaces of collective expression and action, spaces that only obliquely critique Republican cultural nationalism and its raced and gendered preoccupation with Islam by "making a new conversation," in Widad's terms. The quotidian pervasiveness of the racial project of Republicanism and its articulations around Islam has become the backdrop to an arena of social activity in which engaged Muslims elaborate alternative visions for collective life. The first part of this book focuses on some of these alternative visions.

"SEPARATISM" AND STATE REGULATION OF MUSLIM COLLECTIVE LIFE

It is not only political commentary on Islam in France that tends to be overwhelmingly framed in terms of perceived tensions between French secular norms and Muslim practice. Academic research on French Muslims has also often been framed in terms of the question epitomized by John Bowen's title: *Can Islam Be French?*[32] The significant political controversies that have marked the social experience of French Muslims over the past thirty years have demanded nuanced anthropological and historical examination and critical analysis.[33] As many scholars have observed, public discourse on Islam in France tells us much more about the contradictory entanglements of secularism and Republicanism with France's enduring colonial legacy than it does about Islam or about Muslims themselves.[34] Recent scholarship has astutely unmasked the ongoing "racial project of France"[35] that is manifested through the "contradictions of secularism"[36] and recurrent "moral panics"[37] that expose "the unresolved tensions of an imperial project."[38] The ongoing weaponization of political secularism against French Muslims has resulted in a tendency for Muslim French discourse and practice to be read in terms of Republican identity politics and in terms of an analysis of secularism—even while the aim of much of this work is to unmask the contradictions and colonial legacies of current secular politics. This has had the paradoxical result of continuing to frame Muslim France in terms of the obsessions of the state and in terms of a distance from secular culture. *Fraternal Critique* begins from the grounding assumption that French Muslims are French—not simply in terms of nationality, but in terms of cultural norms, participation in certain forms of secular ethics, and political belonging.[39] Young engaged Muslims do not see their Frenchness as something to be proved or achieved, or even asserted as an identity claim. Rather, Frenchness, including secularism, is taken for granted as a part of their moral and cultural inheritance. The first part of this book portrays a scene of religious activity that seeks a new set of terms for engagement in French culture, beyond the state-driven opposition between secularism and Islam.

At the same time, the state is an unavoidable actor in the formulation of Muslim community. Not only do individual politicians constantly invoke the specter of Muslim "communalism," but the state seeks to regulate Muslim collective life on multiple fronts, both by seeking privileged interlocutors and representatives, and by dissolving entities such as mosques and community organizations that do not meet with its approval. While I initially tried to follow Widad's invitation to ignore the political issues and to write a book about Muslim collective life that went against the grain of the overwhelming focus on the state and on state secularism in France, I eventually found it impossible and indeed irresponsible to overlook the role of political actors in shaping the conditions of Muslim community formation. Accordingly, the second part of this book focuses on the post-2015 transformations in the way that different branches of the French state, from the courts to Parliament to the Ministry of the Interior, manage Muslim collective life and the concept of "moral community." They do so not only through regulating the way that Muslims can express community but also through a thick concept of *French moral community*, what Vincent Valentin calls a "communitarian conception" of secularism and national identity.[40]

In 2020 and 2021, the French government unilaterally closed a number of mosques and Muslim organizations, including the Collective against Islamophobia in France (Collectif Contre l'Islamophobie en France; CCIF), the charity BarakaCity, and the publishing house Nawa Editions, whose books were accused of being "anti-universalist and in direct conflict with Western values."[41] Government agencies placed the bank accounts of religious organizations, the schooling practices of Muslim families, and the research agendas of university faculty under more intense scrutiny. In concert with the French Council for the Muslim Religion (Conseil Français du Culte Musulman; CFCM), the government produced a controversial Charter of Principles for French Islam to be signed by all Muslim religious leaders. State actors expressed particular suspicion of links between Islam, decolonial thought, and anti-racist organizing, calling for the investigation of critical race theory in academic contexts. All this surveillance, according to the French government, aims to identify a perceived Islamic "separatism" from French society that purportedly threatens "public order."

State officials have justified this policing of Muslim religious life as a response to recent acts of violence. But the true anxiety at the heart of these measures is not about fringe violent actors. Instead, it is about Muslim "integration" into French society—the fact that more and more descendants of immigrants are breaking barriers in every domain of professional and cultural life, from elite French universities to journalism to law, while continuing to claim their Muslim belonging and practices and their condition as racial minorities descended from colonized people. These claims contravene the French racial frameworks of integration and color blindness, according to which socioeconomic "insertion" in the capitalist and Republican order should be accompanied by the abandonment of other forms of difference. Further, young Muslims are drawing on their French norms and traditions to critique racial and religious discrimination and what they perceive as neocolonial relationships of power. As sociologist Hichem Benaissa put it, "Islam has progressively become a problem to the extent that it has become French."[42] It is precisely the increasing "integration" of Muslim immigrants and their descendants in France, Benaissa argues, that has produced sharp reactions from French elected officials and media elites. My interlocutors in this book, mostly members of an educated and often upwardly mobile pious Muslim French middle class, pose a particular threat to the self-image of the Republic. Indeed, their "integration" and relative success (while not relinquishing their deep Islamic investments) are, perhaps paradoxically, more threatening to the national mythology than the intergenerational socioeconomic marginalization of many of their peers. And the state's reactions to this perceived threat have focused on the very community organizations that, as Nadia Marzouki has demonstrated in the US context, increase participation in national civic life.[43]

The most recent wave of state action against "separatism" was prompted by a murder that horrified France. In October 2020, schoolteacher Samuel Paty was killed by Abdoullah Anzorov, an eighteen-year-old Russian who had come to France at the age of six as a refugee. Anzorov's violence came in response to Paty's decision to show caricatures of the Prophet Muhammad in a class on freedom of speech, recalling the fatal attacks in 2015 at the offices of satirical newsweekly *Charlie Hebdo*, which had initially published the caricatures. Anzorov's trajectory reveals an increasingly isolated individual. He sought online connections with fighters in Syria but was not part of any network or organization. His family and peers reported that he had become reclusive in the months leading up to the murder. When an online campaign was started against Paty by a student's father, who was incorrectly led to believe that Paty had asked Muslim students to leave class while he showed the caricatures, Anzorov latched onto the incident.[44]

In stark contrast to the isolation of Anzorov and other violent actors, however, the government's measures have deliberately targeted spaces of Muslim collective life as well as Muslim ideals of community and solidarity. As the government itself admitted, there was no relationship between the perpetrators of violence and the settings, people, or ideas that have become targets of state sanction. In the words of Interior Minister Gérald Darmanin, the targeted communities and organizations were not linked with any act of violence, but were those "to whom we wanted to send a message."[45] Minister of Education Jean-Michel Blanquer spoke of so-called Islamo-leftists as "intellectually complicit" in Paty's murder, arguing that scholars and activists should be targets of state intervention alongside perpetrators of violence.[46]

CONTESTED IDEAS OF COMMUNITY

As with every other episode in France's long history of constructing and managing racial and religious difference, all these measures are animated by the fear of "communalist" identity politics and "separatism" from the national body. Most often associated with ethnic enclaves or identity politics, "communalism" and "separatism" increasingly apply to all ethnically and religiously specific organizations and to patterns of socialization within ethnic and religious groups. These terms, however, have never applied to the exclusive enclaves of the white or wealthy. This is in spite of the fact that demographer Patrick Simon has shown that on the whole, immigrants and their descendants are considerably *more* likely than the white French population to have close relationships with people of other races and ethnicities—it is white French who are most likely to socialize exclusively with people who are racialized like them.[47] Communalism and separatism are terms of moral panic that serve to stigmatize and criminalize any space of gathering or shared consciousness among France's non-white populations, Muslims in particular.

Current public discourse in France, among Muslims and non-Muslims alike, makes systematic reference to France's "Muslim community." But is it intelligible to speak of a "French Muslim community"? How might this community be circumscribed, found, or forged? If it exists, how can it be molded, revived, improved, or transformed? Do all self-identified Muslims in France belong equally to this community, and is their belonging equally legible? These questions are complicated by the fact that in France today, the idea of "community" itself is deeply fraught, linked immediately to the specter of "communalism." As sociologists Marwan Muhammad and Julien Talpin put it, "communalism" is "a term for a set of fears,"[48] fears about forms of identification, whether religious, racial, ethnic, or based on gender and sexuality, that are felt to threaten what should be citizens' supreme identification with the national community. In practice, the fear of communalism applies overwhelmingly to racial, ethnic, and religious minorities, categories that are often conflated through the racialized idea of the Arab Muslim from the banlieues. Communalism applies to Muslims, to immigrants and their descendants, and to the geographical spaces where they are assumed to be concentrated—the banlieues, the "sensitive urban zones," the "difficult neighborhoods." The term is not used to describe the exclusive enclaves (whether in Paris proper or in the wealthy banlieues) that are inhabited overwhelmingly by white elites, even though these neighborhoods and communities are far more homogeneous and isolated, by any metric, than the supposedly "communalist" banlieues.[49]

The rhetoric of communalism anchors identity-based fears of "multiculturalism" in a Republican political mythology according to which identity is a zero-sum game and citizens' participation in moral communities of various sorts necessarily detracts from their unalloyed allegiance to the national community. To publicly claim an investment in the state of the Muslim community in France is automatically politically fraught. It is perhaps because of this fact, rather than despite it, that so many young Muslims remain invested in the idea of a "French Muslim community" that they also simultaneously call into question. The idea of "Muslim community" is not only compelling to those who are drawn to intensified personal piety. Young inheritors of postcolonial migration in the twenty-first century grew up in an environment where "Muslim" had become the primary racialized category of difference in French society, and many have only thin connections to their parents' or grandparents' countries of origin. The idea of "Muslim community" has therefore become a key resource in locating themselves in the broader landscape of French society, in relationship to an inheritance of ethical norms, cultural patterns, and forms of sociability, but also colonial violence and structural disenfranchisement. Religious engagement, in this landscape, both draws from and exceeds the forms of pious mobilization that marked the "Islamic revival" of the 1980s, 1990s, and early 2000s.

Accordingly, like many French Muslims, I take "French Muslim community" to be a constantly contested and aspirational community, one that is perpetually being brought into being by a broad set of actors.[50] I understand French Muslim community to exist through and because of its internal debates, including those debates that call its very existence into question. Indeed, many of these arguments are underpinned by a shared concern for the moral and spiritual state of "the community" and a commitment to improving it. French Muslims like Hamza and Dounia who are profoundly invested in the moral development and improvement of their community are building a civic culture of literary salons, media outlets, arts initiatives, volunteer organizations, student clubs, and professional networking groups. These spaces are founded and run by people motivated by Islamic social ethics and oriented toward Muslim publics. These organizers sometimes shorthand their projects as "communalist," appropriating the term to designate initiatives that are predominantly formed by and addressed to Muslims. However, this moral project of shaping the Muslim community is far from being a closed project with an insular focus, as those who invoke communalism in France claim to fear. Rather, it is a dynamic set of moral aspirations that often orients Muslims toward civic institutions and social forms—including but not limited to critique, protest, and resistance. Throughout these organizations, events, and networks, the direction and the moral and spiritual health of the Muslim community remains an important concern—even if activists regularly throw up their hands in exasperation at the internal divisions of this community and the ambivalence of many of its members. Some remark deploringly, dismayed by the challenges of organizing, that the so-called Muslim community doesn't even exist.

For different reasons, many scholars would agree. In an effort to calm the general fervor over communalism in the aftermath of the 2015 terrorist attacks, sociologist Olivier Roy reassured the French public in the pages of *Le Monde* that they were "afraid of a community that does not exist." Despite the unceasing political discourse about the "Muslim community," Roy asserted, "There is no Muslim community. There is only a Muslim population." After all, he continued, "There is no Muslim vote. There is no network of Islamic schools. No crowds are marching in the streets for Islamic causes, and there are hardly any grand cathedral mosques—nothing but a proliferation [*pullulement*] of little neighborhood mosques. The supposedly representative organizations have no local legitimacy. In fact, the so-called Muslim "community" suffers from an extremely Gallic individualism, and remains reticent in face of the Bonapartism of our French elites. Which is good news."[51]

Roy is correct, of course, that there is no "Muslim vote" and no legitimate centralized authority in French Islam—quite the contrary. And yet, my own research leads me to a slightly different conclusion than Roy's "good news" that Muslim community does not exist. Disagreement with and skepticism toward authorities are antithetical to community only if we assume that community is defined by shared consensus or allegiance to leadership. It's true that there is broad diversity in ethical views, political orientation, and ways of life among French Muslims. But I argue that community is defined in large part by the arguments that people keep showing up for and the vectors of disagreement that continue to matter.

These conversations take place with acute consciousness of the ubiquity of state and media discourses that portray Islam as a threat to French culture, to political secularism, and in particular to women's rights and sexual liberties. French Muslims have been mobilizing for decades to combat these discourses, in increasingly visible and effective ways. The broader political context therefore shapes, to a certain degree, the sphere of Muslim intellectual and activist culture: as long as jogging headscarves and modest bathing suits are the stuff of political spectacle, they will remain themes of discussion and activism among the communities that are directly impacted. At the same time, Muslim community discourse has long flourished in France along lines that are wholly outside of the concerns emphasized by French politics and media. Muslims discuss how to live rightly and well, and how to shape a social fabric—a family, a neighborhood, a community, a society—

that supports this pursuit. In these discussions, they draw on eclectic moral frameworks, ranging from classical Islamic jurisprudence to Jean Piaget's developmental psychology, from twentieth-century Islamic reformism to the very "Enlightenment values" that are so often contrasted with Islam in public discourse. These conversations are anchored by moral priorities that are not framed by the logic of the state or by any contrast between Islam and secularism: priorities such as how to form stable, loving marriages and raise children who are healthy, successful, and connected to their heritage, how to improve socioeconomic mobility and develop professional skills among young people from disenfranchised neighborhoods, and how to develop outlets for cultural and spiritual expression and joy. Debates on these and other topics constitute Muslim collectivity in a way that is not dependent on consensus, centralized leadership, mass mobilization, or even shared understandings of what "Muslim community" is or ought to be. The overwhelming political (and scholarly) focus on women's modest dress, halal food, and violent radicalization obscures understanding of this rich field of discourse among French Muslims.

PARIS-BANLIEUE

The people and places we will encounter in this book are scattered across the Paris metropolitan area. Paris proper, composed of twenty districts (*arrondissements*) with a border—now an elevated highway known as *le périphérique*—that has not changed since 1860, is encircled by several rings of suburban towns, or banlieues. Together these make up the Paris metropolitan area. As Elayne Oliphant observes, Paris "has become less of a site of revolutionary eruptions," and "stands more frequently as a reliable connection to the past."[52] As Oliphant's analysis of art and Catholic materiality in Paris demonstrates, the city is suffused with a "banal" Catholicism that is a key ingredient in the "culture" that makes Paris the most visited city in the world. The Paris metropolitan area concentrates twenty percent of mainland France's population and over thirty percent of its economic activity in only two percent of its territory. As of 2020, the population of Paris proper was approximately 2.15 million, whereas the population of the whole metro area was 12.28 million.[53] The banlieues thus dwarf Paris proper in terms of human capital, though not in terms of material or cultural capital, which remains heavily concentrated within the city limits and in its exclusive western banlieues. These wealthy western suburbs are not included in the term "banlieue" in the popular imagination, which overwhelmingly indexes the poor and working-class towns to the north, east, and south of the center city, areas that are home to disproportionately high populations of immigrants and their descendants.[54]

The gradual neoliberalization of the French economy since the 1980s, which has significantly accelerated since the 2000s, has simultaneously brought about the metropolitanization of greater Paris (that is, the conglomeration of Paris proper and its banlieues) and its increased socioeconomic stratification, including the gentrification of the center city.[55] Middle-class and socially engaged French Muslims, like all who inhabit this stratified metropolis, are shaped by the capitalist and neoliberal direction of the city and the nation as a whole. Julie Kleinman describes recent West African migrants to Paris as subject to what Nicholas de Genova calls "inclusion through exclusion," or being assigned a subordinate social role that functions to incorporate them into the capitalist economy while restricting them from accessing social and material capital.[56] In a related yet distinct way, my middle-class interlocutors are more likely to face "exclusion through inclusion," that is, conditional access to a certain degree of capital and spatial mobility through processes such as the rental market or employment search that simultaneously produce their social exclusion along racial-religious lines.

The distinction between Paris and its banlieues is often drawn quite starkly, both in visual representations of the city, in the media, and in social science literature on France. Tourist maps, for example, depict Paris as if the banlieues do not exist, and even city street maps, designed to orient pedestrians, represent the banlieues as a blank uncharted territory, contrasted starkly to the crowded streetscape of central Paris. Media and scholarly representations frame the banlieues as the "other France," essentializing and reinscribing them as a land apart, consolidating race, class, and religion as axes of difference from the white, bourgeois center-city norm. The lived experience of engaged Muslims, however, frequently belies these representations. A focus on the banlieues, or indeed any sharp opposition between central and peripheral Paris, distorts the contemporary landscape of Muslim life, which cuts across the périphérique. The boundary between Paris and the banlieues is, of course, extremely porous. It is crossed daily by many thousands of people by rail, car, bicycle, and foot. As Kleinman has shown in her ethnography of West African migrants hanging out in the Gare du Nord train station, city-center sites can simultaneously function as stringently policed border zones and as sites of migrants' mobility, creativity, and "meaningful integration" into the fabric of French society. Kleinman's deliberate use of "integration" here offers a provocation and a challenge to the exclusion that undocumented or precarious new arrivals otherwise face.[57] For still others, the city border itself is a place of residence. Since 2015, a fluctuating population of one to several thousand people on the move, asylum-seekers and other migrants from the Middle East, Africa, and Central Asia, have lived in tent cities underneath the périphérique, their presence testifying to the endurance of France's struggles to address large-scale global inequalities in its peripheries and borderlands—and indeed, in its very heart.

The banlieues continue to be framed in scholarly literature as the primary geographical and cultural backdrop for the development of Muslim communities in France, while city-center sites such as the Mosquée de Paris or the Institut des Cultures de l'Islam are interpreted through the lens of French state management of Islam.[58] To be sure, the history of Muslim presence in France in the twentieth century has been bound up with the history of the rapid urbanization of the banlieues of major French cities during the postwar years of economic expansion known as the *Trente Glorieuses*. During these thirty "glorious" years, many immigrants arrived in France, especially from its colonial or formerly colonial territories of the Maghreb (North Africa), responding to a metropolitan thirst for manual and technical labor to build the infrastructure of postwar France. They were housed—first as individual migrant laborers, then as families—in shantytowns (*bidonvilles*), dormitories (*foyers*), then finally the "mushroom cities" of the banlieues, so called for the way they sprang suddenly from the ground. Through successive waves of immigration, the banlieues came to be seen as the primary territory of France's Muslim population, especially Seine-Saint-Denis, the large suburban district to the north of Paris, often known in reference to its postal code as "the 93." However, Islamic activity has not been circumscribed by the banlieues. Today the city center of Paris is home to dozens of Muslim intellectual and cultural events, Islamic schools and community organizations, and chic halal restaurants. Many of the youngest generation of French Muslims have refigured the banlieues as a homeland, from which they establish new migratory patterns of flux, into and out of the middle-class France from which they have historically been excluded.

Many young middle-class Muslims were born and raised in the Parisian banlieues, but others grew up in the countryside or provincial cities, and only came to the Paris area as young adults for study or work. For these individuals, "migrating" to the Paris metropolitan area was not only a pursuit of advanced study or a better-paying job, but also a move toward the institutional and cultural heart of Muslim France. The highly centralized French government and cultural institutions make Paris several orders of magnitude larger and more influential than any other French city. Correspondingly, the Islamic sites and institutions of metro Paris, scattered across a diversity of neighborhoods that are often held to exemplify both the greatest capital and sharpest failings of the Republic, are disproportionately influential for the French Muslim population as a whole.

THE RACIALIZATION OF MUSLIMNESS

The economic stratification of urban space in the Paris region overlaps with ascriptions of racial and religious difference. In 1984, novelist Tahar Ben Jelloun described France as a "land of asylum and exile where immigration is a nationality unto itself."[59] This has only become more true in the intervening decades. Indeed, it is often how young French people of color are termed in contemporary political discourse: *les jeunes issus de l'immigration* (youth of immigrant origin), trailing off into an ellipsis that often does not specify any "origin" in particular. Perhaps it is assumed; perhaps it is considered irrelevant. "Immigration" itself is a place to come from; it is the fantasy homeland that unites those who must have "an origin," *some* origin, regardless of their birthplace, their nationality, or those of their parents. The categories of "Muslim," "Arab," "immigrant," and "banlieues" are frequently collapsed in French discourse and are used nearly interchangeably to mark "origins" alien to authentic Frenchness. Marxist sociologists have argued that this elision is principally a tool for masking class hierarchy and undermining class solidarity between white French workers and immigrants and their descendants, and some hold that social analyses based on race, ethnicity, or religion only serve to reinforce this "culturalization" of capitalist power and economic hierarchy.[60] And yet, immigrants and their descendants are not all working class, and, as Jean Beaman has demonstrated, neither higher education, nor professional employment, nor secular values and lifestyles have erased the definitive impact of racial parameters for national belonging.[61]

As Sahar Aziz and others have shown in the US context, "Muslim" functions as an indelible racial category in France, always linked to but not consubstantial with "Arab," marking a form of alterity that cannot be divested.[62] Even drawing this comparison with Aziz's US-based analysis might invite the familiar European critique of US intellectual imperialism, according to which "American" concepts such as race are transposed to Europe, where they ostensibly do not apply. But, as Fatima El-Tayeb observes, race is "native to contemporary European thought," and "Muslim" is one of the key figures of racialized otherness, not only in France but across Western Europe.[63] In this vein, for political theorist Sadri Khiari, "Muslimness is not about belonging to the Islamic faith, it is a social relationship. . . . A relationship of struggle. A political relationship. A relationship of power."[64] Engaged Muslims negotiate Muslimness as a political "relationship of power" alongside their understandings of Islamic faith, tradition, and eclectic forms of piety. Following Sylvia Chan-Malik's work in the US context, I argue that many French Muslims construct a "racial-religious" self-understanding, striving to make religion and race legible as co-constitutive social conditions in a political context that denies the very existence of race and attempts to sharply circumscribe religion.[65] Furthermore, I argue that the current articulation of public order in France constitutes the elaboration of an ongoing "racial-religious" project. Despite their avowed race-blindness, French political elites have long used "Muslim" as a fused racial and religious category, or what Muriam Haleh Davis calls a "racial regime of religion"—an indelible embodied form of political difference that was forged in the colonial period.[66] This racialized experience of Muslimness has motivated some young people to work to shape the "Muslim community," since they are not easily able to leave it. Rather than attempting to pull apart these diacritics of social difference and identifying either race, class, or religion as the most fundamental fault line in French society, I am interested in how their amalgamation functions for those living at their intersection.

AN ETHNOGRAPHY OF ETHICAL CULTURE

Fraternal Critique is based in over thirty months of immersive ethnographic research in a wide range of Muslim contexts in metropolitan France, spread over the course of more than a decade. I conducted research from summer 2012 to the end of 2014 in the Paris area, but this project began to be formulated during a year of fieldwork in Toulouse in 2008–9, and has been sustained through regular follow up visits to Paris through 2019. As part of this fieldwork, I became involved in multiple community organizations, helping in whatever ways I could be useful—teaching, tutoring, and translating, participating in organizational meetings, publicity events, and the many social gatherings that surrounded the world of volunteerism. In addition, I attended classes at eight different institutes of Islamic higher learning, participated in three different study and reflection circles, regularly attended Friday prayers, classes, and other events at four different mosques, and attended innumerable short-term seminar series, one-time conferences, fundraising galas, political protests, artistic and cultural events, and social gatherings. Throughout these various forms of engagement, I met and interviewed students, teachers, activists, imams, and others, including some who were on the periphery of these religious networks. As one of my interlocutors put it, after quizzing me about my research methods, "So you show up somewhere, pull a thread, see what happens, and *voilà*, a book, is that it?" He wasn't that far off. Through this process of repeatedly showing up and pulling threads, I formally interviewed forty-five individuals, many of them more than once, and had extended informal conversations with dozens of others in my capacity as a researcher.

While I did not keep detailed demographic statistics about the individuals whom I encountered and interviewed, the large majority of them were in their twenties or thirties. Most were French-born grandchildren or children of immigrants from the Maghreb, with significant minorities of descendants of immigrants from West Africa as well as people who had themselves emigrated as children or teenagers from North or West Africa, from South Asia, or from the Indian Ocean region. I also came to know a number of white European converts to Islam, mostly French but some from other parts of Europe. They had grown up in a wide range of neighborhoods and regions of France, and lived primarily in the Parisian banlieues, although some lived in the eastern arrondissements of the center city. My interlocutors tended to describe themselves first as Muslim, as French, and occasionally as racialized (*racisé-e*), rather than in terms of their specific family immigrant origins, although these histories emerged quickly in our conversations.[67] In the religious settings where we primarily interacted, there was often an effort to downplay these lines of internal difference that had historically been important, in the name of fraternité. All of my interlocutors are referred to in the text by pseudonyms—in some cases, names that they chose themselves— and their identifying details have been changed. In addition, I have given pseudonyms to the organizations that I worked with, and in a couple of instances to individual banlieues, when the name of the banlieue would make a mosque or organization and its leadership directly identifiable.

While some of my interviews and research relationships were relatively formal, in other cases I developed warm friendships with people I met across Paris. As is typical of ethnographic research, some of these individuals have remained friends of mine over the intervening years. During these years, we have shared experiences of weddings, pregnancies, babies, graduations, moves, divorces, unemployment, losing parents—in short, we have shared our lives. These intimacies shape the appearances of some of their voices in the pages that follow, although I have always endeavored to err on the side of preserving the privacy of friendship.

During my fieldwork, I recurrently encountered a fascination with US Islam, whether through the amateur documentary "Californian Muslims" that screened to packed audiences across France in 2014, or through educational trips to the Bay Area organized by French Muslim nonprofits and hosted by US mosques.[68] The widespread interest in US Islam framed the way that I, as a white US Muslim "in transition,"[69] was interpolated in different settings throughout my fieldwork—the questions that were posed to me, the ways that I was called upon to give back to the communities I was involved with, and the forms of accountability and relationship that developed between me and my interlocutors. Equally impactful on my fieldwork was my transition from being a student in my early twenties to a married mother of two young children. Marriage and parenthood markedly shifted how I was received as a researcher. I spent large parts of two pregnancies conducting research in France, one with a toddler in tow, and my maternal body was a part of nearly every ethnographic interaction I had during these months. Fellow mothers saw me as a peer, rather than a young woman to be mentored, and younger women sometimes saw me as a mentor, rather than a peer. Ethnography is an embodied practice of knowledge production. Together, nationality, race, religion, gender, and family structure shaped the ethnographic relationships that inform this book.

I left France at the end of a long research stay only a week or so before the attacks of January 7–9, 2015, on the satirical weekly *Charlie Hebdo* and the kosher supermarket HyperCacher. These attacks, and the response to them, intensified already existing dynamics of widespread securitization and suspicion of Muslims, and a retrenchment of Republican nationalism. French Muslims have expressed complex responses to the *Charlie Hebdo* attacks and the subsequent mass attacks of November 2015 in Paris and July 2016 in Marseille. There have been moments of searching internal scrutiny—could the Muslim community, if such a thing exists, have done anything differently? How could these profoundly alienated and angry young men be identified early and reached, and their trajectory averted? There has also been deep frustration at the mediatized rush to demand all Muslims "apologize" and individually denounce terrorism, pain at the rise in Islamophobic incidents, and righteous anger at the political framing of ordinary preferences of some Muslims—such as not swimming in gender-mixed environments, wearing modest dress, or minimizing exposure to popular culture—as "risk factors" for violence.[70]

This book does not deal in great detail with the string of attacks and their immediate aftermath, since they fell outside the scope of my main period of ethnographic research. These attacks constituted a "discursive turn and critical juncture" in French political culture.[71] The second part of the book is based on political and legal sources from the post-2015 increase in regulation of Muslim life. These sources illuminate the new permutations of longstanding political dynamics that have emerged since these events—increased surveillance of mosques, imams, and Islamic organizations, heightened fervor in the opposition to women's modest dress in many social settings, and the mainstreaming of far-right conspiracy theories about Muslim conquest of Europe, as well as genuine concern about the tiny margin of young French people who are attracted to violence. For their part, engaged Muslims have become even more motivated to change the conversation around Islam and Muslims in France, within Muslim community contexts but also for broader French and international publics.

CHAPTER OUTLINE

Part I, "Forming a Contested Community," focuses on "Muslim community" as an aspirational project of ethical formation among French Muslims. Chapter 1, "An Ethics of Discontent," develops the role of debate, disagreement, and critique in the Paris-area Muslim scene. This chapter shows how broad frustration with the existing Islamic institutional landscape has motivated engaged Muslims to build an eclectic religious culture that can address intersecting moral challenges and malaise. We see how eclectic sites of social engagement are primary places for transmitting, expressing, and debating Muslim ethics. The ensuing two chapters take up specific strands of these debates. Chapter 2, "The People of Knowledge," shows how class has become central to Muslim social ethics in two divergent ways: as both an aspirational resource and an inheritance of moral accountability. Despite structural inequalities and historical exclusion, growing numbers of Muslim "inheritors of immigration" are focused on elite French educational, professional, and cultural contexts as sites for cultivating both spiritual and material excellence. Simultaneously motivated to improve their community through socioeconomic advancement and accountable to their working-class inheritance, engaged Muslims debate if, when, and how to pursue socioeconomic achievement and cultural capital at a time of rising inequality.

Chapter 3, "Sisterhood and Its Obligations," focuses on Muslim women's organizing around gender issues and on feminist terms. Acutely conscious of the incessant scrutiny and politicization of their bodies and behavior, and of the way that feminism is often contrasted with Islam, Muslim French women debate how to situate their activism in relation to feminism. Embedded in this question is a more fundamental concern of how to inhabit the framework of rights, choice, and liberty that structures feminist politics in France. This chapter shows how Muslim women negotiate the "constraints of choice" produced by dominant French discourses on Muslim women's dress.

Part II, "The Politics of Muslim Solidarity," turns to the construction of "Muslim community" as an object of regulation by the French state and political elites, focusing on the period since 2015. Chapter 4, "The Specter of Communalism," details how the political rhetoric of communalism is being used to justify unprecedented restrictions on the freedom of association and restrictions on Muslim practice more broadly. While communalism is a political term that only emerged in tandem with the current form of political Islamophobia in the early 2000s, the term is used to critique all forms of organizing by socially marginalized groups, including anti-racist and LGBTQ organizing. However, there is a particular anxiety around the concept of the "umma" and values that transcend the moral claim of the nation. This chapter draws on the 2021 "separatism law" and the 2021 Charter of Principles for French Islam, among other sources, to unpack why the idea of Muslim community is seen to pose such a particular threat to Republican political culture. Chapter 5, "From Secularism to Public Order," traces the transformations in the political discourse of French secularism over the course of the early decades of the twenty-first century. This period has seen the enlargement of the legal principle of secularism to encompass private entities and the general public sphere. Where the legal framework of secularism has proved inadequate to regulate Muslim life in the ways desired by political elites, the language of "public order" has been amplified to extend it. The new "immaterial conception" of public order is a revival of older legal languages of *bonnes moeurs* (good morals) and aims to enforce a shared moral worldview and conceptualization of human dignity. In the conclusion, I return to the concept of fraternal critique as it emerges in Muslim responses to the state policies and discourses analyzed in part II. I ask what the future might hold, in the face of the collective "fragilization" caused by the attempt to monopolize and impoverish the very notion and practice of community.

I
FORMING A CONTESTED COMMUNITY

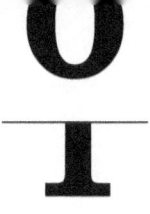

AN ETHICS OF DISCONTENT

NESSIMA: COMING OF AGE WITH ISLAMIC CULTURE

Nessima's car rolled slowly up to the Villevoque[1] commuter rail station on a rainy summer morning. She leaned over, cranked down her passenger window and called toward the group of idlers outside the station. "*Allo!* Which one of you is Kirsten?" I hurried out from under the awning, slid into the car, and introduced myself. Nessima was in her late thirties, petite, brusque, and energetic. She wore green cargo pants, a beige cardigan, and a practical jersey one-piece headscarf. Her car was full of the sticky miscellany of young children. "They're with their dad today," Nessima explained, although I hadn't asked. "We're separated." She eyed me silently, checking for a reaction.

Villevoque, where I met Nessima that day, is a working-class suburb of about thirty-thousand residents in the banlieues south of Paris. I was meeting Nessima that day so that she could introduce me to its largest mosque, Mosquée Arrahma, where I would later come to know a whole network of individuals, including many of Nessima's childhood friends. I was interested in the mosque's educational initiatives, including a new elementary school and evening classes for adults, and the president of the mosque, Ismaïl, had put me in touch with Nessima, who had agreed to be my guide. "She has a master's degree," he explained over the phone. "She will understand what it is you are doing." Ismaïl, whom I would only meet much later, seemed both proud and relieved to be able to pass me along to someone whom he perceived to be better equipped to handle curious foreign researchers.

In the span of our ten-minute drive from the station to Mosquée Arrahma, Nessima narrated the history of the mosque, gave a demographic overview of immigration in Villevoque, and dissected my nascent research plan. "I studied sociology, you know," she said. "It seems to me like you need a more precise research question. Well—we can go over that later."

Nessima had grown up in the Towers, a large housing project at the center of Villevoque that was now in the process of being torn down and replaced with smaller duplexes and rowhouses. Nessima arrived in Villevoque in 1975 at the age of six weeks, when her father got a job that would allow him to bring his family from Algeria and install them in a small apartment in Tower 17. The number of Muslim families in Villevoque grew rapidly, and the nascent community found a vacant basement storage space, two towers away from Nessima's family's apartment, which they repurposed as a makeshift prayer room. Nessima remembered this room from her childhood as the site of ponderous and rather ineffective classes in formal Arabic, which she nevertheless took for years at her parents' insistence.

Over the course of the 1990s, the community of the Tower 19 prayer room began working painstakingly toward a new, purpose-built mosque. For her part, however, Nessima was anxious to leave Villevoque. A star student, she was one of only a few of her circle of peers to pursue higher education. After completing her degree in applied sociology, she landed a middle-class job as a civil servant, in Lyon. "I was the very image of success," she reminisced. "Whenever I came back for a visit, the neighbors all brought their children around and told them 'Look at Nessima. Look how she succeeded. Do like she did.'" But in Lyon, isolated from her friends and family and burdened at her job, Nessima experienced a spiritual crisis. One morning, after a long night and a gripping dream, she went out and purchased her first French translation of the Qur'an. "It was only then that I began to discover my religion," she explained. "And I began to call everything in my life into question."

Nessima turned down a promotion that would have kept her in Lyon. She quit her job, moved back home, and enrolled full-time at an institute of Arabic and Islamic studies in Saint-Denis, an hour-long journey by public transit from Villevoque, if all the trains were functioning. Her parents and siblings were delighted to have her back home, even though she was growing into a form of piety that they did not always understand. To many of her relatives, religious study was for shaykhs and scholars, and the hijab was for older married women. They had trouble understanding why Nessima, a young woman with professional opportunities, would spend her twenties so focused on religion. But in Saint-Denis, Nessima found a group of girlfriends from across the broad Paris metropolitan area who shared similar life trajectories: young women, many with postsecondary educations and professional experience, who felt called to reorient their daily lives around renewed religious practice and the search for "authentic" Islamic knowledge. Together, they frequented Islamic lectures and conferences at sites around the city.

Nessima began leading a study circle, or *halaqa*, first in her home, then eventually at the nascent mosque in Villevoque. She would go on to lead this study circle for nearly a decade. These were whirlwind years. In the midst of her studies and her teaching, Nessima got married, had two children, and threw herself into the fundraising efforts to build a "real mosque" in Villevoque. By the time I first met her in 2012, she was the newly appointed co-chair of the Women's Committee of Mosquée Arrahma, having personally convinced the all-male mosque board that such a committee should exist in the first place. She overflowed with energy, determination, and dreams for Muslim life in her community, and the events she helped organize at the mosque drew women from across the metropolitan region.

In many ways, Nessima's experiences during these years were typical of engaged Muslims during the period of Islamic revival that marked the 1990s and 2000s in France. A generation of Muslims born in France, along with university students from Muslim-majority countries, developed a robust Islamic culture in France as part of a global resurgence of Islamic identification and activity. The increasing consolidation of "Muslim" as a primary vector of political and social difference in France during the 1990s further contributed to the development of an Islamic sphere, as a critical counterpublic to dominant French culture. The generation that came of age during this period often described themselves, as Nessima did, as having rediscovered or even "reverted" to Islam as teenagers and young adults, despite having been raised in Muslim families.[2]

This scene of religious activity was characterized by a dual emphasis on individual piety and institutionalization. The emphasis on individual piety and "revival from below"[3] was a prominent feature of global revivalist movements during this period.[4] But the institutional emphasis of the French Islamic revival was especially pronounced, given that this movement took place in a relative aporia of local Islamic institutions. The founding of the Union of Islamic Organizations of France (UOIF) in the mid-1980s,[5] including its marquee annual gathering of French Muslims in the Paris suburb of Le Bourget, inaugurated a period of Islamic institutional development concentrated in the Parisian banlieues, Saint-Denis in particular. The European Institute for Human Sciences (IESH), an Islamic theological school training imams and other religious intellectuals, was founded in the village of Château-Chinon in 1992, and opened a branch in Saint-Denis in 2001. In the mid-1990s, the

Center for Research and Study in Islamic Sciences (CERSI; now Oussoul Eddine) was founded in Saint-Denis, offering French-language instruction in Islamic sciences for an audience that was not literate in Arabic. Nessima began her studies at CERSI and eventually continued at IESH. Along with the Centre Tawhid, a local mosque and community center active since the late 1980s, these schools anchored Paris-area Islamic culture in Saint-Denis. Regular weekend lectures by popular spiritual leaders such as Tariq and Hani Ramadan, Hassan Iquioussen, and Nassima Prudor drew audiences of young Muslims from across the entire metropolitan area. Éditions Tawhid, a publishing house focused on Islamic literature for a francophone public, opened in 1990, and its books filled the shelves of Islamic bookstores along the rue Jean-Pierre Timbaud and boulevard de Belleville in Paris's eleventh and twentieth arrondissements. A generation of young people sought in these institutions a new framework for relating to their religion. This new framework of Islamic education was systematic, presenting Islam as a comprehensive and universal tradition, global and diverse, rather than embedded in the cultural practices of any one region. At the same time, as John Bowen notes, it was quite eclectic: entrepreneurial religious teachers with diverse types of professional and theological training "engaged in a kind of pedagogical bricolage to construct a suitable way of teaching their new students."[6]

The establishment of these anchoring institutions was accompanied by many local efforts to construct purpose-built mosques, in an effort to transition out of the various provisional spaces that had been appropriated for worship, which many found inadequate and undignified. While some observers in the 2000s described this trend as "a race for mosques,"[7] this wave of mosque construction was in fact quite protracted. In Villevoque, for example, the local Muslim community acquired a piece of land in 1998, broke ground on a foundation in 2001, and assembled each portion of the building only as the local community could raise funds to pay for it: first the framing, then the exterior walls, then the roof, windows, plumbing, interior walls, and finally the carpeting and decor. By the time that the then interior minister Nicolas Sarkozy called, in 2003, for Muslims to leave "the basements and garages, [which] do a great deal of harm to Islam, [and] live in the light of day, free of foreign influences and respectful of French culture and traditions," the Muslims of Villevoque had been slowly but persistently working toward a purpose-built mosque for over seven years.[8] At the time of Sarkozy's now-famous 2003 address, France had 1,600 sites of Muslim worship, including both mosques and simpler prayer rooms. By 2012, France had over 2,200 mosques, with around 200 more under construction.[9] Like Mosquée

Arrahma, many of these newer mosques were built by long-standing communities of worship that painstakingly raised funds from their local populations over the past decade. As they were built, the material structures of the mosques reshaped the engagement of their members. At Mosquée Arrahma, local members brainstormed fundraising strategies, canvassed in the twice-weekly local street market, printed the names of donors on a poster outside the prayer room, and voted on what to call the new mosque. Some worked with banks, negotiated with contractors, and met with government officials. The patterns of Muslim community life thus shifted to include a whole range of administrative responsibilities, in anticipation of the "real mosque" that would come.

EXPANSION AND DISILLUSIONMENT

By the time I first visited Mosquée Arrahma in 2012, the mosque had established a charitable endowment, or *waqf*, and was in the process of articulating an expansive vision for the future. The administration of Mosquée Arrahma had responded to the 2008 economic crisis by seeking a long-term solution to the fundraising fatigue that had hit their community particularly hard, after over a decade of raising money to build the mosque. Their ambition was to place the mosque at the center of a mixed-use urban development that would include a private elementary, middle, and high school, apartments for individuals and families, small commercial businesses, a day care, and a pharmacy. At a community celebration that summer, the emcee invited the audience to "subscribe to the house of God" in the same way that they subscribed to a mobile phone plan.

"The mosque belongs to you now," the emcee emphasized, framing his pitch through references to consumer culture, hoping to prick the consciences of a young and upwardly mobile imagined audience. "You all have flat-screen TVs at home, right?"

"No we don't," whispered Fadoua, a childhood friend of Nessima's who had also grown up in the mosque and in the Towers, and who worked in a day care in Villevoque.

"You all have the comprehensive cable package to go with them," he continued, building steam. "No we *don't*," Fadoua whispered again, impatiently.

The emcee's polished and confident appeal seemed carefully oriented toward a socioeconomic evolution of the local neighborhood. But like

Fadoua, some in the community found the mosque's ambitious expansion and fundraising to be too commercial—*trop business*. The architectural drawings of the planned development were impressive to many who frequented the mosque, but the heavy administrative work involved in growth on this scale had led, perhaps inevitably, to personality conflicts and divergent visions.

A little more than a year after our first encounter on the rainy day at Mosquée Arrahma, I met Nessima on her lunch hour at a vegetarian restaurant in the thirteenth arrondissement of Paris, in the heat of July. I had been to a packed event at Mosquée Arrahma the previous weekend, but I hadn't seen her there.

"I thought I might have run into you at the mosque the other weekend," I commented. "Were you on vacation?"

Nessima shook her head and frowned. She had resigned her women's leadership role at the mosque and had pulled her children out of the mosque's elementary school. I gathered that words had been exchanged, although she didn't want to go into much detail. Several factors had motivated Nessima's decision. First, she had experienced the burnout that plagues many volunteers and unpaid community organizers. Having taken a full-time job in Paris after her divorce was finalized, she now had far less time to dedicate to teaching and organizing at the mosque. Second, she had become uncomfortable with how the mosque culture was developing, and the internal politics were time-consuming. Nessima shrugged. "It's not the mosque that makes you Muslim, after all! But at the same time, it's disappointing."

Nessima's frustration with the rest of the mosque leadership, as well as her disillusionment with the broader institutional project of the mosque complex, was indicative of a broader trend among Muslims of her generation in France, similar in many ways to the "unmosquing" of American Muslims documented by Ahmed Eid.[10] For Nessima and many of her peers, enthusiasm for improving Muslim collective life coexisted with deep frustration and disenchantment with existing institutions. The very individuals who dedicate the greatest effort to religious engagement are often the most pessimistic about local institutions, leaders, and the future of Muslim collective life. While dissatisfaction leads some to abandon institutionalized religion, for many, their dissatisfaction and frustration become a distinct mode of renewed religious commitment.

Even though she had left her hometown mosque, Nessima doubted she would ever fully withdraw from investments in Muslim collective life. She began volunteering with an Islamic charity serving unemployed and unhoused populations around metropolitan Paris. Involved with her sons' school, she also connected with an advocacy group focused on defending the right of women to accompany field trips with their children's classes while wearing a headscarf. She regularly attended group coaching sessions run by a Muslim therapist, and took her sons on a ski trip with an Islamic tour group that integrated evening *dhikr* sessions with long days on alpine slopes. She found new communities, beyond the mosque, the institutes in Saint-Denis, and her old study circle.

The arc of Nessima's still-evolving religious journey highlights the way in which the many Muslim communities and organizations across the Paris area are, for all but their most senior leaders, way stations along a winding path. Ethnographic studies of individual religious communities rarely capture the transience that characterizes many people's participation in these communities, places through which people pass during a season of their life to learn, develop, work, or teach, and then move on. As we saw with Nessima, this transience and flux are often bound up in dissent and dissatisfaction.

This widespread dissatisfaction has been highly generative. Restless circulation anchors and strengthens the organizational fabric of the Paris-area Muslim community, rather than fragmenting it. Like Nessima, many of her peers are disillusioned with existing Islamic institutions, from national organizations to their local mosque, and many have become impatient with the moral emphasis on individual virtue, which they see as inadequate to the ethical and political challenges faced by Muslims today. Instead, they are investing energy in the development of a new Islamic cultural scene: a sphere of social action and intellectual activity that is defined in terms of an "ethical framework" (*cadre éthique*). Like Nessima, many engaged Muslims are driven by a simultaneous dissatisfaction and craving for rootedness. A chronic pessimism about the condition of the French Muslim community is entwined with the persistent hope that this community, or at least some element of it, might soon begin realizing its enormous potential. Discontent has become the engine of a critical restlessness that aims to use cultural change to substantively impact the collective situation of French Muslims. Broad frustration with the existing Islamic institutional landscape has motivated engaged Muslims to shift their focus to building an eclectic religious culture that can address the intersecting moral challenges and malaise faced by French Muslims, both personally and collectively. Moving beyond mosques and Islamic schools, these actors seek to develop a renewed intellectual culture animated by an ethical framework of "fraternal critique."

In the remainder of this chapter, I delve further into this atmosphere of discontent, showing how it is contributing to an intellectual and cultural renaissance of Islam in France. I show how collective frustration is ethically thematized through reference to both "French malaise" and an Islamic "ethics of disagreement." Then I show how this frustration has motivated the development of Muslim social initiatives beyond existing institutional models such as the mosque and Islamic school. Finally, I show how debate and critique are becoming centerpieces of this new ethical culture.

COLLECTIVE FRUSTRATION

"Well, we're French too, you know!" The shaykh's tone was serious. I waited as he paused. It was our first conversation, and I was anticipating a speech about the Republican belonging of second-generation French Muslims.

"We're French," he repeated, "so of *course* we're never happy!" We both laughed heartily.

"But in fact it's true," Shaykh Ahmed continued. "If we see so many young people moving from one institute to the next, one teacher to the next, one organization to the next, this is because there is a discontent in our community that is very typical here in France. In Paris above all, no one is allowed to be satisfied!" I smiled at Ahmed's reference to the common self-deprecating stereotype—Parisians often wryly consider themselves to be the "champions of pessimism."[11]

"Yes," I ventured, "it does seem like people are constantly searching for something."

"Well, from an Islamic point of view, from a spiritual point of view, we are called to be perfectionists. We are not supposed to be happy or content with things as they are today, or with ourselves as we are today. So in fact it's a very *good* thing if people are dissatisfied. And after all, look around! Things as they are right now—what should anyone be satisfied about?" I didn't have an answer for the shaykh, and his question—as well as his quip—stayed with me for a long time.

Shaykh Ahmed, an affable and energetic scholar in his late thirties, with a particular passion for early Islamic history, had recently cofounded an institute of Islamic learning in center-city Paris. His comments about discontent had come in response to my question about why there were so many new institutes forming at the time. For decades, the banlieue of Saint-Denis had been the hub of Islamic learning in metropolitan Paris, anchored by IESH, Oussoul Eddine, and the Centre Tawhid. Since 2010, the oldest schools in Saint-Denis have seen ever-increasing demand, expanding into online learning to serve new student populations for whom the long commute to Saint-Denis is prohibitive. At the same time, dozens of new institutes have arisen in many different regions of the city, including in central Paris. Many of these new institutes have particular thematic emphases, such as Qur'an recitation or calligraphy and the arts, and others have unique formats, such as concentrated weekend intensives or online videoconference classes. As these schools have expanded and multiplied, their clientele has expanded to include students of all ages, backgrounds and professional trajectories. Like Nessima, the students who came of age with the first wave of Islamic institutions in France in the 1980s and 1990s tended to be young people born or raised in France with parents who had immigrated from the Mahgreb, and who were in search of a new and "authentic" relationship to Islam, linked with a global movement of Islamic revival.[12] But in recent years, the population seeking Islamic education has become more diverse in terms of race, ethnicity, and relationship to immigration, and in terms of their approach to religion. Some describe themselves as "on a religious journey," others say they are "not exactly practicing, but interested." Still others are non-Muslims who are interested in learning more about Islam. Increasingly, many of these students go on to integrate their Islamic education with other professional qualifications to develop vocational trajectories that draw on their religious formation, for example in psychotherapy or personal coaching, community nonprofit work, private Islamic elementary and secondary education, or academic research.

Shaykh Ahmed's unique contribution to this rapidly changing world of Islamic education was to combine online coursework with regular spiritual retreats at a comfortable lodge in the French countryside, to deepen the bonds of friendship and solidarity among students, and to offer a taste of the companionship (*suhba*) that historically characterized the relationship between teacher and student in Islamic tradition. "People aren't just in search of knowledge," he explained. "There are all kinds of ways to get 'knowledge,' quote-unquote. Now you can ask Shaykh Google anything you want to know. But students, when they come to learn from a shaykh, among *tullab al-'ilm* [advanced seekers of knowledge], they are really in search of *fraternity*. Fraternity, which is very precious and difficult to find today." For Ahmed, the urban environment demanded an atomized, fast-paced, individualistic lifestyle. It was only by creating a rupture with this environment that seekers of knowledge could find the fraternity and companionship that he understood them to desire.

I had seen this burgeoning landscape as a sign of great enthusiasm for Islamic learning. Instead, Ahmed identified it as a sign of deep collective frustration. Behind every new institute, he explained, was a story of disappointment or conflict. Perhaps there had been splintering leadership, students who felt alienated from their teachers, an inability to pay the utility bills—or just a feeling that something was missing from the available ways of engaging with Islamic learning in greater Paris. New initiatives, whether in the form of a school, a community organization, or a political project, came out of the potent combination of passion and vision for the Muslim community and total exasperation with its current state. These patterns of disengagement and reengagement in collective religious life were themselves key sources for ethical reflection. Shaykh Ahmed's line about being French and therefore never happy put this broad dissatisfaction in an interesting light. He recognized and named the collective frustration, but he didn't lament it. On the contrary, Ahmed described discontent as not only a natural reaction to the exclusion, discrimination, and alienation experienced by many French Muslims, but also as both a typically French state of mind and a pious Muslim attitude. Rather than calling for a spirit of contentment, he argued that it was *discontent* that should be encouraged and refined. Shaykh Ahmed identified discontent as a crucial moral resource. His ethical thematization of discontent drew together a diffuse sense of "French malaise" with a reappropriation of classical Islamic ethical concepts, including the ethics of disagreement (*adab al-ikhtilaf*).

There are four main reasons for the pessimism and discontent that Ahmed identified in the Paris-area Muslim scene. First, there is an elective affinity between activism and frustration, enthusiasm and pessimism. The people who are the most passionately invested in something are often also the most critical, the most likely to be frustrated when they feel that something they care about is not realizing its potential. Second, as Shaykh Ahmed alluded to, there is a widespread sense of malaise in French society at large—a feeling, shared across many strata of society, that "France is doing badly"—*la France va mal*. Third, many French Muslims are exhausted by the incessant political instrumentalization of Islam, alarmed by the rise of far-right populism across Europe, and frustrated by persistent and systemic inequalities and discrimination based on race, ethnicity, and religion, whether in education, employment, housing, access to cultural capital, or everyday interactions at the supermarket. Finally, most French Muslims have little confidence in the most prominent and long-standing Islamic institutions and supposed representatives, particularly the French Council of the Muslim Religion, or CFCM.[13] There is a strong feeling that French Muslims need new organizational models, new spokespeople, new activists and new philosophers.

"THE FRENCH MALAISE"

The idea of a characteristic national pessimism, or *malaise français*, referenced by Shaykh Ahmed, was originally formulated in the 1950s and was revived during the late twentieth century. This concept has seen a worried resurgence since the 2007–8 economic crisis, although it does not necessarily correlate with lack of economic well-being, as noted by Hervé Le Bras.[14] The analytic of "French malaise" intensifies and politicizes the trope of discontent, evoking a nationwide pessimism with numerous intersecting societal causes.[15] Like Émile Durkheim's classic analysis in *Suicide*, the idea of French malaise rests on the integration of individual dissatisfactions—underemployment, ill health, loneliness, lack of purpose, anomie—into a sociological framework. It also marks a strong identification between the individual and the Republic. The persistent refrain that "la France va mal" expresses the strong sense that personal destiny and national destiny are bound up together. If French malaise is, in the words of political historian Pierre Rosanvallon, "the expression of a void, the difficulty in projecting oneself positively into the future, an absence of horizon," it is experienced simultaneously on the individual and the collective level.[16] The difficulty of projecting the *Republic* positively into the future becomes entwined with a personal "absence of horizon."

While "French malaise" is often framed in terms of nationalist nostalgia, it is not the exclusive province of the white working class. French malaise is most often portrayed as a malady of the working- or middle-class white French citizen—squeezed by rising economic inequality, enraged at out-of-touch political elites, and perhaps nostalgic for bygone empire. Whether French malaise is understood in terms of neoliberal reforms and increasing precariousness, in terms of the story of cultural and racial supremacy offered by the far right, or in terms of the perceived fragmentation of French society, the anxiety that not all French participate in the same "national myth," immigration and its discontents are at the center. And yet, in this respect as in so many others, the inheritors of immigration are "as French as everyone else."¹⁷ Too often identified as a *cause* of "French malaise," Muslims are also discouraged and pessimistic about the future of their country, in a way that is bound up with personal malaise. They too are concerned about their economic security, their retirement, their children's education, and the moral direction of the nation. As Shaykh Ahmed highlighted, the diffuse discontent that has animated the Paris-area scene of Islamic activity is a particularly *French* malaise, even if Muslims' affective relationship to the Republic is constituted through tension and exclusion rather than nostalgia.

In his first book, *Foul Express*, prominent French civil rights activist Marwan Muhammad narrates malaise in a way that connects his childhood loneliness to an adult critique of the structural inequalities and racialized politics of French society. Muhammad is especially attentive to how material and spatial inequalities shape the emotional and spiritual development of children who are made to understand themselves as outsiders to France:

> Lonely children recognize one another. They have that sad glimmer in their eyes and the bottomless heart that God has endowed them with. Few notice it, but they know. He did circles on his bike around the Lac d'Annecy to escape the hard looks of the other children. She constructed an imaginary world to escape her housing project in Noisy-le-Grand. As for me, I prepared for war against this world that didn't love me. Against the popular boys whom everyone liked. Against the teachers who wrote me off. Against France, who didn't want me—who rejected me so firmly and so well that in the end, I didn't want her either.¹⁸

The articulation of malaise in *Foul Express* draws out the affective relationship between the individual, his social circumstances, and the Republic, but rather than being grounded in nationalist nostalgia, this malaise is constructed agonistically with the nation, framed in terms of her rejection rather than her romance. Rather than through a political or identitarian commitment to the French Republic, Muhammad expresses his Frenchness in the register of malaise and dissent. Muhammad's memoir captured the experience of many of his generation, through his conjuncture of emotional isolation, structural exclusion, historical oppression, and the desire to escape Paris. *Foul Express* grew from an independently published book into a multiauthor blog and active volunteer organization, giving voice to the many young people who had recognized themselves in Muhammad's "lonely children." Muhammad himself left Paris to work in Tokyo, until he reached a point of moral crisis regarding his career in finance and banking. He felt compelled to return to France to change the situation of his compatriots and rose to national prominence as the spokesperson and later president of the Collective against Islamophobia in France (CCIF).[19]

Foul Express contributed to a growing body of writing by Muslim inheritors of immigration that has combined a systemic political critique of inequality and discrimination in France with spiritual and moral critiques directed internally to the French Muslim community. As we saw with Nessima, collective frustration has often been oriented as much within the French Muslim community as toward broader French society. Throughout the early 2010s, some young intellectuals argued that the Muslim community had collectively failed to provide a spiritual education adequate to the dramatic moral challenges it faced, from Islamophobia to climate change.[20] In the eyes of many of these emergent intellectuals, earlier generations of Muslim leaders had been deliberately quietist, wanting to distance themselves from the anti-racist activist movements of the 1980s and early 1990s, and focused on personal piety, family life, and working-class survival. This desire to "not rock the boat" no longer sat well with a new generation of Muslim leaders. A new cadre of intellectuals and activists joined local community members in articulating a need for religious discourse and forms of collective action that could offer a moral grounding for the dissatisfactions and frustrations that were broadly shared by French Muslims.

The ethical thematization of discontent by scholars like Shaykh Ahmed and activists like Marwan Muhammad has been part of the development of an Islamic moral critique that responds to contemporary French social challenges. With his insistence that Muslims are "called to be perfectionists," Shaykh Ahmed recalled an injunction, expressed throughout the Islamic tradition, for believers to actively and deliberately practice holding themselves and one another to the highest standard. Through the concepts of "enjoining good and forbidding wrong," the "training of the soul," and "corrective advice," a large repertoire of Islamic ethical texts offers detailed reflection on how to work toward personal and collective aspirations to excellence (*ihsan*). And indeed, in the French context, the "call to be perfectionists" Shaykh Ahmed spoke of was also often termed a "call to excellence." For many, this call to excellence was understood as a religious imperative to perform at the very highest level of one's capacity—not only in the moral and spiritual domains, but in the academic and professional ones as well. The fact that we are all perpetually found wanting according to this high standard was, for Shaykh Ahmed, precisely the point. Complacency, he argued, was the real moral danger—either with oneself, one's community, or society at large.

AN ETHICS OF DISAGREEMENT

The moral valence given to discontent and dissent in contemporary Muslim French culture may be "typically French," as Shaykh Ahmed remarked, but it is far from being *uniquely* French. Disagreement has long played a prominent role in Islamic ethical and legal thought. Human difference and diversity are mentioned repeatedly in the Qur'an as divinely created, offering humans the opportunity to learn from one another. Differences of opinion and interpretation of sacred sources emerged early and often in the Islamic tradition, and became structural to Islamic jurisprudence and moral thought as both developed through the eighth and ninth centuries. Differences in practice and interpretation among different regions and schools of law were accepted by the juridical establishment, and in the tenth and eleventh centuries, legal scholars fleshed out an "ethics of disagreement" (*adab al-ikhtilaf*)—a mannerly approach to dispute between jurists that recognized ample room for differing interpretation while prioritizing overarching Muslim unity.[21] Following adab al-ikhtilaf was meant to ensure that no matter how spirited the debates, scholars would participate in the shared goal of discovering and detailing the divinely revealed path for human life, the *shari'a*, to the best of their intellectual capacity.

The ethics of disagreement received renewed attention in the late twentieth and early twenty-first centuries, most notably by Taha al-Jabir al-'Alwani, an Iraqi scholar who emigrated to the United States in the 1980s. Al-'Alwani's treatise on the subject of ikhtilaf opens with a vivid description of the malaise of the global Muslim community:

> The contemporary Muslim world is afflicted by numerous diseases which have spread to almost every aspect of its being. Moral torpor and intellectual paralysis, subversion from within, subjugation from without, the absence of justice and fair dealing, exploitation and corruption, extremes of ignorance and disease, poverty and waste, dependence and insecurity, discord and internecine strife—the list is long and painful. . . . Beset by

such catastrophic afflictions, one wonders in fact how the universal community of believers—the Muslim Ummah—has survived.

Arguably the most dangerous disease which now afflicts the Muslim Ummah is the disease of disagreement and discord.[22]

But if ikhtilaf is the disease of the umma, Al-ʿAlwani argues, *correct* ikhtilaf is its cure. This new adab al-ikhtilaf is somewhat related to the practice of Sunni legal pluralism, or what Ahmed Fekry Ibrahim calls "pragmatic eclecticism," drawing opinions from more than one school of Islamic law.[23] In the contemporary context of hermeneutical pluralism,[24] the legal concept of adab al-ikhtilaf—the ethics of disagreement—has reached new prominence. But rather than offering a "manners for debate" between jurists with broadly shared understandings of the task of ethico-legal reasoning, the new adab al-ikhtilaf actually valorizes the inevitable disagreements among Muslims as a rich inheritance of the Islamic tradition, a diversity to be appreciated and even cultivated. Al-ʿAlwani's text on ikhtilaf was translated into French in 2010 and was referenced several times at events I attended in the mid-2010s.[25]

Indeed, this reappropriated meaning of adab al-ikhtilaf as a moral concept regulating community debate had such widespread resonance in the Paris-area Muslim landscape that recontextualization was often needed to present ikhtilaf as a concept belonging primarily to the *fiqh* tradition. On the first day of an introductory fiqh course at a new institute of Islamic sciences just inside the périphérique, the instructor opened the course with a lecture and class discussion on ikhtilaf. He introduced the concept through a well-known hadith in which the Prophet Muhammad hears of his companions' differing interpretations of one of his instructions and does not favor either of them over the other. In the hadith, Muhammad instructs a group of his companions who are setting out on a short journey in a context of war to pray the afternoon ʿasr prayer when they have reached their destination. Due to an unexpected delay, the time for ʿasr comes before they have reached their destination. Some pray ʿasr at the normal time; some wait to pray it until reaching their destination.

"Which do you think was correct?" the instructor asked the class. "The group of companions who prayed at the normal time, or those who prayed at the destination?" It was the first day of class, so students were tentative to raise their hands. Finally, a girl in the back spoke up. "Both were correct," she said. "The Prophet did not say that either of them were wrong." The instructor hesitated. "A show of hands," he decided. "How many agree that both groups were correct?" The majority of students raised their hands. "But how can this be the case?" he exclaimed.

> It simply cannot be that the Prophet intended for his companions to pray 'asr on the way to the place of Banu Qurayzah *and* once they had reached it—it's not logical. This is a clear example of the division between literalists and those who read for the spirit of the text. The literalists—the ones who delayed their prayer until reaching the village—were wrong to put the exact words of the Prophet before the general principle that prayers should be done on time. The ones who were right are those who read for the spirit, and who understood that they should pray 'asr at the normal time. The Prophet let this ikhtilaf stand only as a mercy, a *rahma*, to his community.[26] He knew it would be too hard for all Muslims to discern the true spirit of his words.

Most of the class, however, disagreed. "I can't see it that way," said my deskmate, Hanane, later. "Isn't the mercy of *ikhtilaf* not just avoiding *fitna* [internal discord], but seeing how *both* interpretations can be legitimate? That there is not just one good way to understand the sources? That maybe there are paths to understand them that we haven't even come to yet? Anyway, in my opinion, that's the lesson of the Banu Qurayzah hadith, and so many disagreements within our community today." Many in the group nodded. For Hanane and her classmates, the ethics of disagreement was thus also a hermeneutical frontier. While their teacher insisted upon the unique validity of "reading for the spirit of the text" over and against literalism, and framed ikhtilaf as an extension of divine generosity toward the ignorant or recalcitrant, the students saw in it a more robust affirmation of the possible coexistence of multiple contradictory interpretations of a source, including, perhaps, interpretations yet to be made. This was a significant methodological departure. Discontent, argument, and critique were described as themselves moral or religious obligations—necessary responses to the present condition of French Muslims, and part of what Muslims owe to one another as brothers and sisters.

The moral valence of ikhtilaf was exemplified at a roundtable debate among five francophone Muslim intellectuals held on a Sunday morning at a mosque in a banlieue just outside of Paris. The event served as a fundraiser for the mosque, which was in the process of raising money for a "real mosque" to replace the repurposed industrial space its congregation currently used. There were several hundred people in attendance, and an abundant picnic was being prepared under tents outside. In the course of a wide-ranging discussion of law and ethics, Shaykh Mourad, an imam, teacher, itinerant lecturer, and widely respected scholar of Islamic law, argued that traditional sources could uphold the ability of qualified women to lead mixed-gender prayers.[27] "But in what mosque of France could I say this?" he asked his audience. "*That's* what intellectual autonomy means." This claim had the intended effect of unsettling his audience, and uneasy murmurs rippled through the crowd. Finally, a man stood up to address the shaykh. A cordless microphone was brought to him. "Shaykh, respectfully, I don't believe you," the man said. "I really don't. But I don't like to think that there are things in Islam, things in our tradition, that are going unsaid because those who have studied them are afraid. I'm no 'alim [scholar]. But I don't think you are right about this. But whatever the case is, I want to know." One of the other panelists, Djibril, a community organizer in his thirties jumped in excitedly.

> See, that's good ikhtilaf! It's mutual critique, critique that goes both ways, the fact that we can all gather here and debate and not be in agreement. It's the proof that the critical method is nothing but another way of entering into the fraternal method. It is a fraternal critique [*une critique fraternelle*]. A method of elevating the level of the community, just like Shaykh Mourad said.
>
> Because that's *our* responsibility, a responsibility that we have inherited from the history of immigration, without which we would never have found ourselves together in this room, having this argument. That history has brought many difficulties, sure. But it has also brought us this opportunity for synthesis, for ikhtilaf, and for fraternity, that for me is very, very precious.

Djibril creatively expands the idea of ikhtilaf to encompass all levels of community debate. He uses it as a broader index of "difference," referencing the internal diversity of the French Muslim community, in terms of national origin, ethnicity, race, and class, among other factors, that has brought "an opportunity for synthesis, for ikhtilaf, for fraternity," and the commensurate moral responsibility, he implies, to fulfill these opportunities. Djibril uses the concept of ikhtilaf to open up a terrain of principled disagreement and debate. He identifies "good ikhtilaf" in both Shaykh Mourad's norm-challenging assertion about women leading mixed-gender prayers, and in the audience member's dissent, explicitly articulated as a desire to better understand the shaykh's argument, and make space for it in community discourse.

Djibril frames all of this as part of the "inheritance of immigration"—the eclectic and plural Islamic discursive sphere that would not exist, he suggests, without the sociopolitical history of postcolonial immigration to France.

As we saw with Hanane and the Banu Qurayzah hadith above, Djibril's invocation of "fraternal critique" is explicitly a question of methodology of religious argument. Some, like the instructor of the fiqh class or the audience member challenging Shaykh Mourad, do seek a single "right answer" rather than an environment of spirited disagreement and debate. But my analytical emphasis lies with those, like Djibril or the students in the fiqh class, who value disagreement for its own sake. I found this value and critical method to be more prominent among a younger generation of engaged Muslims than among older authority figures like the instructor of the fiqh class. In a certain sense, advocates of fraternal critique like Hanane and Djibril can be understood as part of a vanguard, an intellectually influential minority within their larger group, working to form and transform the collective through their embodied social activism and discursive practices. The concept of a "vanguard" has a more specific sense, however, in prominent twentieth-century discourses of Islamic revival. Drawing loosely on Leninist models of social change, influential political reformers such as Egyptian Sayyid Qutb and Pakistani Abu A'la Al-Mawdudi envisioned an authentically Muslim vanguard that would be able to hold itself at some reserve from the surrounding society, while simultaneously working to influence it.[28] Engaged French Muslims do not constitute a vanguard in this sense of Qutb, Mawdudi, or their intellectual heirs—in contrast, they are deeply embedded in their surrounding communities and wider societies. Their investment in improving the "Muslim community" of France takes the form of active participation in collective life, which is directly linked to active participation in French society more broadly.

Engaged Muslims have channeled their "ethics of disagreement" and their frustration with existing models for Muslim collective life in three overlapping ways: reimagining Islamic institutions, engaging in direct social action, and developing a renewed intellectual culture. A thirst for new models of religious community and new formats for responding to urgent moral and political challenges has sparked an effusive experimentation in Islamic associations since the early 2010s. Some of this experimentation has come from within existing institutions, as we saw with Mosquée Arrahma. But much of it has come from new initiatives, outside of the traditional structures of mosques, schools, or national umbrella organizations.

MUSLIM COMMUNITY BEYOND THE MOSQUE

Nadia, a psychologist and mother in her forties, had founded of one of these new initiatives, an organization dedicated to women's self-discovery. Like Nessima, she had been deeply involved in mosques and Islamic schools in her twenties and early thirties, but she too had become disillusioned. "Honestly, I've had enough of mosques!" Nadia gave a half-embarrassed smile and lowered her voice, even though we were in an anonymous café in the winding underground complex of Châtelet-Les Halles, in central Paris. "Every time I go to the market someone is fundraising for a new mosque. Does every single corner of the Paris region need its own mosque? Aren't there other things to be doing with our money, better ways to be reaching the young generation?" Nadia paused and stirred her espresso.

> Well, I'll tell you—the mosques are for old people. Don't misunderstand me, they should have them! They've worked so hard for many decades; now they are retiring and they want a mosque in their neighborhood. At last, they have the time to spend there. They can meet up, they can reflect. Very good! But it's not the future of our community. My dream is to build a center dedicated to the holistic well-being of the Muslim woman. There would be classes, therapy, sports, lectures, and just space and time for socialization, a tea room. And childcare! I don't think we need to go through the mosques to do that. Actually, I don't think that we *can*.

Nadia's dream of a multifunctional community center, a "third space" akin to what Justine Howe describes in the US context, was shared by many engaged Muslims.[29] Some advocated within mosques or religious schools to evolve into more dynamic institutions that met the needs and desires of broad Muslim publics. Others, like Shaykh Ahmed, founded new religious schools. Still others, like Nadia, built mobile nonprofits and community organizations that sought to create pockets of Muslim community in diverse spaces across the metropolis and through social media, in the absence of resources to acquire a physical location. These mobile organizations included women's exercise classes in the back room of a commercial space, a consciousness-raising group in a *salon de thé*, and an improv theater collective in a recording studio rented by the hour. All of these settings were animated by a desire to cultivate an "ethical milieu" (*cadre éthique*) for socialization and collective development among Muslims, and to diversify and deepen the Islamic scene of greater Paris. While many of these organizations are anchored by leisure or cultural activities, they make frequent reference to "respect for Islamic values" as an organizing principle. And just as Shaykh Ahmed noted that many young Muslims seek out coursework in Islamic sciences as much for the fraternity as for the knowledge, leaders of Islamic nonprofits and cultural organizations observe that their members are as interested in religious education as they are in Zumba, in tutoring middle school students, or in theater. These small-scale cultural organizations, part of the rich French social fabric of *associations*, are also sites of learning, teaching, and implementing Islamic knowledge, values, and norms. They can also be vehicles for the accumulation of limited cultural capital by marginalized social actors, as in Catherine Wihtol de Wenden and Rémy Leveau's analysis of a wryly self-described "*beurgeoisie*" emerging from Maghrebi community organizations in the 1980s and 1990s.[30]

Nadia's inspiration to found a community organization, along with her collaborator and lifelong friend, Sara, an art educator, came out of their experience teaching religion classes for young children at a local mosque. This role was the culmination of over a decade of engagement in formal Islamic education and mosque life in their hometown, a banlieue northeast of Paris. But over the course of several years, Nadia and Sara realized that in fact, it was the mothers of their young pupils who were in extreme need of a type of psychological and social support that the mosque was not providing. After unsuccessfully advocating for these mothers' needs within the mosque, they resigned their roles and founded The Reflecting Pool (TRP),[31] an organization "dedicated to the accomplishment and acceptance of the self." Like so many small-scale community organizations, The Reflecting Pool was a relatively short-term project, operating between 2012 and 2017. But during these years, it became a touchstone for a new generation of organizing around Islam and parenting.

"We use the phrase 'reflecting pool,'" Sara explained, "because we wanted women to see their own selves reflected back to them, like a mirror. Not the reflections of others—society, their families, their religious community, etc.—but their own selves on their own terms, in a way they had never seen before." Within a month of the launch of TRP, and thanks to a skillful buildup on social media, Nadia and Sara were inundated with women around the Paris region who wanted to participate in their organization. Going from neighborhood to neighborhood, TRP organized group and one-on-one coaching sessions that use a range of therapeutic techniques and group exercises—role play, trust-building, collaborative mind-mapping—to develop women's self-confidence, self-knowledge, and fulfillment. Particularly oriented toward young mothers, TRP invited a range of perinatal professionals and early-childhood educators to collaborate with Nadia and Sara to offer women a space of informed reflection on their roles as mothers, wives, workers, sisters, and friends, all "through the light of Islam." "I have years of education in Islamic sciences," Nadia explained.

> And it will always be part of who I am. But when it came down to it, faced with a baby, a toddler, a spouse, a career I struggled to maintain, my teaching at the mosque, and then all these pressures, from society, from the community, to be this kind of perfect mother or that kind of perfect woman ... "Breastfeeding for how long?" "Only organic, or is that too *bobo* [bohemian-bourgeois]?" "Oh, you still work—you *have to* work?" But then if you don't, "You're just another oppressed Muslim housewife!"
>
> And I realized that none of my religious education had truly prepared me for the simplest and most complicated thing—how to find and realize my authentic self in the midst of all of that. So that's what we do. Some could call it "empowerment." But it is a fundamentally spiritual project.

Like Shaykh Ahmed's Islamic school and countryside retreats, Nadia and Sara's project of "women's self-development through the light of Islam" came out of a frustration that existing Islamic organizations were not meeting the full moral and spiritual needs of their constituents, not encountering them in the messiness of everyday life. TRP was exemplary of the domain of cultural and leisure activity in an Islamic framework that has emerged out of discontent with the existing institutional landscape.

"ENGAGED PESSIMISTS"

While many people I interviewed described themselves as *musulmans engagés* (engaged Muslims), they often disavowed, in nearly the very same breath, the existence of a rich sphere of Islamic ethical activity in France. During initial meetings with school administrators, nonprofit leaders, students, and imams across the Paris area, I was often told apologetically that there was sadly not much of interest for me to study. The state of Islamic engagement in France was deplorable, people said, and the community should be ashamed. If I really wanted to see Muslims doing something worthwhile, they often asked, why hadn't I stayed in my own country? Everything, they were sure, was being done so much better in the United States.

I began to push back somewhat when I heard this assessment. "How can you say that there is no such thing as Islamic engagement in France," I asked Yassine, an architect and tireless volunteer, "when you are leading an organization of dozens of people invested in social change, and you raise tens of thousands of euros every year?"

"Look, Kirsten," he said firmly, "as long as you keep talking to people like us, you are never going to understand the Muslim community in France." This was a surprise to me, as Yassine seemed to me like a leader in the community.

"In fact, we are so marginal," he continued. "We don't represent the community. We are not the average Muslim [*le musulman lambda*]. The community in general, the average Muslim, they don't understand what we are doing at all. People aren't engaged. People don't even care." Yassine sighed. "It's why we have so much work to do." I observed that this seemed quite pessimistic.

"Yes, actually that's what I call myself. I always say that I'm an engaged pessimist. Frankly, it's the only option." As I spent more time with the community organization that Yassine had founded, I began to hear this phrase, "engaged pessimist," used by other volunteers. It was clearly a term that resonated. This term reflected a delicate and constantly negotiated balance between "engagement"—benevolent social activism as an expression of piety and even hope—and "pessimism"—the malaise or "absence of horizon" that we saw above.

Yassine's point—namely, that focusing on the religiously engaged does not offer a representative overview of all Muslims—is, as he says, crucial for understanding the current state of Islam in France. The network of people who circulate through mosques, Islamic schools, and community activist organizations is, necessarily, an unrepresentative minority of the Muslim population of France. People who do actively participate in collective Muslim life often describe themselves as "engaged Muslims" (*musulmans engagés* or *musulmans actifs*). They sometimes contrast this, as Yassine did above, with the typical or average Muslim, *le musulman lambda*.

In much social scientific literature on Islam in Europe, and in many European Muslim contexts, the category of "practicing Muslims" (*musulmans pratiquants*) is used to demarcate Islamic ritual observance from the simple fact of Muslim identity, the latter being shared by the very devout, less devout, ambivalent, and resolutely secular alike. Many surveys distinguish the large majority who self-identify as "believing Muslims" from those who identify as "practicing Muslims," and then ask about multiple forms of religious practice: completing all or some of the daily prayers, observing the Ramadan fast, paying zakat, and attending Friday prayers at the mosque, as well as markers of personal piety such as abstaining from alcohol or, for women, wearing a head covering.[32] The gradual emergence of "engaged Muslim" as a term of self-identification has replaced this focus on degrees of ritual practice and personal piety with an emphasis on social action—itself understood as an expression of piety and a primary way of practicing Islam.

Engaged Muslims have varying approaches to ritual practice, theological points of view, and trajectories of religious involvement. Some had an experience of spiritual awakening and recommitment to religious practice as young adults, while others have been religiously devout in a consistent way since childhood. Still others might identify as engaged Muslims and participate actively in Muslim community life without scrupulously observing all daily prayers, for example. Their understanding of piety is grounded in action-oriented engagement in their community and in French society at large. The engaged Muslim is distinguished by what she is engaged *in*, or whom she is engaged *for*. Whether she is engaged in the struggle for gender justice, in the fight against Islamophobia, for the human dignity of refugees, or for the educational quality of her children's school, her engagement is inspired by her religious tradition, but not delimited by a single understanding of orthodoxy. As indicated by Yassine's concept of "engaged pessimism," many engaged Muslims are motivated by the sense of collective frustration that we saw above, thematized as a moral and religious imperative. Rather than allowing their dissatisfaction with various aspects of Muslim collective life to alienate them from religion, engaged Muslims are determined to improve the condition of their community—spiritually and ethically as well as materially and politically.

Engaged Muslims emphasize that in order to realize this collective improvement, their horizon of activism must extend beyond Muslim contexts to include French society at large. In the run-up to the 2012 French presidential elections, the Paris-area chapter of the Young Muslims of France (JMF), a national Muslim youth organization linked to the UOIF (later Musulmans de France), released a short video as part of their "get out the vote" campaign, "Bougez, votez."[33] The video was made up of short clips in which smiling, young, and energetic JMF members, in the process of going about their daily lives on the bus, at school, or in the office, held up posters with phrases that combined to spell out a text that read, in part:

I am Muslim / and proud [*Je suis musulman et fier / Je suis musulmane et fière*]
I am Muslim and engaged / I am Muslim and determined

For my community / For our national community
I am confident for my community / I mobilize for my community

Liberty / Equality / Fraternity
are not empty words
We still believe in them

Respect / Work / Giving of oneself / Altruism
Grow my community / Help me to grow myself

I need others / Others need me
I mobilize for them
We are mobilized
—and you?

The JMF video made explicit the values of civic responsibility and orientation toward the collective that inspires engaged Muslims more broadly. It showcased the diversity of the JMF community and the different terrains in which they practice their social engagement—an apartment block in the banlieues, the exterior of a government building, university libraries, workplaces, and a range of streetscapes in Paris and its banlieues. The video highlighted the way that engaged Muslims draw on Republican values while at the same time centering the project of strengthening the Muslim community. In this way, the JMF went beyond the idea of Frenchness and Muslimness as compatible *identities* to insist on Republicanism and Islam as ethical traditions and practices that could reinforce one another. The JMF's explicit acknowledgment that Republican values may sound to many like trite slogans recognizes that many of their peers are deeply disillusioned with politicized invocations of founding French ideals that many find to be selectively applied in practice. Challenging this disillusionment, engaged Muslims claim the mantle of the true defenders of freedom, equality, fraternity, and secularism, all of which, they argue, have been perverted by political elites ranging from the nationalist right to "radical secularists" on the left. Indeed, they disarticulate this commitment to French values from a commitment to the state itself. Addressing themselves to their peers, the JMF issued an explicit invitation to help build a community that is diverse, active, and focused on organizing around a sense of shared purpose. At the same time, by circulating their message publicly on YouTube, they announced all of these attributes as the hallmarks of engaged Islam. In this video, the JMF draws particularly on two of the four repertoires I identified in the introduction, combining a revivalist emphasis on moral activism and dedication to the Muslim community with an engagement with Republican values that both appropriates and subverts state discourses on Islam, secularism, and democracy.

In this appropriation and subtle subversion of Republican values, engaged Muslims tend to work in parallel to, rather than in direct engagement with, more radical decolonial groups such as the Parti des Indigènes de la République (PIR), a political group founded by and for the descendants of people colonized by France, the "indigenized" residents of working-class neighborhoods, and, more broadly, "all those who have a stake in these struggles."[34] (Colonial subjects were known as *indigènes*, or "natives," under the *Code de l'indigénat*, the legal framework that established inferior rights for colonized peoples.) While, as Jennifer Fredette notes, perhaps the single unifying force among French Muslims is their unanimous rejection of political elites' discourses on Islam,[35] groups like the JMF undertake this rejection by cannily *deploying* Republican values, working *within* French civic institutions, and generally advocating greater participation in French public life. As Margot Dazey has observed, the Musulmans de France (formerly UOIF), parent organization of the JMF, deploys a version of pious respectability politics as a strategy in order to rebut and cope with anti-Muslim hostility.[36] This is quite distinct from the pugnacious critique of French universalism of the PIR. I argue, however, that such strategies carve out a space for a civic Muslim practice that is *also* a form of political critique of the hypocrisy and anti-Muslim hostility of state elites. It is worth noting, too, that middle-class engaged Muslims are perhaps not so invested in tearing down "the system" of French universalism precisely because they have been moderately successful within it, despite many barriers. They tend to want to broaden the narrow pathways to success for racially, religiously, and economically marginalized French people, rather than undermining the very idea of universalism.

The positive ethos of productivity, determination, and civic sociability emphasized in the "Bougez, votez" video is held in tense balance with the frustration and even "pessimism," in Yassine's term, that also undergird the broader engaged Muslim scene. As Yassine pointed out, engaged Muslims often feel that they are operating on the margins or at the vanguard of their broader community. Their endeavors are frequently marked by disillusionment, and many move in and out of religious engagement at different periods of life. Despite this, they strive to channel an ethical idealism that calls French Muslims to their most cherished aspirations—aspirations that include a reappraised version of the Republican triptych of *liberté, égalité,* and *fraternité*.

While the JMF is linked to a prominent national Islamic organization, engaged Muslim cultural discourse emerges from heterogeneous sources, often well outside the French Muslim establishment. In 2016, a collective of French Muslim writers, artists, and intellectuals, calling themselves "Les éditions du Grand Remplacement," published a single issue of a literary and cultural review, *Téléramadan*. The magazine's title is a portmanteau of *Télérama*, a popular French media review, and Ramadan. Several key members of "Les éditions du Grand Remplacement" were associated with Bondy Blog, an online news media outlet founded in 2005 to offer the "perspective of the banlieues" through reporting that was rare in mainstream media at the time. *Téléramadan* came out of a similar spirit, wanting to represent Islam and Muslims "in the first person," in a text created "by and for those who observe Ramadan." Although much of its content—film reviews, short fiction, recipes, oral history interviews—rejected the politicized framing of Islam in France, the project did not shy away from provocation. "Great Replacement," the title of a 2011 anti-immigrant text by Renaud Camus, has become shorthand for white nationalist conspiracy theories about France's social and economic situation, according to which immigrants and Muslims, aided and abetted by "Islamo-leftist" elites, are staging a "great replacement" of autochthonous French civilization. The "Éditions du Grand Remplacement" introduced themselves with this statement:

> We are the Great Replacement. But certainly not the one that the crazy people might fantasize. We are a natural great replacement, that of one generation after the others, of the cycle of life. We are the present. We are the Great Replacement of an archaic system that no longer speaks to us, and has never considered us to be its children. We are radical in our ideas; we take beauty to its limits. We will write when you want us to shut up, and we will fight when you have decided that it is time to go to bed. We will reclaim our place, which has been taken by those who have been officially authorized to think.[37]

With this statement, the *Téléramadan* team appropriated the language of white nationalist conspiracy theorists and reframed it through a generational revolutionary spirit that, perhaps unlike the "respectability politics" of the JMF analyzed above, did not shy away from overt antagonism. Throughout

Téléramadan, an eclectic group of contributors combine this tone of provocation and critique with the material and intellectual markers of an emergent cultural elite: a glossy, high-concept magazine with slick design and art photography, Ramadan recipes from celebrated chefs, and interviews with César-winning filmmakers.

The magazine also featured short fiction, original reporting on themes ranging from Ramadan in the Calais refugee camp to sexual practices among unmarried couples observing Ramadan, and an oral history that the writer, Latifa Oulkhouir (later editor in chief of Bondy Blog), conducted with her own mother, who had come to France from Morocco in 1983. The contributors to *Téléramadan*, all Ramadan-observers living in France with an average age of twenty-two, approached the theme of Ramadan from the point of view of its eclectic lived practice in France. They were not concerned with questions of religious orthodoxy, and they sought an expansive understanding of pious and cultural attachments to Ramadan and to Islam more broadly. They wrote articles they would like to read, and featured prominent individuals in French society whose relationships to Ramadan and to Islam they wanted to hear more about: sociologist Nilufer Göle, rapper Médine, actress Maïwenn, and novelist Faïza Guène, among others. The multilayered cover of Téléramadan enacts the peeling back of layers of perception to uncover a different representation. From the outside, the woman is obscured, with only her eyes visible through a cutout. On the next page, she is represented in a black abaya, and finally, another cutout page is turned to show the full image of the model, actress Oulaya Amamra, in a tracksuit, with flowing curls. This triptych of sorts encapsulates the DuBoisian "double consciousness" that many engaged Muslims describe—a perpetual negotiation between representations of Islam and Muslims in French public discourse, in which they are overwhelmingly reduced to headscarves and terrorism, and the effort to articulate their own relationships to Muslimness that are neither defined by nor oriented toward the majoritarian perception.

As Samuli Schielke has observed, "focusing on the very pious in moments when they are being very pious (in mosque study groups, for example) risks taking those moments when people talk about religion *as* religious persons . . . as the paradigmatic ones."[38] Schielke worries that the recent anthropological focus on pious Muslim spaces and ethical subjectivity, influenced by the landmark work of Saba Mahmood, has overdetermined the weight of piety in the lives of Muslims, many of whom are, of course, uneven, sporadic, and skeptical in their religious engagement.[39] In one sense, looking at the broad arena of cultural activity of "engaged Muslims" can address this concern. Being "engaged" in Muslim community often entails a very different approach to religious piety than the one exemplified by studies of mosque culture, Islamic revival, or pious activism, and situates mosque study groups, for example, as only one element of a more expansive social fabric of Muslim life. At the same time, focusing on the religiously "engaged" only through the sites of their most dedicated engagement can also overdetermine these movements and spaces as definitive of Muslim culture in France. This, in part, is what Yassine warned against—the analytical risks of a focus on spheres of intensified activity that by definition can never represent the experiences of as broad and diverse a demographic as Muslims in France. Indeed, the Paris-area scene of "engaged Muslims" that this book depicts is not representative of French Muslims as a population, just as Paris itself is far from representative of France. And yet, in the way that Paris often "stands for" France in both national and global imaginaries, engaged Muslims are disproportionately influential in "standing for" Islam—working to intervene in representations of Islam and Muslims, and endeavoring to shape the way that French Muslims, engaged or not, think about their own religious community. Engaged Muslims are a prominent element of the social landscape of France as a whole, but they are all too often either ignored or misrepresented when approached through a lens that centers the tensions, presumed to be inherent and intractable, between Muslim piety and the secular Republican way of life.

By foregrounding patterns of disappointment, frustration, disengagement, and reengagement, we can put exuberant promotional videos like the JMF's and manifestos like *Téléramadan*'s in deeper context. For the large majority of people who participate in these groups, they are meaningful but temporary waystations on a trajectory of personal development and exploration, marked by patterns of disillusionment, disengagement, and reengagement. Indeed, the groups themselves are ephemeral—*Téléramadan* lasted only one issue, and many community organizations last only two or three years. However, ephemerality does not make these sites inconsequential. On the contrary, these patterns of disillusionment, disbanding, and reengagement are themselves key resources for ongoing ethical development. For some, disappointment and discontent—with their fellow Muslims and also with themselves—are at the core of their moral self-understanding as pious Muslims. Like Yassine, many characterize "engaged pessimists" as a vanguard agitating on the margins of a larger Muslim community from which they could never be disentangled. Engaged Muslims are defined not just by their spheres of socialization or their ethical or political orientation, but also by their self-conscious status as outliers, critics, and even gadflies, often hoping to ignite a spirit of discontent with the status quo. By tracing the relationship between their discontent and their aspirations, we begin to see a model of moral community that is anchored, rather than fractured, by its internal critique.

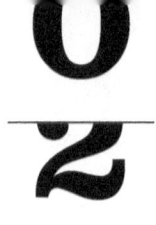

THE PEOPLE OF KNOWLEDGE

For many of the young people seeking knowledge and community in Islamic cultural contexts, a key source of their dissatisfaction lay with Muslim leaders and religious authorities. "Don't be fooled, Kirsten," said Mehdi, an IT professional and president of a community organization who had taken classes at several of the Paris-area institutes of Islamic learning. "In reality, there might be three or four shaykhs in all of France. Of course, we call people Shaykh So-and-So, out of respect and politeness. But real shaykhs? Real people of knowledge? There are very, very few." True people of knowledge, Mehdi argued, would be able to draw on a deep mastery of the Islamic legal, philosophical, and ethical tradition to offer clear, concrete responses to the challenges faced by Muslims in France in the present moment. But he hadn't yet found that type of intellectual culture in any of the institutes where he had studied.

At the same time, many religious leaders are equally frustrated with their publics. Shaykh Mourad, whom we met in chapter 1, deplored what he called the "dictatorship of the masses," which stifled, in his view, the intellectual independence and creativity of Islamic intellectuals. One evening, at the end of a dinner lecture on the life and thought of Imam Malik, held at a small crêpe restaurant in the center of Paris, he elaborated on this tension. The crêperie was packed for Mourad's lecture, the second in a series on the founders of the four schools of Sunni jurisprudence.

For most in the audience, young professionals who worked in the city but lived outside of Paris proper, an evening dinner lecture downtown was an elegant treat, a break from the rhythm of everyday life. To come into the Latin Quarter on a weeknight, hear a rousing intellectual lecture from a highly trained scholar of fiqh, participate in a lively debate on its implications, and linger past midnight over dessert and coffee—all of this was a luxurious moment of repose for the young men and women who filled the restaurant. The time lost in transit and the 10 euro entrance fee was a small price to pay for the warmth and intellectual stimulation of the intimate group that gathered for these regular "Tuesday night seminars." I knew these seminars by reputation for several months before I began attending, as they had been repeatedly recommended to me. "Yes, actually it would be *very* good for you to go to the Tuesday seminars!" said Nawel, a psychologist in her late thirties who had studied with Shaykh Mourad for years. "It would be nice if you university types would pay more attention to places like that when you talk about Islam. They represent Islam too, you know!" Nawel's comment highlighted the fact that places like the crêperie lecture series were not at the center of the public imagination of Islam in France.

For Shaykh Mourad, whose day job as imam of a mosque in a banlieue fifteen miles outside of Paris kept him busy, the opportunity to share his learning with a roomful of eager young students was no less of a pleasure. A handful of those present were the shaykh's private students, who studied individually with him to deepen their knowledge of Islamic jurisprudence and its application in European contexts. Others, like myself, were familiar faces who regularly attended his lectures, either here at the crêperie or at conferences around the metropolitan area. Still others were total strangers, and these, Shaykh Mourad said, brought him the most joy. "Every time I come and speak," he told us that evening, "I see that *subhan Allah* [glory be to God], there are still more young people who are in search of understanding—there is such a thirst, in fact! The question is, are we scholars prepared to meet it? Or are we too comfortable where we are—are we too afraid?" He continued, growing more animated: "Places like this are where the people of knowledge find one another. And you, the people of knowledge, must be the future of the community. This is the problem with us scholars today: we're all afraid of the crowd! If I spoke in my mosque like I speak to you here, what do you think would happen? I'd be run out of town!" Everyone laughed—Mourad's sarcasm was not lost on anyone. He concluded on a provocative note, echoing his intervention at the roundtable some months earlier: "Our intellectual liberty is constrained by the dictatorship of the crowd. The biggest lobby in our community is the masses, and we who are supposed to lead the Muslim community end by meeting their demands. . . . As the people of knowledge, it is up to you to maintain the intellectual liberty of the tradition." The room simmered.

This opposition between "the masses" and "the people of knowledge" was a recurrent theme in Shaykh Mourad's public lectures to a wide range of audiences. Over the years that I attended the shaykh's lectures, sermons, and debates, I came to see reconciling this opposition as his great personal cause. Mourad was passionately preoccupied with bringing scholarship, intellectual rigor, and sharp moral challenges to the mosque, and with urging the younger, educated "people of knowledge" to invest themselves in their local religious communities. In this sense, Shaykh Mourad's "fraternal critique" cut two ways: toward both the "people of knowledge" and the "masses." Mourad saw religious education and secular education as interdependent. He was attentive to the emergent middle class, university-educated young adult Muslim population and saw them as a vanguard full of promise.

In chapter 1, we saw how discontent and fraternal critique were tools for shaping the Muslim community. In this chapter, we turn to diverse educational contexts as key settings for the expression of fraternal critique. These contexts include Islamic educational settings like the crêperie lecture series, French universities and their student organizations, and grassroots volunteer organizations focusing on educational advancement. In each of these settings, we see how class and urban space emerge as key themes for engaged Muslim culture. This chapter focuses on educational and economic mobility as elements of Muslim community formation. As we began to see in the introduction, the place of class in Muslim social ethics is inseparable from the spatial politics of greater Paris, where inequality is mapped onto urban space. For the emergent middle class, top universities and Parisian cultural institutions from the theater to the national library have become sites of Islamic engagement. Grassroots community organizations work to chip away at France's class stratification and shape a "Muslim elite" of the future. At the same time, class is perceived as an inheritance of moral responsibility for upwardly mobile young people who feel a profound accountability to their working-class origins. The organizations highlighted in this chapter carry a critique both of historical patterns of exclusion in France and of the idea that pious practice and elite education are incompatible. They carry out these critiques through building solidarity and kinship, and by making elite institutions spaces for Muslim intellectual development without capitulating to a politics of assimilation.

The ethical formation of the young people whom Shaykh Mourad hailed as "people of knowledge" is shaped and constrained by capitalism and neoliberalization. These young people are working to carve out both material and spiritual conditions of survival, even of flourishing, in the teeth of a capitalist economy predicated on the exploitation of their ancestors and characterized by a level of social mobility that has remained unchanged since the 1970s.[1] Muriam Haleh Davis has shown how in the context of colonial

Algeria, there was a fundamental opposition between "homo economicus" (the "exemplar of European economic modernity") and "homo islamicus" (a racial-religious myth about Muslim fatalism and resistance to capitalist productivism) that "provided a basic grammar that structured debates on colonial policy."[2] Davis argues for the applicability of the analytical frame of racial capitalism to the French-Algerian context, in a way that attends to the local specificities of the "racial regime of religion" that constructed the Muslims as economically unfit and therefore ripe for expropriation and marginalization.[3] In postcolonial France, the particular labor relations and conditions are quite different, but Muslims' "presumably ill-adapted culture" is still frequently blamed for their subaltern economic positions.[4] Those who seek to produce alternate narratives and social formations, such as a "Muslim elite" or a consonance between Islamic and secular knowledge traditions, must navigate the intertwined legacies of colonial racism and capitalism.

INHERITORS OF IMMIGRATION

Rahima is a financial services professional in her early thirties, working for a bank and living with her parents in La Courneuve, a neighborhood of Seine-Saint-Denis, north of Paris. She grew up in the Islamic culture that was the result of the revivalist institution-building of the 1990s, listening to recorded lectures by Tariq Ramadan, enthusiastically attending the annual gathering of Muslims at Le Bourget, and participating in a young women's study circle at her local mosque. Her religious path evolved, from a period in her youth that she later described as "rather Salafist" to a period of deep engagement in French Muslim civic life during her undergraduate years to a period of relative distance from organized religion. Rahima explained that "Islam has always been the same. But my way of living it has changed over the years."

Despite these changes in her way of living, Rahima felt an abiding constancy in her piety, and in her connection to spaces of Muslim collectivity. Over dinner at a halal Thai restaurant in eastern Paris, she spoke of this piety as an affective inheritance from her family. "I learned to love the mosque from my grandfather. I loved him, and he loved the mosque, and I wanted to spend time where he found peace. He used to do spiritual retreat there during Ramadan, and I thought, you know, how beautiful that must be, to live in that atmosphere, that feeling of the mosque. I like to think that I have inherited that feeling from him." She described similar feelings of serenity in many mosques, at certain religious lectures and conferences, and in informal discussion circles of Muslim women. While she had moved among different approaches to the Islamic tradition as an intellectual and ethical project, Rahima experienced constancy, both personally and intergenerationally, in her pious affective inheritance of tranquility and love, emotions that were evoked by religious gatherings and spaces of congregation.

Like many North African men of his generation, Rahima's Moroccan grandfather had worked in France for decades. "This generation built France's roads, her buildings, took the jobs that French people didn't want in the postcolonial period," she explained. "These French people or foreign residents who paid taxes just like everyone else. These people who just wanted to live in peace, who sowed their sweat and only harvested disdain." The love and respect that Rahima held for her grandfather was bound up in her family's history of migration and manual labor as well as his practices of devotion. While the Islamic revival in France has often been framed generationally, as a movement of "modern" young people distancing themselves from their parents' and grandparents' "traditional" forms of Islam, Rahima's pious "feeling of the mosque" was closely linked to her filial piety and sense of indebtedness to her grandfather, his labor, and his sacrifices.[5] Her affective experience of mosques and other spaces of religious collectivity, the aspect of her piety that she described as most enduring over the years, was refracted through her family's intimate history of colonization and immigration. For Rahima, social moments and movements might come and go, but what kept her returning to spaces of Muslim gathering was a connection to her affective inheritance and her self-understanding as a daughter and granddaughter of working-class immigrants.

In *The Suffering of the Immigrant*, sociologist Abdelmalek Sayad writes of emigration as "the product of a fundamental break" of colonization. "More so than any other circumstances that are likely to create or sustain bonds of solidarity, the exile into which the emigrant is forced—in other words the minority existence that is forced upon him and which must be endured when he has to live *amongst others* (who are, as it happens, the colonizers)—inevitably forges new and collective thoughts and hopes."[6] Sayad points here to the relationship between the ruptures of colonization and immigration and the forging of "collective thoughts and hopes." While he writes of these collective hopes in terms of postcolonial nationalism, we can also recognize them in religious forms of collectivity. The eclectic spaces of Islamic revival through which Rahima passed were constituted through the intergenerational inheritance of the "fundamental break" that Sayad described in his work.

Rahima's characterization of her affective inheritance from her grandfather resonates with Ahmed Boubeker's framing of the children and grandchildren of immigrants in France as "inheritors of immigration." This locution recalls and reframes Pierre Bourdieu and Jean-Claude Passeron's classic analysis of social reproduction in French higher education in *The Inheritors*.[7] It underscores the rich cultural and affective patrimony bequeathed to the descendants of immigrants, even while these descendants are excluded from the elite patterns of inheritance that Bourdieu and Passeron documented. Boubeker writes of colonization and immigration as inheritances carried by the descendants of immigrants in France, who have become "'perpetual immigrants,' even though they have not been foreigners to French society for quite some time."[8] In this sense, the rupture becomes a continuity, as each generation inherits the "disdain," in Rahima's terms, that their forebears harvested. As Boubeker observes, the inheritance of immigration is not simply the inheritance of a racialized status of perpetual alterity to the nation-state. It is also the inheritance of "racial-religious" forms of collectivity and mobilization.

Young engaged Muslims like Rahima are drawing on four major repertoires of inheritance from earlier generations to construct a new field of Muslim discourse and culture in contemporary France. First, they are reappraising what has been framed as the "traditional Islam" of North African and West African (and in a few cases Indian Ocean) contexts. This results in a reappropriated understanding of heritage and patrimony—not only the patrimony of ancestral countries of immigration, but also the French patrimony that was constructed by the first generations of migrants whose labor facilitated the modernization of France in the postwar years. Second, they draw on the Islamic revival of the 1980s and 1990s, during which many of the older members of this movement came of age, with its emphasis on personal piety and virtue-oriented morality, and its understanding of Islam as a universalist frame. The institutional legacy of the Islamic revival—from the national federation Muslims of France (MF), formerly known as the Union of Islamic Organizations of France (UOIF), to the associated Muslim Students of France (EMF), to the wave of mosque-building in the early 2000s that we saw in chapter 1—has in many cases been the infrastructure for the emergence of new, postrevivalist articulations of Muslim culture.

Third, they draw selectively on the legacy of French anti-racist movements, beginning with the 1983 "March for Equality and against Racism," and including a subsequent lineage of francophone decolonial thought and leftist anti-racist politics.[9] Prominent national anti-racist organizations such as SOS Racisme have tended to maintain a sharp distinction between racism and anti-religious bias. Efforts to address the absence of attention to racialized religious discrimination led to the creation of the Collective against Islamophobia in France (CCIF) in 2005, an organization dedicated to combating Islamophobia and anti-Muslim racism. The CCIF and its many volunteers and supporters became an important voice in the broader anti-racist movement, facilitating cross-pollination and coalitions between some elements of anti-racist activism and some observant Muslim circles. (The CCIF was shut down by the Ministry of the Interior in 2020, in a crackdown on Muslim organizations discussed in the introduction.)

Finally, engaged Muslims draw on and respond to French state discourses of secularism and integration, at times redeploying these discourses in order to critique what they perceive as the instrumentalization of secularism in media and politics. As select political projects aim to promote social diversity in educational settings, young people of color from Muslim families who attend elite French institutions of higher learning can find themselves both tokenized and isolated. These young people are achieving academic and professional success in a wide variety of fields, from literature to architecture to medicine and engineering. Some frame their aspirations for the broader Muslim community in terms of these trajectories of mobility and achievement within the hierarchical French system. However, race and religion—and the ways in which they are inextricable from one another—complicate this narrative. The socioeconomic advancement of some has not meant, as French politicians long assumed and hoped, that inheritors of immigration are assimilating completely into French lifestyle norms and abandoning their various religious commitments and frames of reference. It has meant, however, that many young Muslims have complete ownership of their French cultural, intellectual, and political inheritance. They draw on all these resources to engage in immanent critique of the loudest current invocations of secularism, Enlightenment values, and the demand for integration.

MUSLIM PLACEMAKING IN THE METROPOLIS

Some young middle-class French Muslims are invested in the formation of the collective subject, the Muslim community of France, through educational advancement and class mobility, and development of cultural critique. These practices entail a new Muslim placemaking, a moral geography that cuts across the périphérique. While Islam is stereotypically associated with the working-class banlieues in the popular imagination, the lecture series at the crêperie was only one of many sites of Muslim community formation in center-city Paris. Islamic schools, cultural cafés, arts events, lecture series, and student organizations flourished across Paris during the 2010s. As Lara Deeb and Mona Harb described in Beirut, this Paris-area Muslim scene offers a "moral leisure"—an atmosphere of fun and entertainment framed by moral registers—for young adults, especially university students and recent graduates.[10]

Following Su'ad Abdul Khabeer's analysis of young Muslim activists in Chicago, this chapter shows how these spaces reflect a project of Muslim placemaking that intervenes in the racial ideology of the metropolis.[11] Unlike what Abdul Khabeer describes in Chicago, however, Parisian Muslim activists are increasingly producing Islamic culture in spaces that have historically been racialized as white and elite, but in a way that goes *against* the logic of integration. I draw on my interlocutors' engagements with Parisian space to show how class mobility has become central to Muslim intellectual culture in two divergent ways: as both an aspirational resource and an inheritance of moral accountability. Zareena Grewal uses the concept of "moral geographies" to describe young US Muslims' relations with the nation and the imagined elsewhere known as the "Muslim World," which functioned for them as a "utopic moral countercategory."[12] French Muslims also engage and subvert "moral geographies" of the metropolis (and by extension the nation) that associate class, knowledge, and merit with city-center institutions and spaces, in contrast to the banlieues so often associated in the public imaginary with Islam.

For those who grew up there, the Parisian banlieues are not only a geographical terrain, but also an imagined nation and birthright. For many middle-class French inheritors of postcolonial migration who grew up in the Parisian banlieues and went on to seek higher education and professional lives in the city center, this territory becomes an "origin," a marker of exclusion from cultural and political capital, of the significant gap between their life experiences and those of their parents, and of intimate acquaintance with the consequences of structural disenfranchisement of immigrants and their descendants in France. They identify as *banlieusard*, shaped by the milieu of the *quartiers populaires*, their rhythms of life, expressive cultures, and ethos. Notably, their upward socioeconomic mobility often does not involve relocating outside of the banlieues. In addition to being prohibitively expensive, living in Paris proper is often not desirable for young inheritors of immigration, especially those who are close to their parents and comfortable in their neighborhoods. At the same time, the banlieues themselves are changing, experiencing gentrification in certain areas. Despite their continued residence in the banlieues, perhaps even in the same building in which they grew up, the social mobility of some engaged Muslims instantiates a cultural distance that prompts some to describe themselves as having "immigrated within France." The banlieues are thus still imagined as a territory apart, even as they stand in a quite porous relationship to Paris proper. Islamic organizations and social actors engage in multiple ways with this imagined geography of the banlieues, often recasting it in spiritual or moral terms.

At the same time, the French state is also engaged in multiple initiatives to reshape the economic landscape of the banlieues and thereby indirectly intervene in the reproduction of class inequalities that persistently characterizes the Paris area. In 2007, the then president Nicolas Sarkozy introduced a vision for the substantive reorganization of urban and administrative space in the French capital. This vision was known as the "Grand Paris" project. The name hinges on a wordplay between Paris and *pari* (wager), underscoring the "great risk" that the state presents itself as taking in investing in this cross-metropolitan infrastructure and vision. With the stated aim of increasing cohesiveness among the many diverse neighborhoods that make up the metropolitan area, and spurring "multinodal" economic development that spread financial and cultural capital beyond the bounds of the périphérique, Grand Paris includes a major transit expansion, financial incentives for corporations that base themselves in economically marginalized zones, an aesthetic and architectural intervention, and an administrative reorganization with electoral implications. Grand Paris was intended to jolt the city out of an aesthetic, economic, infrastructural and moral stagnation and decline, marked by the "museumification" of the center city, widespread gentrification of its outer arrondissements, and rising economic and educational inequality.[13] In the framework of Grand Paris, the economic stagnation of the banlieues has been attributed in large part to their "enclosure" and isolation from the centralized sources of financial and social capital.

The proposed reforms are therefore intended to further "a certain idea of solidarity" by enacting the *désenclavement* (opening up, "de-isolation") of the banlieues to create "the image of territorial equality."[14] In the words of President Sarkozy, "Grand Paris will cease to be an agglomeration in order to become a city where *one no longer speaks of the banlieues.*"[15] Explicit in this urban planning initiative is the moral project of using economic development to combat the "communalism," "isolation," and "enclaves" that are imagined to characterize the banlieues—all code words for political stereotypes about Islam. Sarkozy's desire for Paris to become a city where "one no longer speaks of the banlieues" expressed this impulse to dissolve and assimilate the banlieues and their residents into the urban totality.

Muslim residents of greater Paris are negotiating this centralized project of gentrification in multiple ways. On the one hand, as Eric Hazan writes, "Grand Paris already exists; it is here in front of our eyes."[16] In other words, many residents of the banlieues regularly traverse the whole metropolitan area in the course of their professional, political, cultural, and spiritual formations, traveling against the grain of the highly centralized transit system. In the words of French rapper Médine, "*C'est nous le Grand Paris.*"[17] In a sense, through their search for knowledge, community, and political engagement, young residents of the banlieues produced "Grand Paris" before the state ever thought to. Many also cautiously welcome economic investment in their neighborhoods, particularly the expansion of transit networks to areas that have been grossly underserved. At the same time, they recognize the targeted nature of this state project of "economic uplift," keenly aware of its explicit framing against Muslim "communalism." They are suspicious of neoliberal reforms of population management through urban planning while also seeking the material improvement of their communities and neighborhoods, a pursuit that is often entangled with neoliberal institutions. Engaged Muslim social actors are working to intervene in the moral geography of metropolitan Paris, pushing far beyond the imaginary of the "banlieues de l'Islam."[18]

A MUSLIM ELITE?

It was a typically rainy Paris winter evening when I attended my first formal dinner organized by Le Réveil, a Muslim community organization focusing on educational achievement where I had recently begun volunteering. Le Réveil was headed by Mehdi, whom we met at the beginning of this chapter. The sparse organization offices, on the garden level of a large, utilitarian office complex just outside of the périphérique, had been transformed into a banquet hall. Mothers, grandmothers, and aunts had been conscripted to prepare rows of hors d'oeuvres, vats of fruit juice cocktail, and heaping platters of food, while the desserts had been brought in from local patisseries. The tables were decked out in silver and purple, and the members of

Le Réveil were identifiable by the coordinating purple touches in their outfits. As a brand-new member, I had dug out my only purple article of clothing, a vintage sweater, in an effort to fit in, but immediately upon arrival I realized that I was rather underdressed, in a crowd of suits and silk scarves.

I worked with Le Réveil for nearly a year and a half, teaching English to high school and *prépa* students,[19] administering English admissions tests and practice baccalaureate exams, advising students on applying to anglophone universities, and participating in the mentoring, evaluation, and management of students. I participated in biweekly planning and debriefing meetings, brainstorming sessions for new projects, fundraising galas, celebrations, social events, religious study, and collective worship.

Each of the seventy-five or so attendees at that evening's dinner had been invited because of their high educational achievement. Nearly all were Muslim young adults who attended or had graduated from one of France's *grandes écoles* or top universities—the prestigious institutions that educate an enormous percentage of the country's economic, scientific, and political elite. As we went around the room introducing ourselves, each attendee listed their diplomas, laid out their professional trajectory, and shared what they felt they could give back to the French Muslim community. The members of the group were acutely aware of their exceptional situations: having come largely from working-class families, they were among only nine percent of their peers to have parents who were working class.[20] Many of them were the only two or three French students of immigrant background in their classes of three hundred or more. An evening like this one was therefore an extremely welcome opportunity for socialization.

Beyond the social aspect, the main attraction of the evening was a lecture by Shaykh Abdelaziz, a religious leader and lecturer. Shaykh Abdelaziz has been active in preaching in France since the 1980s, and enjoys a large following. Dressed casually in a shirt, tie, and sweater, Shaykh Abdelaziz spoke in an intellectual register befitting his early career as a school teacher. His lecture drew from scripture, classical theological sources, French philosophy, and a wide sweep of Islamic and Western history, elaborating on the moral responsibilities, historical failures, and dangerous pitfalls of the "Muslim elite." While his tone was sober, his message was piercingly directed to his audience.

> You *are* the Muslim elite. Do you understand? The responsibility is a heavy burden. But it is well worth carrying. Oh yes. The Muslim community will only emerge from the quicksand in which we have been buried since the

beginning of our presence in France if—and I do mean *only if*—you all get to work. Individual success, always with the community in mind. What can I contribute to my community here where I am? . . . You can all, on an individual level, change the world. That is, if you really want to, and if you believe that you have been called by God. And you *are* called by God. In all societies it has always been like that, it's two percent of the population who pulls the rest toward righteousness. That's right. Two percent. Not everyone is made to lead, to influence. It's not the case. God created human beings differently. And you, *you* are this two percent.

Shaykh Abdelaziz's exhortation sparked many questions in the audience. What did it mean to see oneself as part of an elite or a "two percent"? What kind of responsibility did that entail? What relationship, if any, did being part of a professional or economic elite have to religious knowledge or spiritual development? Shaykh Abdelaziz was clear that the "elite" he referenced had inherent responsibilities to the collective. Having been nurtured by Muslim communities, these young people were also committed to reinvesting in the future of the coming generation. Through my ongoing work with Le Réveil, and my fieldwork in a wide range of other contexts of Muslim education and activism, I came to realize that some Muslim social activists have turned to the development of a small but deeply dedicated "elite" as one potential way to transform large-scale social inequalities.

These efforts are a form of fraternal critique, constituting a critical intervention in community norms and expectations, and they also elicit fraternally critical responses from some Muslims, who remain suspicious of the project of constructing an "elite" in the terms of majoritarian French society. While the activists who seek to foster a "Muslim elite" understand their work as part of a social justice project geared toward the improvement of the collective, rather than the success of the individual, others in their communities perceive a fundamental tension between the notion of valorizing an "elite" and aspirations for equality. In an interview, sociologist and memoirist Kaoutar Harchi observed that "the capitalist model demands social *success* of us. But [this demand] is nothing more than a way to make capitalism itself succeed."[21] While Harchi's 2021 memoir is sometimes interpreted in terms of the figure of the *transfuge*, meaning "class defector" in the sense of experiencing upward socioeconomic mobility, she insists that this is a "white concept" that ignores the endurance of racialization and the persistence of social inequalities even for those with elite university degrees.[22] Harchi's analysis, and her refusal of the framework of class "defection," is quite pertinent to the experiences of the young people I worked with. While these students and activists work to turn social and material "success" into a community resource, they also express an unresolved anxiety about the ways that their economic roles may perpetuate the success and the legitimacy of the capitalist model.

While the organizational structures that are nurturing this "Muslim elite" date to the mid-2010s, the idea of a class of educated elites of immigrant background is far from new. In 1988, sociologist of immigration Abdelmalek Sayad was asked in an interview about the possibility of speaking of an emergent "elite" among university students from second-generation immigrant backgrounds. Sayad responded in the negative:

> AS: I think that it is navel-gazing or nostalgia to speak of an "elite" just because one is a university student coming from an immigrant background. The proof is that these students all end up back in a miserable situation. An "elite" making minimum wage? Elite for whom? Elite among immigrants?
>
> INTERVIEWER: Yes, why not? . . . The position of an "elite" that does not have the means to distance itself from its milieu of origin, this creates the problem of a social rift.
>
> AS: Is it a social rift? A splitting certainly, but a rift, no. We must not engage in vocabulary inflation. There is neither a cultural rift nor a social rift. These are journalists' metaphors. There is a social gymnastics, but not a rift.[23]

Three and a half decades later, it is no longer the case that university graduates from immigrant backgrounds all end up making minimum wage, although significant inequalities persist in the French educational system and job market along racial, ethnic, and religious lines, and there remains significant difficulty for non-white university graduates to translate their diplomas into stable, remunerative careers.[24] But Sayad's refusal of a "social rift" and his analysis of a "social gymnastics" remains apt as a framework for analyzing the condition of the upwardly mobile youth who Shaykh Abdelaziz addressed as the "two percent." Far from being cut off from their social contexts of origin, these young people are engaged in a lively gymnastic exercise, whether figured as a balancing act or an obstacle course, of holding together the multiple versions of France that they simultaneously inhabit. Some shuttle between their parents' apartment and the lecture halls of their central Paris university. For others it is the modest neighborhood mosque where they invest their time on the evenings and weekends, and the corporate high-rise office where they remove their headscarf each morning before entering. The Muslim student groups and mentoring organizations that we encounter in this chapter are striving to make this "social gymnastics" less taxing in two main ways: on the one hand, by combating the social structural and demographic conditions that make highly educated young professional French Muslims continue to feel isolated in their educational institutions and workplaces, and on the other, by developing the potential of these institutions as sites of ethical development for French Muslims as Muslims. Both of these measures constitute forms of fraternal critique.

A number of activists intertwine the idea of a socioeconomic elite with that of a moral and spiritual elite. They do this deliberately, in order to achieve their goal of a generation of French Muslims whose access to what is referred to as the nation's "social elevator" will strengthen, rather than dilute, their ties to their religious community. Through this emergent generation of "elites," these activists hope to definitively change the terms of national conversations about Islam and the role of French Muslims in their society. The pervasive idiom of the "social elevator" is an excellent illustration of why many people argue that the disadvantaged status of French Muslims can only be addressed through the cultivation, beginning at a young age, of a small educational and consequently economic elite who will eventually be able to finance large-scale benevolent activities and perhaps even influence French society at the highest level. Unlike a ladder or staircase, the "social elevator" evokes an automated ascension.

In order for young people to board this "social elevator," then, they must start at a very early age. While some mosques and religious organizations take the approach of providing basic scholastic support and tutoring to the widest possible number of young people, others, like Le Réveil, invest an enormous amount of resources in five to ten young people per class, chosen from among many applicants, in order to ensure that these select students achieve not simply a good education and stable career, but the *best* education and *most* impactful career that the Republic has to offer. The fervent hope of these activists, and of the donors who support them, is that that this emergent "elite" will understand that they have succeeded thanks to the deep investment of the Muslim community, not despite the community's skepticism or recalcitrance. Le Réveil illustrates these ties in a promotional video, where a man in a suit comes upon a small clay mosque offering jar. Shaking it and noticing that it contains only pocket change, he takes out his checkbook and a nice pen. However, his folded check is on such a different scale that it does not even fit into the coin slot on the jar. Outsize benevolence is thus portrayed as an intrinsic part of the image of the upwardly mobile Muslim.

VOCATIONAL COUNSELING IN
MUSLIM CIVIL SOCIETY

Le Réveil is far from the only organization working to cultivate educational mobility in terms of Islamic values. In the Paris area, the Young Muslims of France (JMF), a branch of the national organization Muslims of France (MF),[25] organizes France's longest-running and largest vocational fair targeted at a broad young Muslim public. At this fair, which takes place near Saint-Denis, members of JMF as well as a wide range of Muslim young professionals offer presentations on their career pathways, the concrete steps involved in preparing for these pathways, and their experiences as Muslims in various professional settings. They also offer mock interview sessions and on-the-spot résumé and cover-letter editing. In an environment characterized by sharp skepticism for the project of "orientation" as it exists in the school system,[26] the JMF career fairs offer an alternative that foregrounds the viability of a range of professional careers for young people who grew up in the banlieues. The "orientation" process of the public school system is infamous for tracking boys and girls of immigrant background into vocational training programs rather than academic paths that would lead to more remunerative careers. By stepping in to supplement the vocational counseling of the public school system, the JMF claims a space of civil society for Islamic organizations, a role that is neither limited to facilitating ritual activities nor purely charitable in nature. Increasingly, branches of the JMF and/or Muslim Students of France (EMF) are also invited to mosques or Islamic centers, to host career and educational fairs for young people in the community surrounding an individual mosque. In addition to the goals of the broader JMF fairs—offering role models of young professional Muslims who themselves grew up in the banlieues, and dispensing practical advice on how to prepare for and navigate postsecondary education—these mosque-based events are an opportunity for the young activists to argue strenuously for the meritorious and even obligatory nature of secular education in religious ethical terms. These critical arguments are directed not only at the middle and high school students themselves, but also, more obliquely, at their parents.

At one professional orientation event that I attended at an Islamic center in Saint-Denis, five young people gave detailed presentations about their studies, their childhoods, their careers, and their professional goals, and then concluded with a Qur'an recitation. Ayoub, a graduate student in physics, recited the first portion of Sura al-Ra'd (The Thunder), and then slowly read the translation in French. The passage highlights various features of the natural world—sun and moon, land and water, clouds and thunder, from which the name of the sura is drawn—as signs of God's omnipotence and sustenance. When he had finished, Ayoub called attention to a phrase that is repeated in several variations in this sura and throughout the Qur'an: "in this there are signs for people who reflect," "in this are signs for people who reason." "And what do you think this reflection is?" Ayoub asked the audience. "In fact, it's everything we've been speaking to you about today: higher education, advanced study, and comprehension—clear comprehension, through advanced study." Earlier in his presentation, Ayoub had described his work in the physics laboratory as:

> Almost a real spiritual practice, an avenue of approaching Allah. Because the more you learn about the universe, you realize, subhan Allah, what we have been given—we have been given the universe itself, and the capacity to comprehend it. And then you realize, if we abandon this work of comprehension—if I abandon it myself—it's moral negligence!

Another presenter, Mohamed, an accountant, jumped in:

> A scholar no less than Ibn Taymiyya—some of you have heard of him?—a very influential scholar, a great scholar, and he wrote that if there is any domain of knowledge that is neglected by Muslims, as a community, then it is a sin upon all of us. It is a communal duty to gather everything that can be learned from all domains of knowledge, all sciences. When you apply yourself to your studies, in whatever field it is, that is exactly what you are doing: you are accomplishing this communal duty on behalf of all Muslims in France—on behalf of all Muslims, in fact.

Both Ayoub and Mohamed underscored one of the refrains of such events: the ways in which working on one's studies and toward one's professional goals should be understood as a devotional practice and religious obligation. At the same time, they enacted a version of Sayad's "social gymnastics," working to counteract a segmentation of Muslim French life that would seem to keep Ibn Taymiyya and physics laboratories in separate universes of reference.

As we saw with adab al-ikhtilaf in chapter 1, Mohamed borrows the legal concept of collective duty (*fard kifaya*) in order to frame educational and professional advancement not as individualistic projects of personal success, but as projects of religious and communal obligation. His reference to Ibn Taymiyya might have been intended to preemptively dismiss any possible objection that an enthusiastic investment in French higher education could be in tension with a traditional vision of Islamic piety, deftly navigating the waters of community debate on this issue. Mohamed and his fellow volunteers took pains to rebut any impression that the paths of higher education and professional advancement they were encouraging would end in lapsed observance. Like the activists with Le Réveil, these young professionals were committed to helping the youngest generation of Muslims succeed *because* of their Muslim community belonging, not in spite of it.

MUSLIM STUDENT ORGANIZING IN THE GRANDES ÉCOLES

Beginning in 2010, Muslim students in French institutions of higher learning, and particularly in the elite grandes écoles, have also begun to form student organizations within their universities, independent of the EMF and JMF, although not necessarily in opposition to them. Within the grandes écoles, student organizations pertaining to Islam have become spaces through which Muslim students can build a sense of community and a collective visibility and anchor conversations among their peers. The first such organization, Salaam Sciences Po, was founded in 2010, with the explicit intention of bringing together Muslim and non-Muslim students who were interested in topics related to Islam. Salaam Sciences Po was quickly joined by Islam-oriented student groups at numerous other institutions.

The embryonic Muslim student culture of the grandes écoles has emerged in the context of two dynamics that are both convergent and opposed. First, as we saw above with Le Réveil, a wide range of Muslim social actors are acutely concerned with increasing the number of young French-born Muslims from working-class backgrounds who achieve high educational success and socioeconomic mobility. Importantly, they seek to strengthen the ability of young people to integrate their religious development with their academic and professional achievement. These organizations valorize success within the hierarchical French system while also seeking to transform it from within. At the same time, there is a certain desire among some school administrators to create a multicultural politics of diversity on their campuses, in order to defend their claims of France's meritocracy on a global stage.²⁷ Students of color and students of working-class backgrounds, which includes most Muslim students, are expected to visibly prove the institution's inclusivity while remaining invisible in other ways.

Both Muslim social activists and state and corporate actors have a disproportionate focus on the grandes écoles. As Natasha Warikoo has argued about the Ivy League in the United States and Oxbridge in the United Kingdom, the grandes écoles are at once highly specific environments for the cultivation of elite values that often diverge from widespread national values, and they simultaneously play a disproportionate role in broad public ideas about merit, equality, and the image of the nation.²⁸ As Warikoo further points out, the more exclusive a school is, the more entrenched are the beliefs in its meritocratic structure. Muslim student life on these elite campuses is caught up in all of these dynamics.

At the same time, Muslim student life at elite schools is also the result of the activism of young people seeking to create spaces of refuge. The students who have been founding these organizations were born in the 1990s, and they inherited the fruits of an earlier generation of Islamic organizing and religious revival.²⁹ Many of them grew up and came of age in the context of active religious communities, Qur'an schools, and mosque-building efforts, spearheaded by their parents' generation. As university students, they often feel pressed by their peers and professors to, in the words of Karim, a twenty-three-year-old management student, "explain Islam, defend Islam, be an expert on the Maghreb, the Middle East, immigration, oil, Iran, radicalization, and so on! In short, have all the answers." Further, Muslim students experience multiple intersecting forms of discrimination on campus and in the job market. These organizations have thus emerged out of a desire to "open a conversation about Islam," on the one hand, and on the other, out of an acute consciousness of broad educational inequalities. Muslim student groups provide spaces to negotiate these experiences. They seek to reset the conversation from the scrutiny of women's dress or the pressure to "explain" that Karim describes, refocusing campus conversations on Islam around their own priorities—human rights, Islam in the workplace, Islamic finance, and above all, the "ethical dimension" of the business world.

Assya, a twenty-one-year-old student in accounting, arranged for me to visit the offices of the Muslim student group she had cofounded. The office belonged exclusively to the Muslim students' organization, which had been founded in 2013. The office was a small, windowless room, furnished with an Ikea loveseat, a meeting table with six chairs, and a set of lockers. "Before, we sometimes prayed in the hallways," Myriam, one of the students, explained.

"You would never know who could see you, what they would think, what they might say. Each one of us has had remarks. Not every time, but it happens. It's so nice to have a place where you can take a breath and be at ease." "But that's not the only reason we founded the organization," Assya interjected.

> It's not principally about prayers, it's about ideas—ideas that connect our Islam to our studies. After all, there are an enormous number of students here, Muslims, Christians, Jews, atheists, they all want to know more about Islam in the world, they want to understand the relationship of Islam to business, to commerce, to economics, not only here in France but all over the world. And those are the conversations that we are trying to have, building a community around those conversations that are important to us, as Muslims and students, but also of interest to our colleagues and to the public.

These conversations included speaking about ethics, spirituality, and above all, about how to combine a career in business with the search for "meaning." The young people in these student organizations were trying to work out how to flourish in capitalism—how to have careers that would afford them greater financial security than their parents, while simultaneously seeking a sense of "meaning" either through or, more likely, beyond their work. "After all," in the words of a speaker at one of the organization's events, "it's not your résumé that they're going to engrave on your tombstone!" These young students were caught between the fervent desire to break glass ceilings and achieve financial stability, on the one hand, and the nagging sense that their projected future roles in corporate France might not be in line with their ethical values, on the other.

As I learned more about the history of Assya's organization, I saw that both the spiritual and the intellectual had been part of the impetus for the founding of a Muslim student group. In recounting the events of that year, Assya explained to me, a bit sheepishly, that she had repeated her first year in the bachelor's program, after an initial year during which she had struggled a great deal to find her footing as a university student.

> In the second week, there was a new professor, his class met for the first time. And at the end of class he called me up to speak with him. He asked me—and with ostentatious politeness!—he asked me if I wouldn't be so kind as to take "that cloth on my head" off in his class. I told him that I couldn't do that, that I had the right to wear it, now that I was at the uni-

versity I had that right! We had a few exchanges but I remained very firm. And he said "Very well, okay. But just know this, I don't like it. I don't like it, I object, and in my opinion it has no place in my classroom."

For the rest of the term, I could barely think in his class. I never dared to speak—and you know normally I'm the first one to answer a question! In fact it confirmed everything I had feared, the things people had told me before I came, and I had told them no, no, it won't be like that, you'll see. And it got inside my mind [*pénétré mon esprit*].

Over the course of this tumultuous first year, Assya slowly began to connect with other Muslim students in her entering class and in the university as a whole. Toward the end of the year, Assya had two simultaneous realizations: First, she would have to repeat her first year of study, since she had missed a good deal of class and had not done well on several exams. Second, she came to learn that religious student groups already existed at her institution, which had sponsored a Catholic student organization since 2008, and had long been home to a branch of the national Jewish student association, the UEJF. She began to see the repeating of her first year as the perfect opportunity to found an organization of Muslim students and invest in cultivating both a community to support one another in the face of incidents like the one she had experienced, and a school-wide discussion about Islam that would invite faculty and peers to see a different perspective than that offered in the media. More broadly, Assya saw the formation of a Muslim student group as the opportunity to "humanize" her studies: "At this school, we operate almost exclusively in the concrete and technical domain. No one here tells you to reflect, to think more deeply. My major professional ambition, if I can put it like that, is to bring the human element, the human scale, into the world of business. I don't know where it is going to take me, how I am going to manage it. But that is my life mission: humanizing business. And our group, it's one small way of doing that, you know?" By "humanizing business," Assya referred to two dimensions. First, she and some of her peers were interested in small business entrepreneurialism on what they called a "human scale," rather than working for a large multinational corporation. As a woman who at the time wore a headscarf, Assya faced significant barriers and discrimination in private employment. For her and numerous other young women, founding their own business was seen as a path to employment that accommodated their religious expression and was a way of building economic independence within the Muslim community.[30] The high failure rate of small businesses should call our attention to the way this aspiration to entrepreneurship may only reproduce economic precariousness. Nevertheless, the business school student group fostered these entrepreneurial aspirations.

Second, Assya referred to an anxious desire among many of the students to apply their business educations in ways that aligned with their moral conscience, in positions that *somehow* did not depend on the maintenance of oppressive and extractive capitalist hierarchies. Their student group provided a forum for their struggles to articulate these ethical visions and combine them with professional aspirations while caught between competing pressures, expectations, discrimination, and state surveillance. This "humanizing" work allowed Assya and her peers to pursue questions of ultimate meaning and ethics in a professional environment that otherwise seemed to her exclusively oriented toward profit and efficiency. They found their non-Muslim peers to be also quite receptive to these questions, particularly when framed as a conversation among fellow business students.

These new university-based Muslim groups have produced forms of gathering that respond both to the intellectual and social priorities of their constituent members, and to the interests and questions of the broader non-Muslim publics of their institutions. For the young people who move through these organizations during their student years, they are a major source of religious community, socialization, and moral support. As we saw above, they also provide a space to connect lessons and pedagogies of the university classroom to questions of ethical development in an Islamic framework. Given that these groups are nearly all in their early years, their members carry an enormous self-consciousness of their status as pioneers and role models for younger generations. "No one will ever again come to this institution thinking 'I am the only Muslim here,' like I did in my first year," Karim said. "That is part of what it means to have a real student organization, you know, not just a group of people who get together, who socialize. We are part of the culture here now. We are leaving our mark." These groups exemplify the search of young French Muslims for forms of solidarity and ethical discourse within capitalism, as they strive at once to succeed in the dominant system and carve out spaces of refuge from it.

FORMING THE FUTURE "MUSLIM ELITE"

The most commonly proposed answer to the question of what university students and young professionals can give back to the French Muslim community is a call for these individuals to invest their expertise, energies, and status as role models in the development of the next generation of Muslim students. In addition to the tutoring programs run by JMF and EMF, numerous other mentoring programs aim to provide a combination of intense academic preparation, personalized guidance and orientation, and Islamically grounded moral education.

Le Réveil and several similar organizations work to select, inspire, and nurture a pipeline of young Muslims, beginning as early as middle school, who will have the intensive academic preparation as well as the cultural capital necessary to succeed in the most elite prépas and grandes écoles. Le Réveil has identified four barriers to the socioeconomic flourishing of French Muslims, which organization members outline in a polished and engaging "pitch" that they practice, hone, and deliver, in one-on-one meetings and to audiences of hundreds, in a wide range of Muslim contexts. These four barriers are: (1) a lack of knowledge among Muslim families of the pathways and pipelines to high-level academic success; (2) a lack of accompaniment and mentoring of promising young people, modeling the attainability of academic and professional achievement for a young French person of Muslim culture; (3) a lack of the cultural capital that facilitates academic, social, and psychological success in elite environments; and (4) financial limitations that prevent young people of modest means from pursuing certain degree programs, require them to work alongside their studies, or prevent them from going abroad to develop their English and gain international experience. It is worth noting that none of the four barriers explicitly references racial or religious discrimination in education, housing, or employment. When I asked them, the leaders of Le Réveil did not deny that such discrimination exists. They believe, however, that the Muslim community needs to focus both their energies and their rhetoric on factors over which they have more immediate control.

As a whole, the organization works to intervene in each of these four barriers, with the overarching aim of cultivating a "Muslim elite," who will be able to channel their financial, social, and cultural capital for the improvement of the Muslim community at large. To accomplish this goal, these young activists provide intensive academic enrichment classes each weekend and during all of the school vacations, including throughout the month of August. For prépa students, they also provide tutoring several nights a week. In addition to the classes and tutoring, students are each paired with an official mentor, who develops a one-on-one relationship with them, on the model of an older brother or sister. Two professional psychologists volunteer with Le Réveil to provide support to students and their families, both as a matter of course and on a more intensive basis in difficult times. Le Réveil also engages students socially, through weekend team-building retreats, outings with Paris-area benevolent organizations that serve unhoused populations, cultural trips to the theater or debate competitions, and sporting events—regular soccer games for the boys, and cardio kickboxing for the girls. Religious observance, notably regular prayer and weekly mosque attendance for boys and girls, is structured into the educational program. After five years of developing their pedagogical model, Le Réveil was achieving the results they aimed for. Their alumni secured spots in the most elite of the grandes écoles, and in the *classes étoilées* of the top Parisian prépas. Just as importantly to the activists, the majority of these program alumni are, as promised, reinvesting themselves in turn in their roles of "big brother" or "big sister" to younger members of their communities.

The members of Le Réveil are a group of about twenty young French Muslim students and young professionals between the ages of twenty and thirty-three, all volunteers, many of whom were educated in one of the grandes écoles or peer universities. These volunteers dedicate an enormous amount of time, in some cases thirty hours a week alongside a full-time job, to the organization. As a result, the familial and fraternal model of relationship between the organization members and its young students thus extends to the relationships among the members as well, who constantly refer to the organization as a proxy family.

When I first began teaching with them, Le Réveil operated out of a repurposed two-bedroom apartment on the ground floor of an apartment building in a distant southern banlieue of Paris, a fifteen-minute bus ride from the RER. This space was loaned to Le Réveil by an Islamic school that used it for classes during the week, and was typical of the types of makeshift spaces that have been sites of worship as well as community organizing for French Muslim communities since the 1980s. Over the course of several months, Le Réveil moved their operations to an independent location, much more conveniently accessible from Paris, which they had outfitted with movable soundproof walls at considerable expense, so that a relatively modest space could accommodate either five study rooms and an office, or a dinner or lecture space for one hundred or more. This move was facilitated by donations gathered from among the French Muslim community at biannual fundraising galas and regular mosque fundraising appeals, indicating a significant level of community buy-in for the Le Réveil project.

At the same time as their pedagogical efforts, Le Réveil works to raise the consciousness of the Muslim community as a whole about the benefit of the prestigious trajectories to which their students aspire, and the sacrifices that these trajectories often entail on the part of students and their families. They refer to this consciousness-raising process as *sensibilisation*. Le Réveil's sensibilisation work is focused on mosque presentations, vocational fairs such as the one we saw above, maintaining a visible presence at the annual Muslim gathering at Le Bourget, and the production of video clips that circulate via social media. More than simply an informational effort, however, sensibilisation is an ongoing practice of role-modeling and persuasive argumentation that works at once to demonstrate the compatibility of religious observance and professional success for men and women, and to suggest and model norms and attitudes that would make this compatibility less of a "social gymnastic," to return to Sayad's phrase.

The moral education of Le Réveil is thus fourfold: not only are they (1) educating young French Muslim students to understand their studies as a site of religious ethical formation, a way to please God, and (2) educating them to spend their lives channeling their individual successes for the greater good of the community; they are also (3) trying to intervene in the moral norms of the mosque-centered Muslim community and individual Muslim families, and (4) shaping the moral sensibilities of the activists who are positioning themselves as role models and guides to young students and their parents alike.

REIMAGINING THE CLASSROOM

If their public schools are often experienced by Le Réveil students as a battlefield,[31] the space and classrooms at Le Réveil are deliberately organized to offer a contrasting environment. Shoes are removed at the entrance to the building, "so that the whole space is a place where anyone can feel free to pray at any time," Mehdi explained to me. "Carpets are not necessary, and no specific room. We don't have enough rooms for that!" Aside from the injunction to remove shoes at the door, students and instructors dress as they wish. Tea and snacks are always available for breaks, a refrigerator and microwave are available to reheat food, and a growing library is available for student use. When necessary, especially when facing a long trip home after a late night of study, students occasionally sleep in the classrooms. They are encouraged to have both ownership of and responsibility over the space, cleaning the bathrooms, vacuuming, and managing the trash. In class, small groups of students sit around a common table with an instructor, who opens each session with a moment of informal conversation.

The content of the classes was largely structured around developing the skills that would be necessary to succeed on the *bac* and in prépa. In French and philosophy classes, the students worked extensively on textual commentaries and argumentative writing, revising multiple drafts, accumulating mental libraries of citations to deploy at the right moment, and developing commentarial strategies appropriate to each literary genre. But the instructors also had broader goals, Ilyès, a twenty-five-year-old law student who taught philosophy, put it this way:

> More than anything, I want to erase from their minds any idea that philosophy is the enemy of religion, the enemy of Islam, that it is there to make them atheists. There are plenty of people who say that, Muslims who say that! People who think that it is a course of indoctrination in secularism and free thought. That's false, completely false! The students are learning a set of tools to better reflect on their beliefs, better express their beliefs, dialogue better with people who do not share them, and the ones who share them too. You have something to learn from everyone, absolutely everyone.

Accordingly, Ilyès's philosophy classes were environments of spirited intellectual challenge, where students were encouraged to write and analyze from both within and outside of their own moral and theological points of view. "You have to know how to write in order to do well on the bac, but then you have to know how to write in order to *think*," Ilyès continued. "And there is a limit to how much you can think if you leave your convictions to the side at the door of the school."

ACTIVISM AS A SITE OF MORAL EDUCATION

Many of the members of Le Réveil had foregone their own formal educations in Islamic sciences in favor of their volunteer work. Particularly given the significant distances in transit required for most of us to reach either the Le Réveil offices or the major Islamic schools in Saint-Denis, it was nearly impossible to combine both of these engagements with an active professional life or full-time study. In response, Mehdi and the rest of the leadership team decided to invite a shaykh to offer in-house classes in Islamic sciences for members of Le Réveil. We began early on Sunday mornings before the young students arrived, and worked through topics in creed, jurisprudence, and theology. This type of traditional Islamic education was sometimes contrasted to the Islamic education produced by activism itself. Late one evening, after spending hours in an organizational meeting, several women who had been members of the organization for over a year were asked by a newer member, "What does it mean for you to be a member of the Le Réveil family?" Amel, a twenty-six-year-old medical student, was the first to respond. "It means exhaustion!" she exclaimed, laughing. Everyone joined in.

> No, but seriously, what it has been for me, since I joined Le Réveil on September 17, 2012—oh yes, I can tell you the exact date—what it has meant? It has meant learning more about my religion in one year than I could have learned in ten years at an institute, studying Islamic sciences. Patience, perseverance, reliance on God, serving others, good character— all of the values that they tell you about, that are throughout the hadith— how could I have learned in a classroom or from a book how much *work* those values require? No, I would never have understood. It is when you feel the eyes of our young students watching you, evaluating you, imitating you, that is when you learn what it means to refine your character.

Amel's observation—namely, that it is not as a student but as a *teacher* that one learns most efficiently to adopt certain virtues—is a striking inversion of much theological reflection about imitation as a form of ethical pedagogy, across religious traditions. Rather than focus on the moral work of the student or initiate who imitates their teacher, master, or prophet, Amel underscores the moral work impelled in her by her role as a model for young students. Although she contrasts her moral education with Le Réveil to learning ethics "in a classroom or from a book," in fact her work with Le Réveil has also largely taken place in a classroom and with a book—a classroom with her at the head, and a chemistry textbook to work from. Amel's insight here is the core of the moral pedagogy that the Le Réveil members imposed on themselves and one another: at every opportunity, we were reminded that "our younger brothers and sisters are watching, they are depending on us, they are learning how to behave from us, they expect a great deal from us, and we have to be *à la hauteur* [up to the task]."

This drive among young Muslim educational activists to be à la hauteur—

to live up to the very moral, academic, and professional expectations that they are simultaneously attempting to instill in their little brothers and sisters—animates a vision in which socioeconomic mobility within French institutional structures and deep personal investment in local, national, and transnational Muslim communities are held to be mutually reinforcing, rather than in tension. The project of cultivating a "Muslim elite," by insisting on the compatibility between individual success and community-mindedness, aims to make an intervention in the French educational system that is at once structural and moral. In response to histories and structures of exclusion of which they are keenly aware, these activists produce ethical discourses of virtuous achievement "within the system" and amass local repertoires of expert knowledge, in order to counteract this exclusion not thanks to any government policy, but thanks to Muslim community initiative. In response to ethical pedagogies that oppose the character of the Muslim student to the secularism of the public schools, these activists develop a counter-pedagogy that aims not only to surpass public education at its own game (from vocational counseling to philosophy instruction), but also to create independent civic structures that can gradually change the condition of Muslim students since they cannot change the public schools—yet. In short, Muslim students and educational activists engage in fraternal critique of both Muslim and secular discourses that question the compatibility of elite professional trajectories with piety and religious engagement. Far from being a way of distancing themselves from either Muslim or French belonging, these critiques are ways of participating fully in Muslim and Parisian spaces.

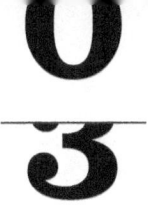

SISTERHOOD AND ITS OBLIGATIONS

I met up with Houda and a few others on a Sunday early afternoon at the Alhambra, a restored Art Deco theater not far from the Canal Saint-Martin, a rapidly gentrifying neighborhood. At night, the theater hosted standup comedy and music from metal to reggae. On this Sunday, we arrived to find a line of hundreds of women of all ages stretching around the block, many in abayas, many in jeans. The neighborhood's regular brunch-goers and boutique shoppers peered curiously at the crowd from the opposite side of the street, and many of the women in our line peered back at them. The theater-goers, a large number of whom had arrived in Paris on buses departing from mosques across the metropolitan area, admired clothes and handbags in shop windows and then widened their eyes at some of the listed prices. As we entered the theater, I caught sight of Michel, who I knew from a local new Muslims' study group. "Just finishing up the sound check, then I'm out of here!" he called to me as he waved.

The theatrical production on offer that Sunday was a classical Arabic-language musical with projected French subtitles, titled *Al Bouraq, The Night Voyage*. The show was produced, directed, and staged by an all-female cast for an all-female audience. In elaborate costumes, occasional drag performance style, and with careful choreography, a cast of forty amateur actresses presented the beloved Qur'anic story of Muhammad's night journey to Jerusalem. The acts were interspersed with short comic vignettes about everyday life—marriage, family politics, female friendships, and motherhood. The production was curated in order to never portray the person of Muhammad or other prophets, and the female-only production ensured the comfort and modesty of actresses and audience alike. The packed theater was filled with cheers, cries, laughter, and tears of emotion.

Al Bouraq was put on by a group of French women who had met through a local institute of Islamic learning. It was the group's second production, after the resounding success of their first show, *L'Étoile Brillante*, which was staged at sites throughout the Paris region during 2010–2012, to audiences totaling in the thousands. The script and music for both shows had been borrowed from a Syrian production.[1] Building on the success of *L'Étoile Brillante*, *Al Bouraq* had moved into a larger and more expensive center-city venue.

At the end of the nearly three-hour production, our group compared *Al Bouraq* to an amateur film festival that several of us had attended a few weeks earlier, Les Mokhtar. The film festival, which described itself as "Islamophile" rather than "Islamic," had the twin goals of using arts to show alternatives to the politicized image of Islam, while also inviting Muslim artists to use the medium of film to respond to political events in France. Both the Mokhtar festival and *Al Bouraq* were part of the continued efflorescence of what Amel Boubekeur described as an "Islamic society of spectacle"—a "new repertoire for action in an 'Islamic mode,'" offering a "cool" cultural reimagining of older activist and/or revivalist movements.[2] Houda compared the two events:

> Magnificent, *Al Bouraq* was magnificent. The spiritual reminders were really touching, and it's something that will stay with you for a long time. And it's amazing when you think about how much work the sisters put into the production. But in the end, what I appreciated more about the film festival was that it spoke directly to our context here in France, where Islam, I mean Islam from a religious point of view, is one element of the game. But it's not the whole game! And it can be something that can feed a critical intellectual approach, even a revolutionary approach. That's what I find so exciting.

Houda had found the "spiritual reminders" of *Al Bouraq* more situated in an older context of Islamic revival, whereas Les Mokhtar, through its explicit political engagement, reconfigured revivalist forms of identification and offered "a revolutionary approach." As I reflected on our afternoon and on Houda's comments, I also found a form of critique in the non-mixed production of *Al Bouraq* at the Alhambra. The event produced an affective politics that I recognized from other "non-mixed" (i.e., without men) spaces from across the Paris-area Muslim sphere. These spaces cultivated an ethos of what some women called "soeurénité"—the respite of sisterhood—that constituted a form of double critique grounded in practices of being together among Muslim women in France.

SERENE SISTERHOOD AGAINST THE BACKDROP OF *MIXITÉ*

Soeurénité is a portmanteau of the words for sister (*soeur*) and serenity (*sérénité*). I saw this term used in multiple different spaces across the Paris-area Islamic scene. This term offers an alternative feminine counterpart to fraternité, in place of the seldom used term *sororité*. Soeurénité frames sisterhood as at once the embodied practice of socialization among women in non-mixed space and the affective state and ethical virtue that can be cultivated through such spaces. This chapter takes up soeurénité as a social ethic and form of critique. Whether at cultural events like *Al Bouraq*, through movements for women's right to mosque space, or through intersectional feminist activism, French Muslim women are engaging in gender-based organizing in ways that both combat and elide the political essentializations of Muslim womanhood in France. The practice and virtue of soeurénité articulates a pious ethos of rights, freedoms, personal development, and spiritual solidarity. Soeurénité marks the historical exclusion of women from fraternité, while also expressing the joys and the refuge of non-mixed spaces.

Fraternity has always been a gendered concept, even if this aspect has not always been apparent, concealed within the conflation of the masculine with the universal. As a political virtue, fraternity is predicated upon the distinction between a masculine public space of political solidarity and a feminine private space of intimate and familial ties. Fraternal critique both echoes and disrupts this distinction. By foregrounding the familial intimacy and the particularity of kinship among Muslims, fraternal critique offers an alternative to the supposed universality of republican fraternity. At the same time, it relies upon the same elision between the masculine and the universal that characterizes the republican virtue and social practice. This elision between the masculine and the universal does not always imply the exclusion of women from politics or solidarity—rather, it implies their presence and participation *as women*, as gendered subjects whose performance of femininity has a particular social function.

In French political discourse, the importance of public interactions between men and women *as* men and women is expressed through the concept of *mixité*. In its primary context, it refers to the intermingling of men and women or boys and girls, often akin to the English term "coeducation."[3] As a social value, mixité is a normative valuation of heterosociality—an assertion that certain patterns and qualities of social interaction between men and women *as* men and women are not incidental, but that these patterns of interaction themselves constitute an important social good, carrying moral benefits for men, women, and shared political culture.[4]

These discourses of women's political inclusion are predicated on discourses of women's exclusion. Joan Wallach Scott has persuasively argued that the discourse of secularism, in France and elsewhere, inscribed gender difference in "a schematic description of the world as divided into separate spheres, public and private, male and female"—spheres that were "both spatial and psychological."[5] It is precisely on the basis of this differentiated and heteronormative idea of gender that mixité becomes so important: "women's morality must tame men's aggression; men's reason must bring women's passion under control."[6] While secularism is often understood as a gender-neutral concept, or even as the guarantor of women's rights against patriarchal religious norms, Scott shows that secularism cannot be understood apart from the gendered and sexual norms that it inaugurated, and the particular moral role assigned to male-female interaction in both public (masculine) and private (feminine) spheres. In a complementary way, Éric Fassin, Nacira Guénif-Souilamas, and other scholars have shown how a colonialist "sexual democracy" has demanded the visibility of sexuality as the condition of women's freedom and equality, framing a state-sponsored feminism as the alternative to the supposed machismo of the *garçon arabe*.[7] The discourse of mixité and visible sexuality has only amplified in France in the twenty-first century, often stepping in where the legal principle of secularism fails to provide adequate justification for the management of Muslim women's bodies and habits of socialization.[8] Against the backdrop of this discourse of heteronormative gender mixing and sexual visibility, homosocial spaces and values generate keen discomfort.

In this heterosocial context, Muslim women have developed a distinctive articulation of sisterhood as a social virtue, grounded in, though not exclusive to, spaces of socialization without men. These practices of *non-mixité* are the subject of intense public scrutiny in a wider context where gender mixité has become a political mandate. Like fraternal critique, soeurénité also offers a form of critique as solidarity, dissent as a way of belonging. In this chapter, we explore different spaces of gendered gathering and organizing among Muslim women, and the ways of thinking about social ethics that emerge from those settings. In particular, this chapter takes up sisterhood as a moral and political concept in French Muslim contexts, and shows how the ethic of sisterhood offers a form of double critique—critique of the patriarchal governance of secular French norms as well as of the marginalization of women in some Muslim community spaces.

In both public discourse and in scholarly literature, Muslim piety and liberal secularism are frequently used as the measures of one another's absence. This chapter foregrounds the engagements of women who challenge this opposition: women whose piety is deliberately anchored in a moral vocabulary of autonomy, individuality, and rights that is often identified with liberal secularism. Values often closely associated with liberal secularism are used in multiple ways in pious Muslim contexts—not to "secularize Islam," as some have argued, but to challenge the secular pedagogy of the French political order and majoritarian culture. The moral framework of free choice and emancipation is not a rhetoric strategically deployed to highlight the hypocrisy of anti-veil policies; it is a pious disposition, an affective relationship with divine guidance and community norms, as well as a form of social critique. I take seriously the ways that pious subjects simultaneously inhabit a liberal ethos of subjectivity, challenge secular political order on its own terms, *and* are perceived as secularism's abject other and lurking threat.

Through attention to spaces of gendered socialization and organizing, we will see how Muslim women in France engage with moral language of choice, freedom, and rights in a way that offers a framework for the intensification rather than the dilution of pious aspirations. At the same time, the centrality of choice in French state discourses pertaining to Muslim women over-determines the language of choice, freedom, and rights by tying them to political secularism. Perhaps because of the way in which they are situated as political secularism's other par excellence, pious French Muslim women may be uniquely well situated to draw out the critical ethical possibilities of secularity. By framing the virtues and utopian potential of non-mixed socialization in terms of choice, freedom, rights, and resistance, the women who cultivate soeurénité self-consciously participate in an ethical sensibility that is heavily identified with secular liberalism and is often instrumentalized by the French state. In so doing, they draw out the potentials of secularity and Islam outside the auspices of the state and the framework of concern determined by political and cultural elites.

Second, we will see how sisterhood as an organizing value produces rich interconnections between movements that explicitly identify as feminist and groups that would refuse or critique that term. While Muslim feminism is often contrasted with an imagined "conservative Islam," there are in fact porous relationships between feminist and non-feminist women's settings. Individual women move among all of these spaces, not only as "consumers" of religious teaching or culture, but also as leaders and organizers.

Muslim women's bodies, families, and habits have been in the crosshairs of political battles in France for generations. The early twenty-first century has seen continued encroachments on Muslim women's sartorial freedoms in Europe, increasingly in the name of maintaining "public order." We cannot grasp the impact of these measures without an understanding of the way that secularism has always been a gendered concept, depending on a binary and complementarian view of the social responsibilities of men and women, and on a pedagogy of mixité. In this context, claiming the choice of modest dress, the right to women's ownership of mosque spaces, and the freedom in non-mixed socialization form part of an "assemblage of heterogenous repertoires"[9] that encompass both pious dispositions and secular sensibilities. Writing on the Belgian context, Nadia Fadil draws on the concept of an assemblage of repertoires to analyze how the performance of Islamic prayers in the workplace draws simultaneously on liberal notions of individual rights, secular understandings of the privatization of religion, pious conceptualizations of sacred duty, and majority/minority negotiations of hegemonic norms. In a similar way, French Muslim women's articulation of soeurénité and their investments in cultivating and defending spaces of sisterhood draw on liberal, secular, and pious repertoires while simultaneously critiquing the patriarchal secularism of the French state.

SORORAL CRITIQUE

French thinkers have rarely engaged with fraternity's feminine counterpart, sororité, as a political concept. Sororité has retained the overtones of popular perceptions of the convent or the American undergraduate sorority—a pledged community of women set apart from society, not aiming to transform it. Against this history, writer Chloé Delaume argues that "we must measure the danger of the concept: with sororité comes independence, even self-rule. . . . For a long time one might have thought that the word "fraternité" had no feminine equivalent—to the point of accepting without batting an eye that at the heart of the French motto, the masculine becomes universal."[10] Delaume rearticulates sororité as "a choice, in which the power of the individual abdicates in favor of a collective force that will soon be ready for action. Sororité is about politics, and has the concrete power to change reality."[11] Delaume understands sororité as a collective force that is not universal, at once a political "choice" and the abdication of the power of the individual.

For Muslim feminist activists like Fatima Ouassak, this political impact of sororité comes through its affective and emotional dimension. Leader of Front de Mères, an organization combating racism, Islamophobia, and sexism in the public schools, Ouassak writes in her contribution to Delaume's anthology on sororité that

> our sororité expresses itself by the love we bear for our children. For yes, we do love them. This love has political stakes above all for non-white and working-class mothers, who are presumed to have borne children out of a religious obligation, out of tradition, because that's how it goes where they're from, for the welfare payments, or in order to live off the backs of their children in retirement. There's no place for love there. . . . But the reality is that these women love their children so much that they are ready to make any sacrifice. Ready for any struggle. And God knows that in France, the political fights of mothers have been undertaken by *these* mothers.[12]

Ouassak's sororité underscores the political stakes of love, of forms of love that are both taken for granted and denatured by white bourgeois apolitical ideals of motherhood and femininity. This affective politics of sisterhood also resonates with the articulation of sororité by the French Afrofeminist collective Mwasi. Mwasi's understanding of sororité, as articulated in their collective work *AfroFem*,[13] is grounded in the "love of ourselves" of African-descended women, entailing transnational political solidarities and the practice of non-mixité of both gender and race: the development of spaces of sisterhood exclusive to African-descended women. These articulations of sororité both highlight the relationship between affect and political mobilization in the face of gendered and racialized oppression.

As we saw above, some Muslim French women have developed an alternate term of sisterhood—not sororité, but soeurénité. (While soeurénité is used to refer to multi-racial and multiethnic socialization among Muslim women, it carries some of the affective politics of Mwasi's sororité, without their specific protocols of racial non-mixité.) This term indexes non-mixed social settings exclusive to Muslim women, the emotional state that these settings inspire, and the virtue of spiritual equilibrium that they cultivate over the long term. Like Fatima Ouassak and Mwasi's understandings of sisterhood as love, soeurénité is an affective political concept that offers a form of social critique that emerges from spaces of solidarity among Muslim women. Soeurénité is a form of resistance to state and majoritarian cultural emphases on mixité. Soeurénité is not primarily expressed in terms of religious norms of sex separation, although those norms form part of the background cultural repertoire from which soeurénité emerged. Rather, by claiming their "right to the mosque" and underscoring the "true freedom" to be found in non-mixed spaces, Muslim women situate soeurénité as a pious politics of resistance.

Sylvia Chan-Malik writes of the importance of "safe harbors" in the lives of US Muslim women. She draws this concept from Toni Morrison, who writes of a space of sisterhood between Black girls in which "they could afford to abandon the ways of other people and concentrate on their own perception of things."[14] French Muslim women's conception of soeurénité is closely aligned with this idea of safe harbor, including in what Chan-Malik marks as the contingency and ephemerality of spaces of solidarity formed against "the continual presence of racist, patriarchal, and imperial violence that necessitate their formation in the first place."[15] French Muslim women engage in what Chan-Malik calls "affective insurgency"—the "continual againstness . . . at the scale of the body, one's community, the nation, and the ummah" that Chan-Malik argues is a "central hallmark of U.S. Muslim women's lives,"[16] and which I argue equally characterizes the lives of French Muslim women. "Affective insurgency" is a form of resistance that "is not, nor has ever been, directed at a singular target; instead, it is a set of affective responses that emerge out of the ways Islam is consistently lived insurgently by women, responses that arise out of the ways U.S. Muslim women engage, navigate, and counter the ways Islam is imagined as an unruly and insurgent political presence."[17] In France, at times this resistance is oriented against male-dominated mosque governance boards; simultaneously, it is oriented against the pedagogy of mixité that is carried out by French civic institutions. In both cases, it re-centers the relationship between the individual, God, and religious community.

Leftist French feminists such as Christine Delphy argue for the political practice of non-mixité on perhaps surprisingly similar terms.[18] Delphy writes that "the practice of non-mixité is very simply the consequence of a theory of self-emancipation. Self-emancipation is the struggle by the oppressed for the oppressed."[19] In this context, non-mixité refers to racial and ethnic affinity spaces as well as women's non-mixed spaces. The "theory of self-emancipation" that Delphy describes is drawn from the use of all-Black spaces in the United States during the 1960s. Delphy's account of non-mixité as a feminist and anti-racist practice (in the case of racially non-mixed spaces) of self-emancipation focuses on the direct relationship between the affective states that are only possible in non-mixed settings and the political projects that can only be gestated in non-mixed groups. This is resonant with the articulation of soeurénité as at once an affect, a virtue, an architecture of social space, and a political resource. Delphy's call for non-mixité does not find favor with mainstream French feminism, however, which remains committed to the moral valence of mixité for both men and women.

SISTERHOOD AS DISSENT AT THE MOSQUÉE DE PARIS

Nassira, a childcare worker in her early thirties, proposed that we meet for tea at the tea room of the Mosquée de Paris, located in the fifth arrondissement. I was accustomed to making the RER trip to her suburban town to visit, but she insisted that this time it would be much more fun to meet in Paris. Neither of us had been to the Mosquée de Paris in quite some time. Nassira explained to me that she liked to suggest the mosque's attached tea room as a location to meet potential marriage partners, but she hadn't had the opportunity to do so in months. We met on a Saturday afternoon just before the midday prayer and went inside to pray.

The Mosquée de Paris is an elaborate structure in the Moroccan architectural style, with a square minaret tiled in green, an internal courtyard, and intricately carved dark wood molding throughout the interior spaces. Constructed as a monument to North and West African colonial soldiers during the First World War, the Mosquée de Paris was "built to reflect [France's] vision of Islam and Muslims."[20] As historian Naomi Davidson argues, the site functioned "as a theater for the display of *Islam français*,"[21] showcasing the embodied materiality that French elites were convinced was especially intrinsic to Islam. In addition to being an institutional hub and symbolic center of Islam in France, it is also a prominent tourist attraction, and apart from Fridays, tourists stroll the main spaces of the mosque's interior before drinking sweet mint tea in the café, going to the hammam, or browsing the gift shop for ceramics and decor.

As Nassira and I made our way through the tourists toward the prayer room, we noticed that the walls were scattered with flyers that appeared to have been hastily printed. The signs read:

Change of Prayer Room
for **Women (Basement)**

Nassira looked at me, baffled. "What's that about?" Previously, women had always prayed in the main prayer hall (now labeled *Salle de Prière pour les Hommes* with the same hastily printed flyers), behind a screen separating them from the men and the imam. We spotted a woman who seemed like she knew what she was doing and asked her for directions. She pointed the way to the staircase that led to the ablutions rooms. When we made our way downstairs, we found a large space lively with activity. Some circles of women were engaged in Qur'an memorization classes, others were enjoying casual conversation. Nassira interrupted one of the circles and tapped a woman on the shoulder. "Excuse me," she asked, "Do you hear the adhan down here?" "Don't worry," the woman reassured us. "There's a speaker. It's not bad." As she had promised, the adhan came within a minute or two, grainy but intelligible. Nassira looked at me and shrugged.

Only a week later, I was interested to read an open letter, addressed to the rector of the Mosquée de Paris and widely circulated in francophone Muslim media, by a group identifying themselves as "Women in the Mosque." The letter read, in part:

> We asked for an official explanation of this new arrangement, and the mosque administrator replied that this decision had been made in response to the request of male worshippers, who were annoyed by the noisy behavior of certain women. This argument did not astonish us, since we too were victims of this situation. We had already proposed, as a remedy to this situation, that the curtain separating the women from the men be pulled back, first because it has no religious basis and has the effect of stigmatizing women, and second, because eliminating this visual isolation would have permitted the "inattentive" women to better concentrate on the activity of their prayers and meditation, just as the men do [*à l'image des hommes*].
>
> By contrast, it was decided to abandon the diligent women to the inattentive ones, in this new space isolated in the basement, which has become a real tea room and day care center, without any possibility of

concentrating and taking advantage of the architectural beauty of this historic mosque, so well adapted to contemplation! Furthermore, there are also men whose behavior is at times bothersome, and yet it has never occurred to anyone to close the main prayer hall to all men!

Finally, this magnificent prayer space is completely underutilized, being 3/4 empty on every day but Friday.[22]

The letter went on to describe the confrontation that had ensued when a group of women went on a weekday to pray 'asr in the main prayer hall as they had been accustomed to. "We were told that it was forbidden, 'haram,' for women to pray in the 'house of men,' 'bayt rajul.' In the face of our religious arguments (namely that the mosque is not the house of men but of God, and that the Prophet (SWS) never imposed a physical separation), calm was restored, however we were threatened by the imam in order to dissuade us from returning." This letter was a strong public statement of dissent, and it pointedly quoted language, like "house of men," that would embarrass the Mosquée de Paris. It also clearly played up the symbolic stakes of the Mosquée as the site of this dissent, with reference to the "architectural beauty of this historic mosque, so well adapted to contemplation," and the sly comparison of the women's prayer room to a *salon de thé*, insinuating that the women's prayer space had been lowered to the level of the mosque's own tourist-oriented tea room, thus eroding the spirituality of the women who had come there to worship.

The authors of the open letter were strategic in their rhetorical positioning. By aligning with the mosque administration in denouncing the behavior of some of the women, and identifying themselves as "victims" of these women's chattiness, the authors ascribed to themselves an unimpeachable piety and seriousness. By arguing for the barrier-free common use of the main prayer hall on the grounds that visible proximity to men would constrain the comportment of wayward women and incite them to behave "just as the men do," the authors appealed to the influence of male authority and example over women's conduct, which was described as degenerating even further when women are collectively "abandoned" to their own devices. I read this supposed critique of women's space as ironic, playing a game of strategic essentialism to negotiate with male authority figures, while taking care to note that "bothersome" behavior at the mosque was found among men as well as among women, with no particular consequences for men's use of mosque space generally.

"The mosque administration responded with radio silence," reported

Saliha, a member of the group Women in the Mosque. "So we returned again to claim our rightful place for prayer. But this time, they were waiting for us. They were ready for a confrontation." Saliha had agreed to meet me only a couple of days after this visit to the mosque, at a Starbucks right in the center of Paris. It was December 23, and the throngs of last-minute Christmas shoppers were out in full force. Saliha had staked out a table in a back corner of the Starbucks, where it seemed as though she had spent most of the day on her laptop and phone, coordinating with the rest of the group via social media. Her phone was constantly buzzing as we spoke.

"It started just after the Islamophobic graffiti," Saliha explained. On November 19, the mosque had been defaced with violent and racist anti-Muslim insults. In the following days, Saliha and a friend had made a special trip to pray at the mosque in order to show their solidarity with this symbolic site of French Islam. "And that was when we became aware of this new policy." Saliha and the other members of Women in the Mosque were thus simultaneously negotiating the violent racism directed toward the mosque and the exclusion they felt within it. They drew strength from their sense of sisterly solidarity and their love for the mosque and for the Prophet Muhammad. "They call us feminists, but we are believers," Saliha insisted. "We are mobilizing for the equality that is described in the Qur'an and Sunna. The women who are with our group, who think like us, they are pious women, women who pray their five daily prayers. They are also women who challenge their subjection at the hands of men, subjection that is totally inconsistent with prophetic example."

After their letter was met with no response, Women in the Mosque planned a return visit. This visit was announced in advance on social media, and the women arrived with a Dutch journalist. "This time we decided to mediatize the incident, in order to say, you know, *stop*," explained Ndella Paye, one of the women in attendance, in an interview with radio station Beur FM. "We were maybe twice the number of people, a dozen. We entered the mosque; they didn't prevent us from doing that. But at the entry to the main prayer room, the one they called 'the men's room,' there were men waiting who said no, you won't enter. At every door. The doors were closed. They tore away our prayer rugs, they got in our faces, without any concern." According to Hanane Karimi, another spokeswoman for the group, "it quickly transformed into a general melee. Multiple women were attacked. In this case, they had no problem touching women!"[23]

The incident was widely covered in French media in the ensuing days, finally forcing a response from the Mosquée de Paris leadership. As reported in *Le Figaro*, they described Women in the Mosque as "a little group of six or seven feminist Islamists,"[24] and claimed that they were "using the term 'basement' in an ambiguous manner, and spreading lies that obviously lead to *fitna* [discord]."[25] The aim of these comments was manifestly to discredit the women, and to imply that their criticisms were misplaced, since the basement (the mosque's own term) to which the women's prayer room had been relocated was a finished and decorated space. These responses neither satisfied nor dissuaded Women in the Mosque, who retained a lawyer and started an online petition that received over a thousand signatures.

A pair of women, Aicha and Selma, returned to for a third time to pray in the main hall. "I was animated by a force that surprised me," one of them wrote afterward, in a statement circulated on social media.

> Animated by love for my sisters. I was filled with energy. The energy of Fatima Zohra, beloved daughter of the Prophet [Muhammad], of Aicha Manoubia, of Aicha As-Sadiq,[26] I invoked all these servants of Allah. In the back of the space, I felt gazes upon me. I made two rakats, for the mosque.... As a Muslim, I felt at home. I protect myself with His name, I seek refuge in His citadel. I need His protection, I know it.[27]

Aicha and Selma draw out the affective registers of sisterhood that animated the Women in the Mosque movement—the love for their sisters, the feeling of home and belonging in the mosque, and the force and energy of resistance.

Women in the Mosque were ultimately unsuccessful in their campaign to restore women's use of the upstairs prayer hall. Their period of dissent exemplified a practice of sisterhood as double critique. They had to simultaneously navigate their pain at the violent Islamophobia toward the mosque and their feeling of exclusion in their space of refuge. They also had to negotiate organizing for women's inclusion in a way that directly refused the term "feminist," knowing that this term would be applied to them pejoratively by mosque leadership. Saliha's words, "they call us feminists, but we are believers," encapsulated the fraught status of "feminist" as a term in French Muslim contexts. The historical imbrication of feminism and Western imperialism, and specifically the degree to which some prominent French feminists have taken leading roles in the legislative restrictions on Muslim women's freedoms, undergirds the understanding among many that "feminists" and "believers" are mutually exclusive categories.

Women in the Mosque drew on other references and traditions to frame their dissent. They cited the precedent of the practice at the Prophet

Muhammad's original mosque, in which hadith reports indicate men and women prayed in a single space without a barrier. They drew on their understanding of mosques as spaces of refuge, and they drew on the significance of the Mosquée de Paris as the central site of Islam in France. "It's symbolic," Saliha insisted. "If we don't have equality here, the equality that is described in the Qur'an and Sunna, where does that leave us? This place remains very important, it's an exemplar for the community." Most of all, though, they drew on their commitment to an agonistic practice of improving their community. "Our ultimate goal is to reform the behavior of men and women in terms of their spirituality and prayer," Saliha explained. "We see this issue of prayer space as something that has implications for the relations between men and women in all areas of life." As Ndella Paye put it in her write-up of the Women in the Mosque, "It is up to each of us to reform ourselves individually so that God can reform us collectively."[28]

The practice of sisterhood of Women in the Mosque exemplifies the agonistic dimension of sisterhood as dissent and double critique. Here, sisterhood was oriented *against* the institutional space of the mosque—and not just any mosque, but the most prominent one in all of France. But this was not the only way that women organized on gender-based terms to claim mosque space. In the next section we will see how women sought refuge in soeurénité *within* the institution at a very different mosque, while still engaging in a form of the "affective insurgency," in Chan-Malik's term, that we saw with Women in the Mosque.

SISTERHOOD AS RESPITE AT THE DAY OF BEAUTY AND WELL-BEING

On a balmy June Saturday afternoon, I arrived alone at Mosquée El-Amel, a suburban Paris mosque that I had visited several times. The mosque was surrounded by an ample, unpaved parking lot, which on this day was three-quarters full of cars. When I reached the entrance gate, color-printed flyers with pink flowers announced the "Sisters' Garden," and directed me to the rooftop terrace. On the terrace, I found several familiar smiling faces staffing a welcome table. Large, professionally printed posters announced the afternoon's activities for the "Day of Beauty and Well-Being": massages, manicures, hairstyling, makeup, tea and pastries, and an afternoon lecture by a Muslim family therapist. Admission was free, and the beauty services were available for a small fee, all of which would be put toward the mosque's *waqf* (endowment) and its planned expansion. The services themselves were donated by members of the mosque community, professional beauticians along with some amateurs. Men had been asked to abstain from the mosque for much of the day, as the high attendance necessitated use of the men's prayer room for the afternoon lecture. "Spend the day in total soeurénité," promised the posters.

I paid 10 euros for a manicure and sat down with a cup of tea to wait for Aïcha, a forty-year-old social worker, who was to give the manicure. A few minutes later, Aïcha emerged from her massage, relaxed and cheerful. While she did not ordinarily wear makeup, she had applied glittery blue eye shadow for the occasion. We entered the "salon," a classroom that had been temporarily rearranged and supplied with mirrors, tables of beauty products, and extension cords to power several hair-dryers. As Aïcha began filing my nails, a small circle gathered around our table, attracted both by Aïcha's skills and by my presence and motivations. By the time my second coat of clear polish had dried, we were engaged in a lively conversation about wedding planning, the challenges of living in the Paris region, and what sites they would most like to visit in the United States. Toward the end of the afternoon, word spread through the mosque that there had been at least two hundred women in attendance over the course of the day. The mosque's reputation for "openness," referenced frequently by women in the makeshift salon, had given it a wide reach.

Events such as the Day of Beauty and Well-Being, sponsored and hosted by individual mosques, are only one element of a rich culture of women-only social spaces in the Paris area, organized by and for Muslim women. Local nonprofit organizations offer low-cost exercise classes from Zumba to boxing, while small women-owned businesses band together to organize shopping days in large event spaces. Childcare is often provided, or women are encouraged to "leave the kids with daddy" and enjoy a day "among sisters." One association, Elles & Dyn, which was active for several years in the early 2010s, described its mission as "offering activities exclusively reserved for women in order to allow them to blossom, physically as well as socially and spiritually." Like many similar associations, Elles & Dyn had hoped to eventually open a physical location dedicated to women's well-being: "A real space of relaxation and leisure exclusively for women. A space where you can come play sports or dive into a swimming pool, but also benefit from the services of a hairstylist and aesthetician, do some shopping, and find a bookstore, a day care, and most importantly a tea room where women can have discussions, aid one another, and connect to one another in friendship."[29] Other women-only associations founded by Muslim women during the 2010s ranged from a collective of entrepreneurs that offered networking soirées and business development coaching, to a series of discussion circles focused on "the accomplishment and the acceptance of the self," to a spiritual reflection group called the "circle of freed spirits." This social fabric of single-sex (*non-mixte*) and predominantly women-of-color camaraderie, leisure, and personal development explicitly aimed to cultivate a set of feminine virtues: psychological equilibrium and emotional well-being, industrious dynamism and energy, invested motherhood, and sisterly solidarity.

Later in the afternoon at the Day of Beauty and Well-Being, Aïcha and I met over coffee and mini-profiteroles in another classroom that had been transformed into a café, with bistro tables and potted plants. As we talked, Aïcha drew an org chart in my notebook to explain the various "poles" through which the women's committee of the mosque organized their activities. They imagined the mosque not only as a source of religious education and space of worship, but as an anchor for the whole community: a place for childcare, mental health care, exercise, socialization, and beauty. Aïcha elaborated:

> We want to have sessions for women to "get in shape," at least once a week. The men have their time slots for sports, and we would like a time slot too, we have a right to that. . . . We want a trained female psychologist to come to the mosque one day per month and hold consultation hours, for women but also for families. We would like to hold these sisters' days twice a year, except that it's a huge amount of work, and we're going to need more help. But we have a lot of ideas!

The ambitious energy for developing a culture of soeurénité at Mosque El-Amel was echoed at other dynamic mosques throughout the Paris region. The financial and logistical support that women had given to mosque-building projects had fortified their sense of having "a right to the mosque," both in terms of its physical space and its financial and cultural resources. As Aïcha observed, "Women expect a lot from the mosque, you know, but then they're not so present on the level of decision-making, but that's changing—it needs to change. And besides, everyone needs to remember that if this mosque exists at all, it's because men *and women* gave, gave so so much money and they [*elles*] keep on giving—so watch out! Women are very invested." This sense of investment of money and time corresponded to claims of rights to the mosque's material resources, but also to expectations that the mosque would be a site for women's flourishing on their own terms. Acutely cognizant of gendered Islamophobia, these women expected the mosque to preserve a space of freedom—not only freedom from harassment, but freedom to enjoy the respite and security of sisterhood—the soeurénité of non-mixed community. As one woman opined during our conversation around the manicure table, "The restrictions on being Muslim in society, the problems at work, at school, or in the street; for me, they just remind me that true freedom is not about doing whatever I want in the world. We have to find the spaces of true freedom somewhere else—like here." Events such as the Day of Beauty and Well-Being invite women to a time and space of fortification for the frictions of daily life. Far from being purely a retreat, this space of freedom is designed to be generative, to reenergize women psychically, spiritually and morally, for their engagements at home and in the world. Unlike the women organizing *against* the institution at the Mosquée de Paris, these women organized *within* the institution to transform mosque culture in order to facilitate their freedom. In the next section, we will see how yet another group of Muslim women chose to organize *outside* traditional institutions such as mosques, building their own spaces and frameworks for the cultivation of sisterhood.

SISTERHOOD AS DECOLONIAL FEMINIST PRACTICE

The value and virtue of soeurénité can even extend to mixed-gender spaces as well. The landscape of gender-based organizing in the Paris-area Muslim scene included mixed-gender events that were also grounded in an ethic of sisterhood and solidarity. On the roof deck of the National Library of France, a vast modernist expanse overlooking the Seine River, about two hundred people from many different walks of life gathered on a long summer evening for what had been announced as a feminist iftar. The iftar was organized by a recently founded Muslim feminist collective and had been broadly publicized on social media. The crowd of attendees was young, like the founders of the collective. As the gathering grew, more picnic blankets were produced, extending the "table" along the length of the esplanade. An adjacent wall had been bedecked with festive pennants to mark the space. Nearly everyone had brought a dish to share, whether it was a homemade salad or a pizza from around the corner, and the organizers were prepared with ample bottles of water and fruit juice. Although it was already 9:00 p.m., the lowering sun still cast a rosy glow over the group, as people began to chat with their neighbors.

Before eating, we were invited to break up into circles of eight to ten individuals. Malika, one of the organizers, stood up with a portable microphone and announced the evening's themes of discussion: "What does feminism mean to you? What is decoloniality anyway? And what does any of it have to do with Islam?" People looked nervously at one another. A man in our circle wondered aloud if he was supposed to leave. Conversation began haltingly in the groups, made up almost entirely of strangers, Muslim and non-Muslim, male and female, with many different frames of reference and personal connections to these questions. But half an hour later, as the organizers passed out dates and water in anticipation of sunset, the chatter was deafening. Dozens of cell phones sounded a tinny collective adhan, and the dates vanished. Some paused to pray; others didn't. All manner of food was passed up and down the esplanade. The boardwalk lights came on, and conversation continued late into the night.

The feminist iftar was different from the first two events in a couple of ways—first, obviously, it wasn't in a mosque, and second, it was prominently identified as feminist. The collective that organized this iftar hosts both mixed-gender events like this one and events for women only. They rarely partner with mosques, instead focusing on creating new spaces. They reach out to an "unmosqued" Muslim population as well as to engaged Muslim youth, inviting them to strengthen their stake in religious community—to find or develop meaningful ways of engaging with traditional knowledge or practices, ways of formulating religious commitments. Like Women in the Mosque, this collective is highly public and oriented toward the media. However, unlike the rhetoric of Women in the Mosque, they cultivate an image of activist engagement and gregarious socialization in which piety is one animating presence, but not the singular focus. And while both the decolonial feminist collective and the Day of Beauty and Well-Being are focused on building positive cultures of women's socialization, the collective foregrounds explicit political commitments and challenges participants in each of its events to engage with them. Akin to Justine Howe's description of the Webb Foundation in suburban Chicago, this collective is a dynamic "third space" outside of the mosque and the home for the enactment of Muslim belonging and solidarity. As Howe notes in Chicago, and as we saw briefly in chapter 1, "third spaces" such as community organizations and clubs "fulfil social and religious needs that members believe are missing from mosques."³⁰ Their desire to offer a sometimes-critical alternative to more traditional spaces of religious gathering, however, makes them no less important as expressions of investment in Muslim community.

As an organization, the decolonial feminist collective describes itself using similar language of choice, freedom, emancipation, and sisterhood that we saw with the Women of the Mosque and the Day of Beauty and Well-Being. In the online event description for the feminist iftar, the organizers wrote that "we are making a world in which women choose in total liberty the means of their emancipation." This language is central to their ethical culture, along with solidarity and sisterhood. They aim to "recreate the solidarities fractured by oppressive systems with the aim of sustaining ourselves. Sisterhood is the immutable link that women can weave through listening, sharing, and love." The collective's conceptualization of sisterhood is affectively grounded and politically salient, at once a form of piercing social critique and a conviviality among sisters that aims to remake the world. Whereas the women at the Mosquée de Paris organized against the institution and the women of Mosquée El-Amel organized to transform the institution from within, these women organized outside of traditional institutions altogether, building their own model for communities they want to live in, and forms of solidarity they want to inhabit. Each of these three positions is part of the broader critique of Muslim institutional spaces that we began to see in chapter 1, for example with Nadia and Sara from The Reflecting Pool.

At all three of these events, Muslim women are engaged in gender-based organizing in order to increase their ownership of and leadership within Muslim and French spaces. They differ in their approach and their priorities—there are disagreements among them and within them as well. But in all three cases, their sharp criticism of Muslim community structures and norms is a way of *belonging* to and *participating* in those structures and norms, not a way of abandoning them. This agonistic orientation and the frictions it produces give rise in turn to new cultural practices and new values, such as soeurénité.

SECULAR SENSIBILITIES BEYOND THE CRITIQUE OF SECULARISM

At the end of *Religious Difference in a Secular Age*, Saba Mahmood asks whether "secularity—as a substrate of ethical sensibilities, attitudes, and dispositions—[can] provide the resources for a critical practice that does not privilege the agency of the state."³¹ The practices gathered through the concept of soeurénité draw on a "secular sensibility" of choice, rights, and freedoms while being diametrically opposed to the political secularism of the state. As individuals for whom the state does not function as a guarantor of personal equality, liberty, or emancipation on their own terms, French Muslim women have pushed the potential of secular sensibilities as critical practice. We have seen how the discourse of the right to the mosque and the freedom of non-mixité exercise a form of double critique, challenging both male-dominated mosque leadership and secular norms. In what follows we will see how the moral language of free choice is likewise simultaneously a "secular sensibility" and a pious, counter-secular discourse. This language of free choice and emancipation, linked to the values of the spaces of soeurénité described above, offers a critique of state scrutiny of Muslim women's bodies and habits. The moral language of autonomy and choice has become especially constraining for women racialized as Muslim in contemporary France. I build on the work of Saba Mahmood and others who have argued that "unruly subjects . . . are crucially formed by operations of secular power even as they challenge many aspects of this operation,"³² but I follow my interlocutors in moving beyond a focus on the disciplinary apparatuses of secularism.

In a high-profile interview in April 2018, French president Emmanuel Macron addressed a topic of perennial anxiety in French politics—the Islamic headscarf, and whether and where it can be worn. Hoping to offer a more nuanced point of view than some of his colleagues, Macron focused not on the requirements of secularism, but on women's inner motivations.

MACRON: It's not true that secularism requires us to ban the headscarf everywhere. Now, me, am I happy to see a woman in a headscarf?
INTERVIEWER: Yes, how does that make you feel?
MACRON: I respect her! But I want to be sure of one thing, that it is her choice.
INTERVIEWER: So it *could* be her choice?
MACRON: It could be. And therefore in the Republic we must tolerate it.³³

This exchange encapsulates a major strand of current French public opinion on the headscarf, especially among those non-Muslim French who consider themselves broadminded toward cultural diversity. The headscarf might not be a "happy" sight, in Macron's words, but the woman who wears it must be respected and tolerated, so long as her scarf meets the standard of having been freely chosen. Indeed, this freely chosen headscarf is read by some

French observers as a beacon, the first step on a teleology of authentic liberation, prodded by civic and cultural forces, and made explicit in the pedagogy of the public schools. In the words of former president François Hollande, "Today's veiled woman will be tomorrow's Marianne. Because if we succeed in offering her the conditions for her flourishing, she will liberate herself from her veil and will become *a Frenchwoman, capable of embodying an ideal*, while still being religious if she wants to. In the end, what are we betting on? That this woman will prefer liberty to servitude. That the veil may be a protection for her, but that tomorrow she will not need it in order to be assured of her place in society."[34] Hollande's language makes quite concrete the state pedagogical project of producing secular subjects. His language of the capacity to "embody an ideal" recalls Charles Taylor's account of secular individuals as "buffered selves" who are "essentially ... aware of the possibility of disengagement" from their social context.[35] This location of transcendence in the subject is, as Hollande recognizes, compatible with "still being religious if she wants to." However, this contingent religious practice must remain subordinate to the pieties of secular society and to "being a Frenchwoman"—a project with key embodied markers.

Conscious of their role in the administration of these secular pieties, observers like Macron and Hollande are especially anxious to discern which scarves are "freely chosen" and which are not. For some observers, this question vexes the mind; it raises philosophical questions of agency and performance while also demanding careful empirical attention. For their part, however, most French Muslim women, especially, but not only, those who dress in religiously-marked ways, systematically describe their performance of religious norms in terms of choice, rights, freedom, and autonomy. Slogans like *Mon voile, mon choix* (my veil, my choice) or *Le voile, ma liberté* (the veil, my freedom), however counterintuitive they may still seem to some non-Muslim French, have been staples of French political discourse since at least the 1990s. Indeed, in the French public sphere, it has become nearly impossible to offer any reason for wearing modest dress *other* than deliberate and autonomous individual choice. And far from a duplicitous understanding of modest dress, on which one speaks publicly of choices and privately of subjection, the language of choice and freedom is an integral part of personal and collective moral cultivation in many Islamic settings. The incessant assumption that women only wear modest dress out of patriarchal coercion has demanded a response in terms of personal choice and autonomy, and the increasing encroachments upon women's sartorial freedom have demanded a response in terms of secularism and equality. This language of autonomy, freedom, choice, and emancipation resonates with the moral vocabulary of all three spaces of gender-based organizing that we saw earlier in this chapter. However, the prominence of liberal moral language in Islamic contexts is no indicator of a teleology of Republican emancipation—of becoming "tomorrow's Marianne," in Hollande's terms. Instead, it offers a framework for the intensification rather than the dilution of religious aspirations.

The moral framework of free choice and emancipation is not a rhetoric strategically deployed to highlight the hypocrisy of anti-veil policies—it is a pious disposition, an affective relationship with divine guidance and community norms. Rather than reading Muslim values of choice, freedom, and rights as evidence either of the "integration" of Muslims into France or of the totalizing effect of secularism, I argue that Muslims are central contributors to the production of liberalism and secularism in France—not as a political project, but as a "way of life."[36]

The secular character of many Islamic discourses has long been recognized, but this secularity has often been analyzed in terms of either a symbolic cultural identity of "secular Muslim," or a rationalized "secular religiosity" that separates essential truths from contingent phenomenal forms, historicizing scriptural revelation and relativizing the importance of rituals, liturgies, or embodied affect.[37] Both of these are typically contrasted to nonliberal forms of piety, embodiment, or scriptural hermeneutics that are often characterized as more "authentic" traditional alternatives to the symbolic use of religion in a secularized frame. The spaces of soeurénité present an alternative to these images of secular vs. authentic Islam. In the French context, the expression of "free choice" has become a political mandate and legal criterion with significant material consequences for Muslim women, and feminism is used as a tool of political oppression. Discourses of liberation are constraining and overdetermined, and many Muslim women in France seek freedom from oppressive deployments of "liberation." In the words of the decolonial feminist collective discussed above, "Don't liberate us, we'll take care of it!"

To fully understand the way in which Muslim French women are often "constrained to choose," I return to Saba Mahmood's classic account of pious agency as a challenge to core assumptions of liberal feminism, offered in *Politics of Piety*. For Mahmood, the women's mosque movement in Cairo offered an important challenge to a liberal feminist model of agency grounded in choice, freedom, and resistance to dominant norms. Normative liberal feminist assumptions, "such as the belief that all human beings have an innate desire for freedom, that we all somehow seek to assert our autonomy when allowed to do so, that human agency primarily consists of acts that challenge social norms and not those that uphold them," universalized a single account of the subject and her relationship to power and authority.[38] By the yardstick of agency-as-resistance, the participants in the Cairene mosque movement would inevitably be found wanting, a judgment with very real material and often violent consequences. Instead, Mahmood argued, we should "move away from an agonistic and dualistic framework—one in which norms are conceptualized on the model of doing and undoing, consolidation and subversion—and instead think about the variety of ways in which norms are lived and inhabited, aspired to, reached for, and consummated."[39]

As we saw in chapter 1, the Islamic revival also shaped the French Muslim sphere in recognizable ways: classes in Islamic sciences filled, male and female religious teachers attracted large audiences, and a generation of young people, most in their teens and twenties, cultivated a new, "knowledgeable" relationship to their inherited religious tradition, with an emphasis on ritual observance, the development of personal virtues, and an "Islamic way of life."[40] Women's engagement in the culture of Islamic revival was instrumental in the construction of the French Muslim landscape. During the period that women's study circles and family activities became part of the life of mosque communities, these communities outgrew the earlier makeshift prayer spaces. Hundreds of projects to finance and construct purpose-built mosques with more adequate space for all worshippers were launched around the country in the 1990s and 2000s, with women taking major roles as fundraisers and donors.

But unlike what Mahmood underscored in Cairo, pious Muslim women in France have long been impassioned and vocal about the fact that their piety, and their ways of expressing and performing it, are *choices*, made freely, deliberately, and individually. They speak about their pious engagement as a "form of emancipation"[41] and female empowerment, opening up avenues of self-discovery and critiques of patriarchal norms. As we saw above, while some distance themselves from both the label "feminist" and the attitudes that they associate with it, others take up the language of feminism while challenging its historical assumptions in the French context.[42]

In a conversation with a group of women at an end-of-school-year celebration at Mosquée El-Amel, the same mosque that had hosted the Day of Beauty and Well-Being, I raised the argument that religious practice might offer an alternative to a secular feminist emphasis on maximizing personal choice at the expense of other ties and commitments. Some of them objected:

"Why should secularism have a monopoly on free choice, or on liberty?" Ahlem, a dental assistant in her thirties, protested.

> To me, Islam has always very clear about the importance of our free choice. There is no compulsion in religion![43] And to me, that means that your religion, how you live your religion, that's *your* choice, and yours alone. No constraints. And it's very important to be conscious of this, because it's only *by* choosing yourself that you are doing it for Allah.[44]

Others nodded, but disagreed somewhat: "Of course, of course," interjected Aïcha, who, in her twenties, had studied Islam briefly in Cairo.

> But also, for me personally, Islam, I mean really *living* my Islam, it couldn't have been anything *but* my choice. What I mean is, I just wouldn't have come to it any other way. I don't know if it's the same for the girls I knew in Egypt—religion meant something different in their families, and then too, they haven't had to deal with France—haven't had to endure it! But me, I had to choose Islam personally, *myself*. Sometimes I still have to choose it every day.

Aïcha paused, smirked, and continued, self-deprecatingly: "Besides, I'm a product of the Republican schools. I like my free will very much, after all!" The group broke out in chuckles and rolled eyes. Aïcha went on to explain that her parents, like many Algerian immigrants, were not particularly enthusiastic about her "turn to religion" in her early twenties. Studying Qur'anic Arabic in the early 2000s, Aïcha had bonded with many of her classmates over their parents' incomprehension at their daughters' newfound interest in religion. Her point that her religious practice "couldn't have been anything *but* my choice" referenced this background. At the same time, Aïcha's understanding of "choosing Islam" as a daily act indexed the constraints of French society that produced this ritual of choosing.

For Aïcha, religious observance causes daily frictions—in her comings and goings between her downtown Paris office and her suburban neighborhood, in her interactions with her colleagues, and in her involvement with her children's school. Each of these moments of friction presents itself to her as a reminder of her choices—both her choice of a certain form of religious observance and what it might mean to choose otherwise. She thus constructs her "choosing Islam" on three axes: against the grain of her parents' expectations, against the grain of French society, and finally, aligned in an ironic way with the pedagogy of the Republican schools.

The emphasis on choice, freedom, and rights made by Ahlem, Aïcha, and others does not correspond to what Mahmood described as a symbolic semiotic of piety, according to which the headscarf, for example, is simply a *symbol* of cultural identity or of resistance to neocolonial power, but nor does it correspond to the understanding of veiling as habituation to divine will that she emphasizes among her Cairene interlocutors. Instead, these women conceptualized free, deliberative choice as its own ethical project— not opposed to or alienated from divine will, not calling into question the pertinence or validity of scriptural injunction, but focusing on the moment of choosing as the site of acquisition of the norm. While their insistence on autonomous individual choice may have been "secular" in Charles Taylor's sense discussed above, it did not align with a rationalized religiosity that reduced religion to a "system of symbols . . . ready for a cultured individual to interpret according to her poetic resources."[45] Of course, it should come as no surprise that the language of autonomy and choice is itself obligatory and constraining, and constrains some political subjects differently than others. Indeed, one hallmark of French secularism is its pedagogical character, including its reliance on the public schools as sites of authoritative moral formation.[46] But just as Mahmood argued about the participants in the Cairene mosque movement, Muslim French women are not caught in a binary of constraint/resistance vis-à-vis the patriarchal pedagogy of French secularism. They also inhabit moral language that they identify as secular, claim it, and reconfigure it.

II
THE POLITICS OF MUSLIM SOLIDARITY

04

THE SPECTER OF COMMUNALISM

As we saw in the first part of this book, cultivating Muslim community is a complex aspiration for many young Muslim social actors. The fraught nature of this aspiration arises in part from the fact that Muslims are constantly accused of "communalism" (*communautarisme*) in public discourse.[1] Through the discourse of communalism, French state elites simultaneously critique Muslims for a supposedly identitarian attachment to the religious collective and seek to manage Muslims *as* a collective, through religious authorities, mosques, and community organizations. As we have seen, in spite of this sharp politicization, some Muslims remain deeply invested in the idea of Muslim community and seek to build it on their own terms. They do so, however, in the teeth of an apparatus of surveillance that focuses its attention on practices, institutions, and ideals of community. Since 2015, and particularly since 2020, the French state has been engaged in increasingly intense scrutiny and policing of Muslim collective life. To account for these dramatic developments, this second part of the book takes up "moral community" as an object of state scrutiny and management. These two chapters show how "communalism" and "identity politics" are primarily practices of the state, rather than practices of Muslim French citizens.

In chapter 1, we saw how Young Muslims of France's "Bougez, votez" campaign drew on Republican values to mobilize for civic participation. In chapter 2, we saw how Muslim student organizers in and around the grandes écoles drew on their religious ethics to seek educational and socioeconomic advancement in French society. And in chapter 3, we saw how soeurénité and sisterhood as organizing values produced rich interconnections between groups that identified as feminist and groups that would eschew or critique that term. All of these forms of ethical investment in community are essential to the social fabric of democratic societies. And yet, French political elites continue to characterize communalism as a "separatist" political project that seeks to undermine the nation. Like the organizations discussed in part I, Muslim community organizations that were forcibly closed by the French government in a crackdown on Muslim "communalism" and "separatism,"[2] such as the Collective against Islamophobia in France (CCIF), also contribute to a democratic public sphere. The CCIF was the central actor of the broader social movement against Islamophobia, as well as a significant part of the tissue of Muslim collective life in France. As Deva R. Woodly has argued, "[Social movements] remind members of the polity that there is a public sphere where politics can and must take place if democracy is to be both authorized by and responsive to the people."[3] Groups like the CCIF, and like other organizations discussed in this book, all work (or worked) to construct, broaden, and expand access to the public sphere in Woodly's sense. In other words, they contribute to French democracy by enriching the space of public discourse. They make it a space where Republican values, alongside other moral commitments, undergird practices of argument as a form of solidarity—what I have followed some of my interlocutors in calling fraternal critique. These practices of fraternal critique are not simply internal to Muslim communities, they are part of the democratic fabric of France.

This chapter details how the political rhetoric about communalism and "separatism" is being used to justify unprecedented restrictions on the freedom of association, and constraints on Muslim collective life and practice more broadly, including the forced closure of many dozens of community organizations, mosques, and prayer rooms.[4] While communalism is a term that only came to prominence in tandem with the current form of political Islamophobia in the late twentieth century, the term is used to critique many forms of organizing by socially marginalized groups, including anti-racist and LGBTQ organizing. However, there is particularly sharp rhetoric that uses "communalism" to delegitimize the concept of the "umma," or Muslim community, and to undermine value claims that might transcend the moral framework of the nation. This chapter draws on the 2021 "separatism law" and the 2021 Charter of Principles for French Islam, among other sources, to unpack why the idea of Muslim community is seen to pose such a particular threat to Republican political culture.

Each of these documents expresses anxieties about communalism and about Muslim community in particular. They each constitute an instance of what Francesco Ragazzi has called "policed multiculturalism," insofar as they both seek to govern the French public through recognition of its religious diversity, in particular through the recognition of Islam.[5] This "recognition of religion," of course, is precisely what the state claims it does not do, in the 1905 secularism law.[6] Nevertheless, and particularly acutely since 2015, the French state has engaged explicitly in the "recognition" of religion: directly engaging with religious authorities, attempting to pedagogically transform religious communities, and soliciting a state-approved version of Islam.[7] The first of the two documents under study, the 2021 Charter of Principles for French Islam, lays out a vision for President Macron's desired "Enlightenment Islam" (*Islam des Lumières*). The second, the 2021 Law to Strengthen Respect of the Principles of the Republic (*Loi confortant le respect des principes de la République*), widely known (including in official documentation) as the "separatism law," complements that vision with the regulation of various forms of cultural practice associated with Islam, and the revision of certain principles of the famous 1905 "secularism law" regulating religions and the 1901 law regulating community organizations. As we will see in the analysis of these documents, the French state seeks to do significant institutional and even theological work managing the boundaries, the nature, and the organization of an imagined Muslim community.

A METHODOLOGICAL SHIFT

Part II marks a methodological shift in approach from ethnography to the analysis of political discourse. While I (and perhaps my readers!) might wish for more ethnographic vignettes to leaven the sometimes dense textual analysis of these last two chapters, my years of in-depth fieldwork actually yielded very little commentary on the sensitive topics of state surveillance and political silencing. Instead, in this second part, I carry forward some of the orienting questions of the first part of the book—How are communities formed across lines of disagreement? What is the relationship between religious communities and the broader democratic societies of which they are a part? How are communities formed in a context of stigma and securitization? I turn to French legal and political texts as key sources to understand the material conditions under which my interlocutors live. I take up laws, charters, parliamentary reports, political speeches, and other forms of discourse, tracing the ideas of Muslim collectivity that we saw developed in a grassroots sense in part I through the mechanisms of state regulation. I do so in order to show the Janus face of "community": a concept that is simultaneously projected onto Muslims as a stigma and instrumentalized as a tool of governing Muslims. The discourse of communalism calls communities into existence and forbids them from existing at the same time.

This second part of the book serves as a sequel to the ethnographic chapters, as the bulk of my fieldwork was completed by December 2014, several years before the political developments that I trace in these chapters unfolded. At the same time, these political developments are only the current, intensified manifestation of long-standing patterns of governance of Islam in France, patterns that already shaped the landscape I described in part I. The rhetoric of communalism, separatism, and public order has deep roots in French politics, entangled with secular governance of religion generally and of Islam in particular. However, the regulations of the past several years have had an especially chilling effect on the sphere of Muslim public discourse in France. The forced closure of civil society organizations like CCIF and the charity BarakaCity, the surveillance and forced closure of mosques, and the passage of repressive policies such as the Charter for Principles of French Islam (discussed below), have all combined to constrain the possibilities for Muslims' public engagement on any terms outside those dictated by the state. In short, the lively arena of discourse and activism that I described in part I of this book appears to have contracted from its earlier form. This chapter will explore some of the reasons why.

Two weeks after I left France at the end of my longest period of fieldwork, the country was roiled by the January 2015 terrorist attacks at the offices of the satirical newspaper *Charlie Hebdo* and the kosher supermarket HyperCacher. Later that year, more than 130 people were killed and more than 400 were wounded in a series of suicide attacks at nightlife and social venues in eastern Paris and Saint-Denis, notably the Bataclan concert hall. In 2016, 90 people were killed in a vehicle attack at Bastille Day celebrations in Nice.[8] Most of these attacks were subsequently claimed by either Al-Qa'eda or the Islamic State (ISIS), a militia based in Syria and Iraq. However, most of the authors of these attacks were born and/or raised in Europe. This violence was thus manifestly a product of French and European society, rather than simply a "foreign" threat.

The 2015 attacks prompted the creation of a sprawling counterterror apparatus in France, with the immediate declaration of an extended "state of emergency" that did not end until the passage of a major policing law in 2017, the "law reinforcing internal security and the fight against terrorism," known as the SILT law.[9] This law made permanent many of the provisions of the ostensibly short-term state of emergency, notably the ability of the prefecture of police to close a house of worship for vindication of or incitement to terrorism, as well as numerous measures related to policing public space and surveillance of individuals suspected of endangering public order. In complement, the 2015 Intelligence Act concentrated powers of surveillance in the hands of the prime minister and Ministry of the Interior, obviating the need for court orders for widespread monitoring of electronic communications. A counterterrorism plan known as Vigipirate instituted a system of alert levels, and a corresponding military program known as Sentinelle increased the presence of the armed forces in policing France's cities. Notably, President Emmanuel Macron called upon the counterterror forces of Sentinelle in 2019 to control the "Gilets Jaunes" (Yellow Vests) demonstrations, a grassroots (nonreligious) protest movement focused on economic inequality.[10]

In short, beginning in 2015, the French police and surveillance state expanded rapidly under the aegis of counterterrorism, and at the same time the country continued to be marked by periodic outbursts of tragic violence. One of these incidents was the brutal 2020 murder of schoolteacher Samuel Paty in response to his classroom display of caricatures of the Prophet Muhammad, which I discussed in the introduction. This murder sparked the most recent round of legislation cracking down on "Islamism," "Salafism," and "communalist withdrawal." These policies have focused almost exclusively on Muslim culture and collective life. To understand these laws and their impact on the fabric of French society, we must first understand more deeply the key concept of "communalism."

"THERE IS ONLY ONE COMMUNITY; THE NATIONAL COMMUNITY"

Sociologists Marwan Muhammad and Julien Talpin write: "There is no word more disqualifying in the contemporary French public sphere than 'communalism.' . . . Since the end of the 1980s, Muslims have incarnated this particular danger to the 'republican order.'"[11] As a term of public debate, communalism refers to an imagined way of life and political philosophy in which people are defined by their belonging to a homogeneous and endogamous collective. Often styled as "communalist withdrawal" (*le repli communautaire*) from (majoritarian) society, it refers both to imagined patterns of exclusive socialization among groups sharing a particular identity characteristic and to claims made in public space by members of a community in the name of that community. In the former sense, communalism is close to "ethnic enclaves," and in the latter sense it is close to "identity politics" in the United States. These two interlinked forms of communalism—the lifestyle and the political—are understood to at once negate individual differences and oppose the ostensibly universal community of the French nation.

While most often associated with what we could call ethnic enclaves or identity politics, "communalism" and "separatism" are increasingly used in reference to all ethnically and religiously specific organizations, and to patterns of socialization within ethnic and religious groups. However, importantly, these terms never apply to the exclusive enclaves of the white or wealthy. This is in spite of the fact that demographer Patrick Simon has shown that on the whole, immigrants and their descendants are considerably *more* likely than the white French population to have close relationships with people of other races and ethnicities—it is white French people who are most likely to socialize exclusively with members of their own ethno-racial group.[12] Communalism is a term that only applies to the minoritized and racialized, never to the homogeneity or exclusivity of dominant French society.

The term "communalism" and its attendant forms first began to be used in the French media in the late 1990s and hit its first peak in the early 2000s with the most prominent "headscarf affair," when the 2004 ban on religious signs in schools was passed. Fabrice Dhume shows how during this period, political and media elites portrayed communalism as an internal-but-foreign existential menace to the "Republican model" of the nation as universal community.[13] The "foreign" nature of the communalist menace is simultaneously figured as Muslim and as Anglo-American. The two foils of communalism are the "separatist" Muslim family and the ideology of Anglo-American multiculturalism, linked through the recent neologism "Islamo-leftism" (*islamo-gauchisme*).[14] Like communalism, "Islamo-leftism" is a term of political anxiety that in this case aims to insinuate an alliance between leftists and Islamists to bring down the Republic. Critics of so-called Islamo-leftism draw a link between "foreign ideas"—multiculturalism and identity politics, seen to come from US university campuses above all—and foreign bodies: Muslims and people of color who understand themselves in terms of a dynamic collective and engage in community organizations and practices. This link between foreign ideas and foreign bodies animates the rhetoric of communalism.

It is a political platitude for the French to say that "there is only one community; the national community." In the aftermath of a 2019 shooting at a mosque in the southern city of Bayonne, the then prime minister Édouard Philippe invoked this saying in a speech before the National Assembly:

> In a mature democracy like ours, in a republic that is sure of its principles, we may all together consider that *there is only one community, the national community*. Every time that someone singles out such and such a religion or such and such a portion of the people, they thereby impoverish what the Republic is. That is to say a union, a nation, a daily referendum [*plébiscite*] of people who are not like one another, who don't believe the same thing, who don't look like one another, but who are united in the values of the Republic and in the respect of the law.[15]

Philippe's statement, which was met with much applause, was at once a rebuttal of the anti-Muslim violence and a rebuttal of those who would single out the Muslim community as uniquely under attack. For Philippe, the Bayonne mosque attack was an attack on France and France alone, and to single out and name the violence as targeting a particular religious community by virtue of their religion would be to "impoverish what the Republic is." The national community, in this style of French public discourse, is the only legitimate form of identification. Identity is conceived of as a zero-sum game, in which forms of committed group belonging—as Black, as Muslim, as queer—detract from the fullness of national identity and belonging.

Conscious of the dangers of this zero-sum logic of communalism, President Emmanuel Macron has tried at times to move away from the language of "communalism" to a language of "separatism." "I am not at ease with the word 'communalism,'" Macron said, in a major speech in Mulhouse in February 2020.

> I will tell you why. Because we can have communities in the French Republic. According to the country that one comes from, each person claims belonging to a particular community. The same is true for religion. However, these forms of belonging should never mean a subtraction from the Republic. In fact, they add something to it. They are forms of additional identity that are compatible with the Republic and that we do not seek to stigmatize here. . . . The problem that we have, it's when people want to separate from the Republic in the name of a religion or a form of belonging, and therefore no longer respect its laws, and thereby endanger the possibility of living together [*vivre ensemble*] in the Republic. In this

regard, when one leaves [the Republic] oneself, one endangers the possibility of others to form it.[16]

Macron distinguishes here between a thin type of collective belonging or identity that is compatible with Frenchness and a type of collectivism that he calls "separatism," which consists of a refusal of *vivre ensemble*, or living together, in the Republic. (We will return to this concept of vivre ensemble in chapter 5.) Later in the speech, he links this in particular to norms of gendered interaction, such as declining to shake hands with members of the opposite sex. In distancing himself from the term "communalism," Macron is making a gesture to pressure from the political left, which has been critical of the instrumentalization of this term. At the same time, he offers a model of community as an additive identity to the core Republican moral framework, reconsolidating national identity as the substrate and precondition of any vivre ensemble.

Despite the pains Macron took in this speech to defend the possibility of French people's legitimate belonging to diverse communities, the Macron administration has continued to mobilize the language of communalism, which remains widespread across the political spectrum. In 2019, the Macron administration requested the establishment of "Centers of Combat against Radical Islamism and Communalist Withdrawal" (CLIR) in each of France's 101 departments, followed by the establishment of a national CLIR in 2022.[17] These departmental centers, of which 83 had been established by mid-2020,[18] were charged with assessing the level of "communalist withdrawal" in their departments and coordinating multiple departmental resources to combat it. By June 2021, the departmental CLIRs claimed to have closed 615 individual establishments or organizations deemed "communalist."[19] These establishments, which have not been publicly listed, include schools, sporting clubs, community organizations, and houses of worship.

The 2021 "Law to Strengthen the Respect of Republican Principles," discussed in detail below, was also promoted through the framework of the fight against communalism. In the impact study that accompanied the proposed law, the parliamentarians defined communalism as "a relativist doctrine according to which an existing community, determined by a certain unity of culture (ethnicity, language, religion, customs), constitutes the *milieu of the full realization of the human being* [*le milieu d'accomplissement de l'être humain*] as well as the condition of his or her identity."[20] Communalism is framed as dangerous precisely because of the way it allows a "full realization of the human being" that is independent of the universalist values of the national collective. This understanding of communalism is linked to the fear, expressed in the impact study, that members of a given community will find their values "superior to others, notably to the national community, its unity, and its norms."[21] Policymakers thus draw on an account of the dangers of communalism and its intensified form, "separatism," that focuses on the possibility that individuals might find the fullest and best expression of their humanity in a specific community, rather than in the nation.

Communalism has also been prominent in politicians' public rhetoric. In late 2020, Interior Minister Gérald Darmanin kicked up a brief controversy with his reference to "communalist cuisine," referring disapprovingly to ethnic, halal, and kosher food aisles of large supermarkets. "That's how communalism starts," he complained.[22] Asked to respond to Darmanin's comments about "communalist cuisine" in supermarkets, the then minister of education Jean-Michel Blanquer told journalist Sonia Mabrouk approvingly that "we must be very attentive to even the smallest details of our collective life, because there are links among these different elements. I am concerned with the intellectual complicity in terrorism." He continued:

> Look, in this affair [of Samuel Paty's murder], there is not just a single assassin, there is an assassin who is conditioned by other people, who are in a certain sense the intellectual authors of this assassination.... And when you have these groups, like those that we are in the process of dissolving through the Council of Ministers, when you see this type of groups that are well established and that obviously don't commit crimes themselves but encourage this intellectual radicalism, they are in fact intellectual accomplices of crime. So we must be very attentive to that, because, as they say, "fish rot from the head down," in other words it is today's ideas, this communalism that comes to us from somewhere else, that comes from models of society that are not ours [that will rot our society].[23]

It is through this logic of the intellectual danger of communalism that the CCIF, a civil rights group focused on combating Islamophobia, became a target of the state during the aftermath of Samuel Paty's murder in 2020. As Blanquer lays out, members of the government drew connections between "even the smallest details of our collective life" and murderous violence, with particular attention paid to groups that appeared to defend "communalism"—that is, groups that organized around collectives as salient elements of the French social landscape, Muslims in particular. Blanquer also references the "somewhere else" of communalism that was discussed above, indexing the relationship between foreign (Anglo-American) ideas and foreign (Muslim) bodies that characterizes much of the rhetoric around communalism.

As Saïd Bouamama has shown, the specter of communalism has a long history in French national myth-making, from the stereotyping of regional linguistic minorities such as Basques and Bretons as unassimilable and antimodern to the stereotyping of Jews as dangerously disloyal to the national project.[24] "Far from expressing any reality," Bouamama argues, "the pseudo-communalism imputed to diverse groups is a political and ideological elaboration that promotes the construction of a credible scapegoat. This scapegoat offers social fears an 'object' to support them, one that works to delegitimize the resistances and revindications of equality of those who are accused of critically damaging national unity."[25] In other words, and as we saw repeatedly in part I of this book, minoritized communities can in fact be means of forming solidarity and mechanisms for claiming liberty and equality—the very values so often arrogated to the state and its national myth-making. These communities are crucial resources for combating discrimination and oppression. But the dominant rhetoric of communalism attempts to delegitimize these essential democratic resources.

"POLICED MULTICULTURALISM"

The idea of communalism presupposes a coherent "Muslim community" in France that competes for loyalty with an also presupposed distinctly different national community. Politicians constantly invoke the idea of a coherent "Muslim community" or "separatist Islam" as a social problem in order to justify policies that aim to repress collective solidarity and group identification among Muslims. These policies have the paradoxical effect of consolidating and isolating the "communities" that they claim to want to dissolve into the national whole. The state uses the idea of communalism to both call communities into existence and forbid them from existing at the same time. That is, alongside Muslims' own eclectic ethical projects of building community, accusations of communalism also construct the idea of "Muslim community" and reproduce conditions of marginalization that only further reinforce collective identification as a form of solidarity and resistance. "Community" becomes a form of governance, in addition to being a moral aspiration, as we saw in the first part of this book. As Mohamed and

Talpin put it, "Elected officials and state institutions bring 'communities' into existence in order to better control them."[26]

Political scientist Francesco Ragazzi has developed the concept of "policed multiculturalism" to account for the ways in which counterterror policies enact the "politics of recognition"[27] of multicultural governance, even as the politicians who enact these policies disavow multiculturalism. We see this "politics of recognition" throughout the government sources analyzed in this chapter, which seek to respond to individual violent acts by conjuring and managing "Muslim community" as a "racial-religious" political entity. Ragazzi argues that "the current forms of everyday anti-terror policing work precisely through what they are trying to avoid, namely a securitized management of diversity along ethno-religious lines."[28] He writes,

> The production and reproduction of distinct communities, far from being an unintended consequence of modern forms of counter-terrorism, is located at the very core of its *modus operandi*. Instead of working through homogenizing practices targeting the individual or affecting society as a whole, I argue that the current impact of counter-radicalisation policies is best described as "policed multiculturalism": practices of the production and management of diversity that remove fundamental questions about pluralism and citizenship from the political debate, casting them instead in the expert, technical, and de-politicized language of security.[29]

Policed multiculturalism operates through laws and policies like those we will examine in this chapter, policies that solicit and construct privileged Muslim interlocutors and collaborators for the state, while simultaneously subjecting large populations of Muslims to surveillance and profiling. Ragazzi points out how this engagement of trusted collaborators from the "suspect population" not only produces a "good Muslim, bad Muslim" dynamic,[30] but also legitimizes the state's actions through the active engagement of members of "the community" in question.[31] In Ragazzi's empirical analysis from the French context, the French counterterror and counter-radicalization apparatus, which is made up of social workers, local government officials, and school headmasters as well as security professionals, deploys a "structuring discourse" of secularism and communalism in its interactions with Muslim youth perceived to be at risk of radicalization.[32] That is, secularism is seen as integral to the process of risk prevention and counter-radicalization, and communalism and identity-based "victimization," in the words of one of Ragazzi's interviewees, are seen as key risk factors for violence.

The French security state and its political elites instrumentalize the discourse of communalism and the concept of secularism as part of national identity in order to manage the religious lives of Muslims in France. They do this through the surveillance and selective closure of mosques, through the expulsion of certain imams for reasons including sermons that "contravene male-female equality,"[33] and through documents like the Charter of Principles for French Islam, which I introduce below. State elites have an avowed agenda of fostering what they call an "Enlightenment Islam" and quashing not only concrete acts of violence but the broad ideologies that they term "political Islam" or "Salafism."[34] What they mean by these terms turns out to be somewhat elastic, with "signs of radicalization" sometimes taken to include Islamic practices as fundamental as praying more during the holy month of Ramadan, or practices of modesty such as avoiding mixed-gender swimming pools.[35]

This project of molding Islamic practice and discourse is distinct from but interrelated with the project of maintaining a secular public space free from religion, and a hierarchical relationship between the state and religion. Casual observers of French secularism often find the state's level of involvement in religious affairs surprising, given the state's avowed religious neutrality and the importance of secularism to French national identity. How can a secular state profess a project of managing religious affairs? In the words of the French Ministry of the Interior, "the state does not recognize any religion, but nor does it ignore any. The nonrecognition of religion does not mean that the state ceases to have relations with religious institutions; it simply means that political powers are autonomous and that religions are free to organize themselves."[36] As many scholars have shown, the active management of religion has long been a part of the secular state project, particularly, but not only, in France. French secularism does not only establish that the state does not "recognize, salary, or subsidize any religion [*culte*],"[37] it also establishes a hierarchy between the state and religions. As Solenne Jouanneau puts it, the French government "aims to definitively impose state rationality and Republican laws upon religious beliefs and practices. In other words, it is a matter of assuring that religious practices, beliefs, or authorities cannot serve as support for the contestation of the political and national order of which elected officials and bureaucrats would like to be the sole guarantors."[38] We will return to the question of the "contestation of the political and national order" in chapter 5. For now, it is enough to note that state management of religion generally, and of Islam in particular, is a long-standing pattern in the French context. Political developments since 2015, including the heightening of "policed multiculturalism," have intensified and in some cases rechanneled this pattern.

THE CHARTER OF PRINCIPLES FOR FRENCH ISLAM

On January 18, 2021, the French Council for the Muslim Religion (CFCM) presented a Charter of Principles for French Islam to President Macron. This charter, solicited by the Macron administration, was to be the foundational document for a National Council of Imams. The National Council of Imams, whose scheduled January 2022 inauguration was delayed due to a COVID wave and then tabled entirely with the collapse of the CFCM, was intended to be a certification body for imams trained in France, rather than abroad, in the vision of "Enlightenment Islam" laid out by Macron and other political actors. There is broad support among French Muslims for training more imams in France rather than recruiting foreign imams, sometimes salaried by the governments of Morocco, Algeria, and Turkey.[39] However, there is much contestation over what role the French state should play in the process of imam training, if any. For some, the proposed National Council of Imams merely replaced the older "consular model" of Islam in France with a nationalist model, exchanging one form of state oversight for another.

The CFCM was itself the product of an earlier wave of efforts at state management of Muslim populations through appointed representative interlocutors. Founded by the then interior minister Nicolas Sarkozy in 2003, the CFCM was the outcome of the French government's desire to have an "official" Muslim interlocutor as a means of regulating religious practices and defining an authorized "French Islam." This project dates back at least to the late 1990s, and takes up the legacy of the colonial management of North African populations through religion.[40] The CFCM was composed of seven independent associations of Muslims in France, including organizations closely aligned with Algeria, Morocco, and Turkey, as well as other organizations. During its tenure, the CFCM was the chief Muslim interlocutor of the French state under the aegis of the Ministry of the Interior. Over the years, the CFCM became moribund with internal strife among the member associations, and had little to no legitimacy for the majority of Muslims in France, whatever their relationship to religion. Most saw it as a bureaucratic arm for France's "Muslim policies."

While the CFCM drew up the Charter of Principles for French Islam, not all of the member associations initially agreed to sign on to it. In particular, the two Turkish federations and the organization Foi et Pratique (Faith and Practice), associated with the Tablighi Jamaat movement, declined to sign the charter in January of 2021 with the other organizations of the CFCM, saying in a press release that certain clauses of the charter "attacked the honor of Muslims, with an accusatory and marginalizing tone."[41] In late December of 2021, these three organizations finally reversed their decision and signed the Charter of Principles. By then, however, it was too late for the CFCM. Due in part to the divisions over the charter, the Ministry of the Interior had ceased to see the CFCM as a reliable interlocutor. In December 2021, Interior Minister Gérald Darmanin declared that the CFCM was "dead" and was "no longer the interlocutor of the Republic."[42] In its place, the Ministry of the Interior announced the foundation of the Forum of French Islam (FORIF), a new organism for state-Islam relations, in early 2022.[43] The members of FORIF, whose names were not made public, were selected by the Ministry of the Interior, and their mandate was, among other things, to manage the training and recruitment of imams and to apply the "separatism law" to religious organizations. I discuss this law in detail below.

Institutionally, therefore, the Charter of Principles has been (for the moment) somewhat orphaned, the product of a quickly obsolete formulation of state-Islam relations. Its content, however, is no less important, for it outlines the Macron-era vision of "Enlightenment Islam," and implicitly expresses the state's anxieties about Muslim discourse and practice, including the ever-present fear of "communalism." The signatories to this charter, in authorizing themselves to speak on behalf of Muslim institutions, also express a vision of the pedagogy of religious leaders over "ordinary Muslims." The charter makes regular reference to this pedagogical influence, reflecting the vision of the state as well as its privileged interlocutors that imams wield significant ideological influence over French Muslims generally. This vision is not borne out by sociological research.[44]

The Charter of Principles for French Islam is at once a political and a theological document. Ironically, this dual nature mirrors widespread assumptions about Islam as lacking necessary boundaries between the religious and the political. Instead of attempting to hold religion and politics separate, the charter deploys their conflation as a form of secular governance. That is, the charter instrumentalizes religion in the interests of secular power. The charter articulates a domesticated "Republican Islam" while repeatedly raising the fear of foreign influence. The document was designed to "frame the ethics and moral rules that should structure the operations of the National Council of Imams"—ethics and morals derived from the state, rather than from the imams' own collective or individual deliberations, informed by their multiple traditions.

The charter invokes the idea of a "pact" that links Muslims, "whether they are [French] nationals or foreign residents," to the French Republic. This "pact," which applies specifically to Muslims, "entails the respect of national cohesion, public order, and the laws of the Republic."[45] The charter repeats this framing of Muslims as somehow external to the national community, aiming to "instantiate peaceful and confident relations between the national community, in all its diversity and plurality, and all Muslims living in the territory of the Republic, whether they are [French] nationals or foreign residents."[46]

These provisions, and in particular the language of a "pact" between Muslims and the Republic, serve to place Muslims outside of the community of the nation, even as the charter admits that Muslims may (technically) be French citizens. This framing is repeated throughout the charter, with its constant concerns that foreign influence and agendas might be expressed through Islamic settings and rhetoric.

The explicitly stated commitments of the signatories to this charter are numerous and wide-ranging: they commit themselves to "reject all crimes against humanity,"[47] to "respect the freedom of thought, of conscience, and of religion,"[48] and in particular to reject the language of "'apostasy' (*ridda*)" or "*takfir* (excommunication)"[49] as ways of managing the boundaries of Muslim belonging. On the one hand, the signatories of the charter reject *takfir*, or the labeling of other Muslims as non-Muslims; on the other hand, they are being called in this very document to manage the boundaries of correct and incorrect Islam. The "freedom of thought" defended by the charter apparently does not extend to all religious commitments, which might include a different understanding of the boundaries of Muslim belonging than the one outlined in the charter itself. The charter asserts that "equality between men and women is a fundamental principle attested by the Qur'anic text,"[50] and commits the signatories to "inculcate respect of this principle in conformity with the laws of the Republic, reminding the faithful, in the context of our pedagogical role, that certain supposedly Muslim cultural practices have nothing to do with Islam."[51] These "supposedly Muslim cultural practices" that contravene gender equality are left unspecified.

The signatories further commit themselves to "refuse to engage in any promotion of what is known as 'political Islam,'" and to neither use nor permit anyone to use "Islam or the concept of umma (community of believers) in a political optic, whether local or national, or for the needs of a political agenda dictated by a foreign power that negates the plurality that is consubstantial with Islam."[52] The charter's particular concern for the nebulous idea of "political Islam," and for the relationship between religion and politics generally, is a way of policing the appropriate role of Islam in society—specifying the kind of Islamic arguments that are acceptable to make and the kind of concerns that are acceptable to take up from a theological perspective. "Our mosques and sites of worship," the charter states, "are reserved for prayer and the transmission of values. They are not constructed for the diffusion of nationalist discourses defending foreign regimes and supporting foreign politics hostile to France, our country, and our French compatriots."[53] In addition to the repeated specter of "foreign politics hostile to France," this passage indicates the assigned role of mosques and sites of worship as fundamentally ritual, not socially active and certainly not politically engaged. At the same time, mosques and sites of worship are being politicized by this very document, becoming spaces of disciplining correct religion as envisioned by political elites.

The linking of the concept of the umma or community of believers with "political Islam" indicates an anxiety over claims of Muslim collectivity—a sense that these claims are automatically linked to a political project that poses a threat to the Republic. There is also an internal contradiction in the way the charter uses the idea of the umma. On the one hand, it is held to be a dangerous concept whose usage should be curtailed; on the other hand, the document presumes and perpetuates the existence of a community of believers who can be educated and influenced by religious authorities.

Article 7, "Attachment to reason and free will," commits the signatories to a process of "guiding the faithful to reflection and helping them to distinguish, among scriptural sources, what is applicable in the context of French society." This process of discrimination is also described as a "harmonious adaptation of these universalist sources to the realities of our country," which will "allow each Muslim to reconcile his or her religious practice and his or her engagement as a citizen, in order to live out both in peace and serenity."[54] Again Islam is presented as being in a fundamental tension with "engagement as a citizen," needing to be "distinguished" and "adapted" in order to align with "the realities of our country"—realities that remain merely implicit throughout the charter.

The charter addresses anti-Muslim hostility and racism as one of these "realities of our country," but quickly turns to defend the French state against any charge of discrimination. "These [anti-Muslim] acts," the charter states, "are the work of an extremist minority that cannot be confused either with the French state or with the French people. Consequently, the denunciations of a so-called state racism, like all victimizing postures, are instances of defamation. They nourish and exacerbate both anti-Muslim hatred and hatred of France."[55] The concept of "state racism" is a phenomenon of considerable public and scholarly debate,[56] but the charter commits its signatories to understanding claims of state racism as not only a "victimizing posture" but also a form of "defamation." "Defamation," the charter goes on to specify, is "a crime, and forbidding it is a moral imperative."[57] In support of this, the charter quotes a verse from the Qur'an: "O you who believe! If a disobedient one comes to you with information, investigate, lest you harm a people out of ignorance, and repent thereafter what you have done" (Qur'an 49:6). The identification of claims of state racism with "defamation" in a charter of Islamic principles calls critical attention to the relationship between Muslim communities and anti-racist organizing, warning that the wrong type of political dissent is both un-Islamic and criminal. This provision in particular shows how the Charter of Principles is not only about Muslims, it is also about citizenship more broadly, and about what kinds of political speech are presented as defamatory of the state itself.

In article 9, the signatories to the charter commit to "privilege the French and francophone corpus to allow the best assimilation of concepts by Muslims of France and the greatest transparency of discourse." They further (and again) "refuse all rhetoric coming from foreign countries that aims, in a total misunderstanding of the realities of our society, to create discord and to divide us."[58] In this, the charter aligns with the widespread desire of young French Muslims to have a francophone religious discourse. In the process, however, it stigmatizes non-French discourses as lacking in "transparency" to French-speakers, and links them to divisive "rhetoric coming from foreign countries." Notwithstanding this repeated concern about foreign influence, this document was composed with the cooperation of religious representatives who are closely aligned with foreign governments, despite the fervent desire of the younger generation of French Muslims to abandon the "consular model" of Islam in France.

In certain ways, both the Charter of Principles itself and its language of a "pact" to "respect national cohesion and public order" echo the famous clerical oath of Revolutionary France. In the winter of 1790, the nascent National Assembly required that all members of the Catholic clergy swear a public loyalty oath to the nation, the law, and the constitution, establishing the primacy of their allegiance to the state and their assent to the Revolutionary reorganization of the Church.⁵⁹ This idea of a hierarchy of commitments, with one's role as citizen always paramount, has been a hallmark of the French approach to religion since the Revolutionary era—long before the elaboration of state secularism at the dawn of the twentieth century. It has also been a persistent theme in France's governance of Islam and Muslims. The Charter of Principles for French Islam, as a prelude to Macron's planned "Council of Imams," is a sort of clerical oath for the twenty-first century, demanding that religious officials *as religious officials* publicly avow their loyalty to public order, which their vocation is presumed to implicitly threaten.

THE "SEPARATISM LAW"

Simultaneously with the development of the Charter of Principles, the Macron administration pursued major legislation to combat Islamism and Salafism. The Law to Strengthen Respect of the Principles of the Republic, or the "separatism law," was proposed in December 2020 and passed in August 2021. The early development of this law by the Macron administration began in the summer of 2020, thus predating the October 2020 murder of schoolteacher Samuel Paty by several months. However, it was after Paty's assassination shocked the country that the separatism law took on new force as well as heightened societal significance.

The broad outlines of the law were sketched by Macron in a major speech in the Parisian banlieue of Les Mureaux on October 2, 2020 (exactly two weeks prior to Paty's murder). In the speech, Macron called for a "Republican reawakening." He organized his response to "political Islam" around a surely-not-coincidental "five pillars," echoing the five pillars of Islam itself. These pillars were: (1) expanding and deepening the secularism of public services, (2) tightening the regulation of the educational system, (3) reforming the laws regulating community organizations, (4) cultivating an *islam des Lumières* (Enlightenment Islam), and (5) nourishing a renewed love of the Republic. In Macron's words, "If we must make the Republic feared, by applying its laws without weakness and reviving the power of the law, if we must reconquer through these pillars that I have laid out, we must also make [the Republic] beloved once again, by demonstrating that it can permit everyone to construct their life."⁶⁰ This call to make the Republic both feared and beloved once again exemplified the carrot-and-stick approach of Macron's proposed legislation. "To radical Islam, brandished with pride,"

Macron said, "we must oppose a confident Republican patriotism, and go even further." His speech in Les Mureaux outlined an approach to legislation that placed the cultivation of identitarian secularism and French identity at the heart of counterterrorist policymaking.

At the same time, in the impact study that accompanied the law, the parliamentarians clarified that the law was not necessarily about terrorism at all. "The present proposed law," they wrote, "aims [instead] to respond to separatist tendencies that constitute a form of antithesis to the Republican project but that do not manifest systematically in terrorist acts, even though they may constitute the ideological substrate of these acts."[61] In other words, the law saw collective practices and norms that the parliamentarians identified as "separatism" as the precondition for and justification of terrorism, without necessarily having anything to do with violence itself.

Much of the final draft of the separatism law closely tracked the first three of Macron's "five pillars," the fifth—love of the Republic—being especially difficult to legislate into existence. (The fourth pillar, cultivating an Enlightenment Islam, was addressed through the Charter of Principles for French Islam discussed above, along with the National Council of Imams.) The first provision of the law expanded the scope of secular neutrality to include private contractors of the state, such as transportation workers. In practice, this means that these workers, although they may technically be employees of private companies, are considered like state representatives in that they are prohibited from manifesting religious belonging, such as by wearing a headscarf. This provision manifested a so-called *laïcité de combat* or "combative secularism," a term reappropriated from French late nineteenth- and early twentieth-century anti-clerical movements to refer to the contemporary deployment of secularism in culture war offensives. The idea that preventing bus drivers from wearing religious garb will contribute to reducing acts of mass violence is typical of this weaponization of secularism, as well as of the creeping privatization of secularism that I discuss in chapter 5.

Other provisions of the law treated Macron's second "pillar," the reform of laws regulating community organizations. These organizations face increasing regulation and expanded possibilities for the state to dissolve them for "seriously troubling public order or attacking fundamental rights and liberties."[62] Most prominently, community organizations that receive any state subsidy, contract with the state, or host youth doing community service (which is most civil society organizations in France) are now required to adhere to a new "Republican contract." It is important to note that France has a rich culture of voluntary associations, often subsidized by the state. These state subsidies, grants, and relationships expose this realm of civil society to potential government intervention.

The "Republican contract" is analogous in some ways to the "pact" language of the Charter of Principles for French Islam. It commits the leaders and members of associations to not engage in any activity that is against the law or causes "serious trouble to public order." They further commit themselves not to draw on their "political, philosophical, or religious convictions in order to liberate themselves from the shared rules that govern their relations with public collectivities. Notably, they commit themselves to not call into question the secular nature of the Republic."[63] This reference to "the secular nature of the Republic" betrays the anxiety about religious organizations that animates this contract, even though it is obligatory for all community organizations, whether faith-based or not. The contract goes on to commit its signatories to refrain from proselytism, to reject racism and anti-Semitism,[64] to take measures to combat sexual violence and sexism, to not provoke hatred or violence, and to not "exploit the psychological or physical vulnerability of their members . . . whether through pressure or attempts at indoctrination." Finally, signatories to the contract commit to respect the flag, national anthem, and motto of the Republic. Organizations found to be in violation of the Republican contract will have to repay any subsidy and may be dissolved by the state. This new "Republican contract" has been the object of significant criticism by a wide range of civil society actors, who see in it both an attitude of suspicion and control on the part of the state, and provisions that could be used to penalize numerous kinds of public demonstrations that might include civil disobedience. As with the expansion of secular neutrality to private contractors of the state discussed above, the Republican contract draws on a *laïcité de combat* in which recognition of secularism becomes a mandate used to manage community organizations.

To address Macron's third "pillar," the educational system, the separatism law made public or private schooling mandatory from the age of three, restricting the authority of parents over their young children's education and development. The law severely curtailed the (quite marginal) practice of homeschooling, now only permitted in very specific cases approved by the state, such as medical needs. Parents' philosophical preferences are not accepted as a justification for home education. The law also curtailed and more intensively regulated private schools *hors contrat*, or without a contractual agreement with the state, which are not bound by state curricula and do not receive public financing. Both homeschooling and hors contrat schools are relatively rare in France, as most private schools are contracted with the state, teach state curricula, and receive public funds. Private schools hors contrat include most but not all Islamic schools, as well as some Montessori and Waldorf schools, and other schools with alternative pedagogical models.[65]

These three "pillars" were far from the only provisions of the law. In addition, the separatism law added an assortment of regulations of gender and family relations, some of which received outsized media attention. These regulations targeted miscellaneous perceived gender inequalities presumed to be related to Islam: forced marriage, an obsession with virginity, polygamy, and gender-differentiated inheritance. The law forbade doctors from issuing "virginity certificates," a practice so rare in France as to be quite difficult to measure.[66] The law gave the state official conducting marriages the power to further scrutinize a couple suspected of engaging in a "forced marriage," and to deny the couple the ability to marry if they continued to suspect coercion. The law reinforced existing regulations denying migrants the ability to obtain a residency permit if they were engaged in polygamy, and amended the law on inheritance to mandate equal inheritance shares for daughters and sons. (This last provision would render illegitimate many shari'a-informed wills, which often leave a greater share of the estate to sons than daughters, in accordance with men's greater financial responsibilities for their families in Islamic jurisprudence.) One notable additional provision that was debated in the National Assembly and the Senate but not included in the final draft of the law would have forbidden minors from wearing headscarves anywhere in French territory, invoking the assumption that girls are coerced by male relatives to wear headscarves—an assumption that has been disproved by ethnographic and sociological research.[67] The law and its surrounding debate thus draw on what Lila Abu Lughod terms "key symbols of Muslim women's cultural alienness"[68] to frame Islam as uniquely oppressive to women, and to link this supposedly heightened oppression of Muslim women to a violent political project perceived to be present in French mosques and other Muslim collective spaces.

The provisions of the separatism law do not stop there. The law adds a new ability for the state to close places of worship for hate speech or violations of "public order" (article 44), and it increases the penalties for crimes of defamation or hate speech when these crimes are committed in religious spaces (article 39). Finally, in one of its most impactful sections, the separatism law introduces a range of new and modified regulations of religious organizations, which are governed by the laws of 1901 and 1905, concerning community organizations and secularism and religious freedom, respectively. Religious organizations of any size and budget are required to undergo an annual "certification of accounts," declaring the sum total of their donations and expenses and the locations of their religious activities (article 33). In particular, they must declare donations of over 10,000 euros from foreign persons or entities. The law strengthens the distinction between *religious* organizations (*associations cultuelles*), cultural organizations (*associations culturelles*), and those that have both religious and cultural aims (*associations mixtes*). Donations for and expenditures on religious and cultural activity must be declared to the state separately, and funds must be held in separate bank accounts. "Cultural" activities encompass anything that is not strictly ritual, including education and youth programming—fundamentals of most mosques and other religious organizations. These regulations will significantly impact most mosques, and indeed most houses of worship of any faith, by creating layers of bureaucratic oversight of what is properly "religious" (*cultuel*) and what is not, and by significantly increasing state scrutiny of their finances.

Taken as a whole, the separatism law regulates Muslim collective life on several fronts and through multiple avenues. The law tightens the state scrutiny of religious organizations, both mosques and community associations, and creates or increases penalties for a range of infractions related to religion and religious speech, including criminal proceedings and permanent closure of religious organizations. Through numerous gendered provisions, it contributes to the specter of Muslim women's singular oppression and to the fantasy, repeated in French lawmaking, that the state can save Muslim women from male tyranny over their bodies.[69] Finally, the law inserts language and oversight of the "respect of secularism" into the law governing private organizations and agencies contracted with the state. This includes the establishment of "secularism specialists" (*référents laïcité*) in various jurisdictions around the country, who participate in the enforcement of the respect of identitarian secularism by lower-level state agencies. This provision of the separatism law allowed the minister of the interior to call a special review of the Grenoble city council's 2022 decision to allow full-coverage bathing outfits in municipal pools, resulting in the Conseil d'État's overturning of this decision.[70] Thus, the separatism law is already being invoked to curtail women's freedom of dress and municipal councils' ability to regulate their own city facilities.

The separatism law has been the object of lively debate and substantial criticism from major French civil society actors. Numerous consortia of community organizations, including the League of Human Rights and the

Citizens' Organizations Collective, signed open letters in protest of the law. They were joined by groups ranging from the National Federation of Street Arts to Greenpeace France.[71] All of these organizations felt interpolated by the constraints on freedom of association contained in the separatism law, in particular the requirement for community organizations to sign, uphold, and enforce among their members a "Republican contract" enjoining respect for secularism and "public order." In the words of one of the open letters, the separatism law "will seriously weaken the Republican principles that it pretends to uphold."[72] The "Republican contract" was singled out in another letter for being a "contract of defiance" against the whole sphere of civil society, which would "grievously weaken the life of community organizations which is, in our country, a pillar of citizenship."[73] The widespread concerns of civil society organizations were borne out in September of 2022, when the separatism law was used to demand a return of state subsidy from Alternatiba Poitiers, a (nonreligious) environmentalist organization that held a festival including "civil disobedience training."[74] Alternatiba Poitiers, a small organization with an annual budget of 21,000 euros, was required to repay 10,000 euros of subsidies to the state as a consequence of organizing this training. This incident manifested the fear of many community organizations that not only Muslim communities are under attack by the state, but that there is also a broad effort to regulate the public sphere as a whole under the aegis of the fight against "separatism."

In addition to civil society organizations, religious leaders of numerous traditions and denominations have critiqued the separatism law, on overlapping but distinct grounds. Muslim representatives from the CFCM critiqued the law to the National Assembly as it was being debated, along with members of other religious groups, including Christians, Jews, and Buddhists.[75] After the law's passage in July 2021, representatives of the Protestant, Catholic, and Orthodox churches in France appealed to the Constitutional Council to call the law's constitutionality into question, but to no avail.[76] While the churches applauded many aspects of the law, notably its gendered provisions, they protested its "spirit of control" over religious life.[77] They contrasted it unfavorably with the secularism law of 1905, arguing that "from a law which enumerates the conditions of liberty and allows that liberty to be exercised, we have arrived at a law of multiple constraints and forms of control."[78] The Christian organizations saw in the separatism law a sweeping attack on freedom of religion, one that would be particularly constraining on religious activities with a "mixed" religious and social mission, such as religious scouting groups or groups that undertake the maintenance of church organs and buildings. But they also saw a particular danger for French Muslims. "How can we hope," they asked, "that these legal provisions will give our Muslim fellow citizens confidence in the willingness of the Republic to permit them to live their faith with freedom and a sense of responsibility, and to practice their religion with the sole constraint of the respect of public order?"[79] The Christian organizations concluded by calling attention to the law's "attack on fundamental freedoms of religion, association, education, and even freedom of opinion, which is already being abused by a thought police that is more and more present in common space." Like the civil society organizations, these religious leaders pointed to what they characterized as the law's broad illiberalization of the public sphere, including spheres of religious activity and community organizing. In the words of a joint group of imams and priests writing in protest against the law, the law "makes believing and practicing citizens exceptional citizens, to be surveilled." It "passes from a secularism that seeks to protect freedoms of conscience and religion as public freedoms to a secularism of controlling religions in the name of values defined by the state."[80]

"A MILIEU FOR THE FULL REALIZATION OF THE HUMAN BEING"

What do we learn about the state's view of Muslim community from reading the Charter of Principles and the separatism law together? We see that the state views Muslim community as a potential threat. The state uses political violence as an excuse for pursuing the admittedly only partly related project of curtailing "separatism," a form of "communalism" that the state argues offers the ideological substrate for violence, even as state actors explicitly acknowledge that this connection is often merely imagined. The state does this by cracking down broadly on sites of worship, schools, and community organizations, and by singling out Muslim religious leaders and enjoining them to sign a special statement of Republican loyalty. Further, the state sees the promotion, expansion, and "respect" of secularism as a central part of its counter-radicalization toolkit, which in practice serves to curtail religious expression in an ever-wider arena. The state identifies increased religiosity with increased risk of violence, and surveils accordingly.

In the Charter of Principles for French Islam we saw how the concept of "umma" was singled out as a potentially dangerous political concept. In the separatism law we saw how community organizations and sites of religious worship are coming under increasing regulation, in what civil society groups argue is an attack on the freedom of association. In both documents we saw how persistent stereotypes about Islam, such as the idea that it is uniquely political in orientation, or that it is uniquely oppressive toward women, continue to animate French policymaking.

This vision of Muslim community contrasts starkly with the way Muslims themselves perceive their religious community, as we saw in part I. Muslims seek religious community as a form of engagement in civil society, as a way to improve their lives and their surroundings, and as a form of collective expression. And indeed, in the words of the French parliamentarians defining "communalism," some Muslims do seek religious community as "a milieu for the full realization of the human being," as a setting that provides the conditions for a holistic moral project, and as a collective form of human flourishing.[81] These Muslims would argue that valuing their communities as milieus for the full realization of the human being is in fact part of the freedom of association that is foundational to the Republic. Current French lawmakers, by contrast, see all this as a form of "communalism" that poses a threat to the moral primacy of the nation. While many Muslim community activists understand community practices to constitute an essential part of democracy and democratic tradition, the state instead places its emphasis on enforcing "respect for Republican values" and the centrality of the Republic as the single moral frame of reference for its citizens. We will expand on this idea of regulatory French moral community in chapter 5.

FROM SECULARISM TO PUBLIC ORDER

As we saw in chapter 4, an identitarian form of secularism is a key element of the increasing regulation of Muslim communities through the framework of "communalism." This identitarian secularism is at once "narrative" and juridical—that is, it operates simultaneously in the register of national identity discourse and in the practice of law. Mutations in the practice of French secularism in the early decades of the twenty-first century have increasingly aligned legal practices with the "narrative secularism" of identity politics.[1] But even as the legal deployment of secularism has expanded, secularism is also being superseded by the language of public order as a means for regulating Muslim practices. This chapter takes us from the "privatization of secularism" to the expanded, "immaterial" sense of public order (*ordre public immatériel*)[2] that is allowing state actors to enshrine a particular understanding of moral community and human dignity into law and authoritative political discourse. Whereas in chapter 4 we saw how the French state targets Muslim moral community for regulation, this chapter shows how the state also uses the idea of *French* moral community to regulate Muslim practices and individuals.

Historically, scholars have distinguished between the strict sense of juridical secularism of the law of 1905, which constrains only the state and its representatives to religious neutrality, and a "combative secularism" of political rhetoric, organized in recent decades around an anti-Muslim animus.[3] However, these distinctions are collapsing as French law and policy takes on the contours of the identitarian, narrative, and combative forms of secular politics, resulting in what some scholars have called a "new secularism" (*la nouvelle laïcité*),[4] or what legal scholar Vincent Valentin has referred to as a "communitarian conception" of secularism—in short, secularism as the identitarian anchor of a moral community.[5] This "communitarian conception" of secularism is the mirror image of the projected specter of Muslim communalism that we unpacked in chapter 4.

At times, the political forces of identitarian secularism have found the legal framework of secularism as articulated in the law of 1905 insufficient to buttress their policy goals of regulating Muslim practice. In many of these cases, political elites have increasingly turned to the language of "public order."[6] "Public order," once understood to refer primarily to a material condition of social peace, is interpreted with increasing frequency to refer to an "immaterial public order," a moral order implicating a particular ethical understanding of human dignity and particular ethical exigencies of collective life. According to Valentin, public order in France "encompasses more broadly a basis of principles and values, for the direction and protection of individuals and society, that the state understands to *supersede individual will*."[7] This immaterial conception of public order is a revival of older legal languages of "good morals" (*bonnes moeurs*) and is sometimes referred to as a "moral public order."[8] It buttresses the enforcement of increasing restrictions on religious expression in the private sphere in the name of a moral order articulated by the state, including a particular account of human dignity that at times notably encompasses a specific understanding of gender parity.

One important element that emerged out of this "immaterial public order" in French (and subsequently European)[9] jurisprudence of the 2010s is *le vivre ensemble* (living together), perhaps best translated as "coexistence." While it is often used in the context of calls to live peacefully in a diverse society, le vivre ensemble has also become a legal rationale for restricting certain individual freedoms in the name of a shared moral project. As Valentin puts it, le vivre ensemble is at once "a subjective right and an objective limit on the exercise of liberties. . . . Le vivre ensemble, like public order, is simultaneously the guarantee of and a limitation on individual freedom."[10] In other words, in the framework of emergent French jurisprudence, the state's admittedly fluid notion of the moral necessities of coexistence can serve both as the grounding substrate of freedom and as a constraint on individual claims to express that freedom, notably a constraint on women's modest dress, perpetually taken as the signature of Islam in public space.

In chapter 4, we saw how the state regulates Muslim community and collective practices through law, policy, and political discourse. We saw that the idea of Muslim collectivity, and especially Muslim moral community, functions as a looming threat in the French political arena. But moral community is not only an object of regulation by the state. In this chapter, we will see how the state also regulates Muslim individual practices through its *own* thickly normative ideas of moral community, as expressed through the three concepts introduced above: identitarian secularism, "immaterial public order," and "coexistence." We will see how French secularism has been privatized, in the sense that it now can be called upon to regulate the behavior of private citizens or the domain of private organizations, rather than only regulating the state and its representatives. We will also see what anthropologist John Bowen has called a turn to "values-based reasoning," a turn to making arguments against various forms of Muslim practice based on claims about shared French values that are held to underpin a democratic society.[11] Importantly, these forms of "values-based reasoning" are not reducible to secularism, either in its legal, political, or philosophical senses. The French state does not only regulate Muslim practice through the legal framework of secularism, despite the disproportionate attention given to secularism in studies of France and Islam. Rather, the state increasingly draws on a diverse repertoire of concepts, and in particular the idea of "public order," in order to police and surveil the practice of Islam. While the ideas of "public order" and of the *police des cultes* were present in the original legislation of secularism, they have developed into novel legal and political frameworks that extend beyond what some scholars have called the "liberal exception" of juridical laïcité.[12]

"THE SECULARISM OF BRIAND AND JAURÈS"

Despite widespread framings of tension between secularism and Islam, many Muslim activists in France have insisted upon positioning themselves *within* the framework of secularism, which they argue has been "radicalized" and distorted in opposition to Muslim practices since the late 1980s. Before exploring how secularism has been "privatized" by the state, it is important to understand how secularism in its "original" sense is understood and claimed by Muslim civil society actors. In a 2016 interview with daily newspaper *La Libération*, Samy Debah, the founder and then president of the CCIF, described his organization as motivated by "the principle of secularism, as it was understood by Aristide Briand and Jean Jaurès."[13] Prominent Socialist politicians of the nineteenth and early twentieth centuries, and cofounders of the left-wing daily *L'Humanité*, Briand and Jaurès were both instrumental in the composition and passage of the 1905 law on the separation of church and state. In referencing these figures, Debah was aligning the CCIF with an originary legal understanding of French secularism. He implied that since the late 1980s, secularism had transformed into a different sort of political concept, organized in particular around the management of Islam. This understanding of secularism is echoed in a number of the CCIF's annual reports. In the opening section of their 2018 annual report, the CCIF wrote that "in order to politically justify their racism, certain people don't hesitate to instrumentalize secularism in order to exclude and reject others."[14] They aligned themselves ironically with President Macron's own critique of the "radicalization of secularism"[15] and included in this annual report an article by Fatma Zragua, a specialist in workplace diversity and inclusion, titled "Toward a Radicalization of Secularism in France?" Macron's term "radicalization of secularism" reads as an intentional redeployment of language that has been systematically used by the state and other social actors to target Muslims, reinforcing the idea of a "moderate" centrist combat against "radicalization" in all its forms. I read the CCIF as borrowing this term ironically because they were long vociferous critics of Macron's policies related to Islam and so-called radicalization, so their usage of Macron's term was more likely intended to call out his hypocrisy than to amplify his logic. By their 2019 report, the CCIF had abandoned the language of "radicalization" and had shifted to the term "pseudo-secularism"[16] to describe this "combative" approach to secularism, which deviated from the secular tradition of Briand and Jaurès claimed by the CCIF. This language still implies an imagined "real" or "true" secularism that can be defended.

The CCIF is far from the only vehicle through which French Muslims have claimed the language of originary secularism against its loudest contemporary defenders. In the words of one Muslim activist, quoted by Amélie Barras, "We are for an interpretation of laïcité in accordance with the 1905 law. . . . Muslims in fact have become experts on the 1905 law."[17] Barras shows how Muslim French activists have "refashioned" secularism, reclaiming and appropriating it away from dominant state discourses. This is precisely echoed by Margot Dazey's research on Muslims of France (MF, formerly UOIF), in which she found that organizational leaders systematically described themselves as "experts on the Republic, on secularism, on [its] history."[18] In a similar vein, Alexandra Kassir and Jeffrey Reitz studied two groups protesting the ban on headscarves for women accompanying their children's school field trips, including Mamans Toutes Égales (All Moms Equal). Kassir and Reitz note that all the women they interviewed who had been involved in these protests "strongly endorsed the *laïcité* principle."[19] At the same time, like the CCIF, these women "consider that it [secularism] has been diverted from its original meaning as stated in the 1905 law and the Ferry-Goblet law on schools."[20] Similarly, Carol Ferrara, in her work on Muslim schools in France, shows how Muslim educators situate the framework of secularism as the very legal and social condition of possibility for their religious activities.[21]

But what exactly is this "secularism as it was understood by Aristide Briand and Jean Jaurès" that the CCIF and other Muslim groups refer back to and claim? How does it differ from contemporary invocations of secularism? Historian and sociologist of secularism Jean Baubérot describes how the development of the 1905 secularism law was a "pact" or a compromise in the "conflict between two Frances"—the anti-clerical Republicans and the loyalist Catholics. By secularizing the nation-state and stripping it of its Catholic identity but preserving freedom of religious organization unimpinged upon by the state, the law shifted the influence of religion from state to civil society. Baubérot argues that figures like Briand and Jaurès, as key architects of this compromise, articulated both "a different future from the conflictual horizon that confined the present" and "the will and the political possibility to act as much according to this utopian future as according to the present conflict, thus reaching a relative pacification" between the Catholic and anti-clerical factions.[22] It is perhaps this utopian vision of secularism as an entente that appeals to some early twenty-first-century Muslim activists, like those from the CCIF or Mamans Toutes Égales. Understanding the law of 1905 (and the preceding secularization of the public school system in the 1880s) to have wrested apart the French state and the Catholic Church, opening up the sphere of civil society as the appropriate domain of the religious and making space for religious plurality in the public sphere, Muslim civil society actors often view their activities as indebted to this law and to the provision of separation that it enforced.

This separation of church and state did not mean that religion was relegated to the individual realm, purely an affair of private "conscience." Baubérot notes that article 4 of the 1905 law, which deals with the distribution of church property, transfers this property to the control of associations that "conform to the general rules of organization of the religion of which they propose to assure the exercise,"[23] thus guaranteeing that, as a notable example, Catholic Church property would go to organizations that conformed to the authority of Rome rather than to independent local or regional authorities. This article was opposed by the radical separatists, for whom the provision was tantamount to state recognition of Roman Church authority. According to them, the state should only recognize *individual* French Catholics, not the "rules of organization" of Roman Catholicism as such, which individual Catholics might, after all, vociferously critique (and they did). But by passing article 4 over prominent opposition, Briand and Jaurès indicated that it was not only freedom of individual conscience that the 1905 law sought to protect, but also freedom of religious association and collectivity.[24] This is important to recognize in light of contemporary invocations of secularism that would confine the religious to the purely individual.

As Baubérot makes clear, multiple conflicting understandings of secularism have long coexisted in France, with different ones taking precedence by turn. The Briand-Jaurès understanding of "inclusive separation" that was victorious in the 1905 law, he argues, has become "dominated" in the present by a model of secularism as French civil religion, together with a new "identitarian secularism."[25] In harkening back to the secularism of Briand and Jaurès, Samy Debah and the CCIF, along with other Muslim social actors, claim a distinctively French political inheritance of secularism as the guarantor of the place of religion in civil society. However, and as Baubérot acknowledges, the history of secularism is not quite so simple as a narrative from originary liberal inclusion of religion to contemporary illiberal exclusion of religion from the public sphere.

Even at its origins, secularism was both an instrument of women's subordination and an artifact of French colonial rule over Muslim populations (in contexts where the law of 1905 did not apply). As Joan Wallach Scott has argued, "the discourse of secularism, despite its promise of universal equality, made women's difference the ground for their exclusion from citizenship and public life more generally." This was not because secularism inherited theological ideas about women's inferiority. Rather, Scott shows, "the apostles of secularism, in France and elsewhere, offered what they took to be entirely new explanations for women's difference from men, rooting them in human nature and biology rather than divine law."[26] In the French anti-clerical tradition of secularism, women were particularly demonized through their purported association with religion, their supposed inherent weakness and susceptibility to the moral seductions of priests. Relying on this association between women and religion, many secularists argued against women's suffrage (because pious femininity posed a danger to the Republican polis) in the same breath as they claimed that secularism guaranteed universal equality before the law. Secularism was thus the grounds for women's exclusion from the realm of politics, and at the same time women's ostensibly greater moral and pious sensitivity was seen as necessary for "civilization"—a complementarianism grounded in the emergent science of the nuclear family.[27] Even with the movements of women's political emancipation, Scott argues, a particular view of the social sphere "cordoned women off from the masculine worlds of politics and assumed further that public attention to welfare issues drew upon a natural inclination or sensibility of women. The difference of sex, still understood as an asymmetric relationship based upon inherent natural differences—men on top, women subordinate in some way to them—and necessarily organized in separate spheres remained, well into the twentieth century, the dominant model for representing gender in modern Western nation-states."[28] This asymmetric relationship relied on political secularism—not only the radical anti-clericalism that Scott cites, but also the more moderate separatist project of figures like Briand and Jaurès, who in practice remained ambivalent on the subject of women's suffrage, despite rhetoric in its favor.[29]

Secularism was not only implicated in this new science of gender differentiation; it was also central to the French colonial project, even though—and indeed, precisely because—the 1905 law of separation was not applicable in colonial territories. Mohamad Amer Meziane argues that the colonial and imperial theaters were pivotal for the development of secularism in the metropole.[30] He traces the history of imperial secularization to Napoleon's arrival in Egypt in 1798, when Napoleon instrumentalized Islamic rhetoric as an (ultimately failed) technique to govern the Egyptian population.[31] The construction and usage of religions by empire as part of a *police des cultes* (policing of religions) gives rise, he argues, to secular universalism, which can supersede and organize all specific "religions" through the engine of the modern state. In Egypt, by speaking in the name of Islam, Napoleon secularized French empire and made religion an instrument of imperial power, and this in the metropole as well as in the colony. No coincidence, then, that when Interior Minister Gérald Darmanin addressed the newly constituted Forum for French Islam (FORIF) in 2022, he quoted Napoleon's letter to the Egyptians, saying, "They will say that I have come to destroy your religion; do not believe them. I have come to restore your rights and punish the usurpers, and I respect God, his prophet, and the Qur'an."[32] By locating himself explicitly in Napoleon's legacy of instrumentalizing Islam in order to attempt to govern Muslims, Darmanin clarified the continuity of contemporary French secularism with Napoleon's vision of religion as a tool of the state.

Rather than reading the development of French secularism as the relegation of religion to the private sphere of conscience, which, as we saw above, is historically inaccurate to the legislation of 1905 and the 1880s, Meziane reads secularization as the articulation of a universal French subject, whose religion is *supposedly* indifferent to the state, in contrast with the racialized Muslim subject of Algeria and other colonies, whose religion is determinative for his or her political condition. He argues that the colonial schools and their "civilizing mission" were a laboratory for what Baubérot describes as the "secular pact" of 1905, as Catholic instructors educated Muslim students in the Republican universalism from which these students were simultaneously excluded.[33] As Baubérot writes, "the two universalisms—the Catholic and the Republican—meet up in an ethnocentric conception of civilization, and a patriotism in which the 'love of the fatherland' supplants love of humanity."[34] This "*catho-laïque*" compromise of the colonial school became a crucial precedent for the compromise of the law of 1905.[35]

So even though Muslim civil rights activists have consistently relied on secularism in their public arguments, the seams of this line of analysis are showing. As Meziane writes,

> Secularization [*laïcisation*] therefore never signified the absence of intervention of the State in the heart of religious practices. The practices of exclusion of Muslims are faces of a secularization [*sécularisation*] exposing its imperiality that are far from being simple exceptions to the regime of secularism imposed by the state. Even if the state no longer finances religions, it regulates and surveils them through an ensemble of practices that section 5 of the law of 1905 describes, in language that is still in force today, as the "police des cultes."[36]

In other words, the secular "pact" of 1905 is an imperial construction born out of the context of colonial rule and the domination of the state over racialized human capital and natural resources alike. It has historically relied upon and reproduced ideas of racialized religious and gendered difference and inferiority.

Today, political elites like Darmanin increasingly interpret secularism in ways that are at odds with the forms of civil rights activism (Muslim and otherwise) that have insistently claimed this history and legal concept as protective of religious freedom.[37] But what many describe as mutations in secularism are arguably a return to its roots. As Joan Wallach Scott and many others have shown, the supposed alignment of secularism and women's rights that is brandished by many of its contemporary partisans is historically unfounded: secularism introduced new discourses of women's inferiority through their association with religion. And as Meziane has persuasively argued, secularism is an artifact of colonial governance in which Muslims were defined as "racial-religious" subjects, not citizens. So we should not be surprised that secularism continues to be useful for state projects of managing Muslim women's comportment in particular. In the following three sections, I return to the concepts introduced in the opening of this chapter—identitarian or "privatized" secularism, le vivre ensemble, and public order—and show how each of them, in intensifying ways, governs the lives of French Muslims through the development of a thick idea of Republican moral community. This regulatory ideal of Republican moral community is complementary to the state management of Muslim ideas and practices of collectivity that we saw in chapter 4.

THE PRIVATIZATION OF SECULARISM

In the 2017 speech in which he pronounced himself "vigilant" about the "radicalization of secularism," President Macron reportedly declared that "the Republic is secular, not society."[38] This maxim would seem to uphold a sharp distinction between state actors and private citizens, supposedly central to the jurisprudence of French secularism. However, this distinction has been belied by a range of recent measures taken by a variety of state entities to expand the realm of secular neutrality from the state to the private sphere. While this mode of regulating religion has always been part of the broader discursive culture of secularism in France,[39] it contravenes the famous compromise of the law of 1905 and marks a shift in French jurisprudence, if not in broader political culture.

French secularism has been understood to require not only the separation of church and state, as articulated in the law of 1905, but also the religious *neutrality* of the state and its representatives. This has meant, in practice, that representatives of the state are strictly forbidden from manifesting any religious belonging in speech, dress, or comportment.[40] In legislation, this historically meant a strict distinction between agents of the state, who were obliged to present themselves as religiously neutral, and ordinary citizens, who were not, even in their engagements with the state. Indeed, the 2021 revision of the "Charter of Secularism in Public Services" reiterates a version of this distinction, although it indicates that the religious freedom of users of public services must remain "within the limits of the respect of the neutrality of public services," an ambiguous phrase suggesting that public services themselves are religiously "neutral" spaces.[41] However, under the influence of either "new" or resurgent interpretations of secularism, the application of secular neutrality to private citizens has expanded. This is what I mean by the "privatization of secularism": the encroaching transposition of legislative secularism from state contexts and actors to private or corporate contexts and actors. While the jurisprudence of secularism has long relied on a purported division between public and private actors, in the terms of Stéphanie Hennette-Vauchez and Vincent Valentin, "New Secularism wants the public to be privatized and the private to be made public."[42] That is, the current trend in the jurisprudence and legislation of secularism in France, to say nothing of the political discourse, minimizes the distinctions between public and private entities and domains that were once central to a liberal understanding of separation, in the vein of Briand and Jaurès.

We have already seen this "privatization of secularism" in chapter 4, with the 2021 separatism law. This law extended the principle of religious neutrality to employees of private agencies contracted with the state, including (but not limited to) bus drivers, airport employees, and health care workers—all employees of private companies whose role as "agents of the state" was ambiguous at best before the passage of this law. This measure was a legislative extension of the judicial ruling of the high appeals court in the "*Baby Loup* affair" of the early 2010s. In the *Baby Loup* case, a day care worker in Chanteloup-les-Vignes, an exurb of Paris, was fired from her position after returning from parental leave wearing a headscarf. The private but government-subsidized day care, Baby Loup, argued, among other things, that it was a "business of conviction," its convictions being notably that a strict implementation of religious neutrality was necessary to "transcend the multiculturalism" of the diverse populations it served, and to preserve the "freedom of conscience" of the toddlers in its care from undue pressure.[43] The case was appealed and referred numerous times to higher courts, ending with the plenary Chamber of the Cour de Cassation, France's highest civil court.

In their study of the *Baby Loup* case, Hennette-Vauchez and Valentin argue that it is paradigmatic of the transformations of the jurisprudence of secularism in the twenty-first century, bringing a version of the principle of neutrality that restricts individual liberties in the private (that is to say, nonstate) sphere together with a "mixture of control and support of religion through public powers."[44] They argue that *Baby Loup* was "the grand finale of the political mobilizations that have, for the past ten years, undertaken to completely redefine the principle of secularism, from being a principle that is imposed on public authorities to enjoin an obligation of strict religious neutrality, to being a principle applicable to private persons as well as public actors and, therefore, tending toward a generalized social obligation of religious neutrality."[45] In other words, the case succeeded in blurring the supposedly bright lines between public domains, where the law of secular neutrality previously applied, and private domains, where it did not.

While the French high court did not ultimately uphold the reasoning that Baby Loup was a "business of conviction," it did affirm the day care's right to impose religious neutrality upon their workers. It did so through a legal sleight of hand, dismissing secularism as irrelevant to the case only to smuggle it back in. At first, the appeals court argued that the case must be judged under private employment law rather than public administrative law, as the lower courts had adjudicated it. These lower courts had effectively treated the day care as an instance of the state because of the fact that it was providing a heavily subsidized "public service."[46] In principle, the high court's switch to the framework of private employment law would mean that legal secularism was not at issue, and that the obligation of religious neutrality did not apply to the Baby Loup workers. However, the court then argued that Baby Loup, a private enterprise, was permitted to impose secularism as an "ethos" onto its workers. They argued further that this restriction on the employee's religious expression was neither disproportionate nor discriminatory, given their significant assumption that religious symbols such as the headscarf were necessarily detrimental to the freedom of conscience and indeed to the general well-being of the children in Baby Loup's care.[47]

At the time of the *Baby Loup* judgment in 2014, the courts had to walk a fine line when allowing the "ethos" of secularism, as opposed to the legal principle of secularism, to apply to private sector entities.[48] However, with the 2021 separatism law, the legal principle of secular neutrality now applies to a wide range of workers with private employers, including those in the childcare sector. The lesson of the *Baby Loup* case is not so much the final ruling, which is now rendered largely moot, serving primarily as precedent for its legislative extension in the separatism law. The point here is that secularism has been diffused and decontextualized from being a concrete legal principle that the courts once held to be strictly limited to the state to being an "ethos" that can be applied by directive in private establishments. Secularism becomes once again an instrument in the culture war over Islam, with an ever-widening terrain of applicability.

This process of privatizing secularism only continues as the separatism law begins to be applied in full. In June 2022, the Conseil d'État, the highest administrative court in France, overturned the policy of a Grenoble swimming pool that would have allowed bathers to wear full-coverage bathing costumes, known colloquially as burkinis. The Grenoble policy also allowed female bathers to bathe topless, or in long-sleeved anti-UV suits, making the intimate decision of swimwear up to the individual rather than state regulators. This policy was flagged by the region's "secularism specialist" (*référent laïcité*). (This role within the Ministry of the Interior was created by the 2021 separatism law, as discussed in chapter 4.) The secularism specialist's argument, upheld by the courts, was that to permit burkinis was in practice to grant a special privilege—the ability to swim fully covered—to members of a specific religious group—Muslims, thereby violating the secularism of the state-run swimming pool. Ordinarily, the *users* of state services, such as the bathers at a public pool, are not subjected to secular neutrality. However, in this case, the Ministry of the Interior argued that the state had "recognized" religion by allegedly granting the special privilege of bathing fully covered to Muslim women. This argument was blatantly specious, ignoring the fact that women of any and no religion were permitted by this policy to bathe in the swimwear of their choice.[49] Nevertheless, it is part of the state's ongoing deployment of secular rationales to regulate the behavior of private citizens. This type of governance, with its ever-expanding bureaucracy of surveillance and oversight, is emblematic of the privatization of secularism. As we have seen, this legal extension of secularism as a regulatory "ethos" of diverse French institutions and spaces serves to further what Vincent Valentin has called a "communitarian conception" of secularism.

COEXISTENCE AS A REGIME OF GOVERNANCE

Despite all this, secularism as a legal concept, even when read expansively and in novel ways, does not always provide support for the type of restrictions on Muslim practices, especially modest dress, that political elites seek to enact. In particular, it does not (yet) support the regulation of religious practice in open public spaces. In these cases, parliamentarians and jurists have turned instead to novel legal justifications, including but not limited to the idea of le vivre ensemble, or coexistence. At first glance, the concept of le vivre ensemble sounds like it should describe the peaceful coexistence of multiple ways of living in a pluralistic society, and indeed this is how the phrase often reads in ordinary discourse.[50] As a technical legal term, however, le vivre ensemble has come to mean almost the opposite: rather than coexistence in diversity, it now refers to assimilation to a specific social ethos and aesthetic. This concept, according to Valentin, "synthesizes the evolution of secularism" through the expansion of the scope of "public order" to include "immaterial" conditions as well as material ones.[51] Le vivre ensemble was taken up as a legal framework because the legislation on secularism could not be used to support the goal of the National Assembly and French president to ban face veils across French territory. Where secularism falls short, the state turns to public order, of which le vivre ensemble is one subtype.[52]

The framework of le vivre ensemble entered into French law in 2010, with the ban on face coverings in all public spaces.[53] This ban, which principally concerned a tiny group of fewer than two thousand French women who wore the *niqab*, or face veil, was passed after a prominent parliamentary group, the Gerin Commission, issued an extensive report on the practice of face-veiling, interviewing dozens of individuals, from philosophers and sociologists to magistrates, although they neglected to include any women who wore the face veil. The result of the report was a new law, stating that "no one may, in public space, wear an outfit designed to conceal the face."[54] The penalty for concealment of the face was a fine of 150 euros and a citizenship class, but the penalty for forcing someone else to conceal their face because of their sex was set at a year in prison and a 30,000 euro fine, both doubled if the person forced to conceal their face was a minor. This second, more stringent, prohibition expressed a fantasy of the state about delivering veiled women from oppressive men. Many eclectic rationales for this ban were offered in the Gerin Commission's lengthy report, including the defense of women's rights and gender equality. But in the end, le vivre ensemble as a component of immaterial public order was the one that stuck, despite the fact that the Conseil d'État deemed the law to be on constitutionally precarious ground.[55] The law was ultimately justified and approved by the Constitutional Council based on "a renewed and enlarged conception of public order, which can be defined as the essential rules of coexistence."[56] One of these rules, the Constitutional Council affirmed, was the mandate that people in public spaces show their full face. The rest of the "essential rules of coexistence" were left unspecified, open to diverse interpretations. This abstract nature of the concept of coexistence has been much commented upon by legal scholars, many of whom worry about the possible uses to which such a fluid concept could be put.[57]

Nevertheless, the framework of le vivre ensemble was upheld by the European Court of Human Rights (ECHR) in 2014 in *S.A.S. v. France*,[58] enshrining this novel concept into not only French but also European jurisprudence. The European court did not detail what "coexistence" might require, but simply stated that they could "understand the view that individuals who are present in places open to all may not wish to see practices or attitudes developing there which would fundamentally call into question the possibility of open interpersonal relationships, which, by virtue of an established consensus, forms an indispensable element of community life within the society in question."[59] On these grounds, the court was willing to restrict the religious freedom of a minority, even while acknowledging that this restriction "risks contributing to the consolidation of stereotypes which affect certain categories of the population"—that is, that it reinforces negative perceptions of Muslim women.[60] The ECHR further solidified its commitment to le vivre ensemble three years later, siding with the state in two Belgian cases in which the Belgian government employed the same rationale to justify its ban on face coverings.

So far, le vivre ensemble as a legal framework has not stretched beyond face veil cases.[61] Yet after a pandemic era of widespread and at times state-mandated face covering, it seems contradictory and puzzling to continue to claim that showing one's full face in public is a foundational legal prerequisite of a functioning democratic society.[62] But le vivre ensemble is not the only way that ideals of collective morality—specific ideas of how to express human dignity and what values underpin our coexistence—become part of state regulation. More broadly, the language of public order, of which le vivre ensemble is one form, is used to regulate religious practice in the name of a supposedly shared moral sentiment. As historian Judith Surkis has observed, "public order is one very crucial way in which the symbolic power and sovereignty of French law is articulated and enacted."[63] As we will see below, the broader register of public order has become a primary vocabulary through which Muslim practice is regulated in France, in the name of a "communalist" conception of common morality.

MAINTAINING PUBLIC ORDER

In 2022, a well-known Muslim preacher, Hassan Iquioussen, was issued an order to leave French territory by the minister of the interior, Gérald Darmanin. Born in northern France in the 1960s to Moroccan parents, Iquioussen had never obtained French citizenship, living instead on ten-year renewable residency permits. However, he had lived his entire life only in

France, and had French children and grandchildren. Active in preaching and Islamic organizing since the 1980s, Iquioussen was a sought-after speaker at conferences, in mosques, and in Muslim community organizations up until the time of his deportation order. As a long-standing prominent member of the Union of Islamic Organizations of France (UOIF; now known simply as Muslims of France [MF]) and as former president of the UOIF youth wing, Young Muslims of France (JMF), Iquioussen was a key figure in the French Islamic revival of the 1990s—a period of resurgent piety and Islamic institution-building that we saw particularly with Nessima in chapter 1. His case prompted widespread support and outrage from French mosques and a broad segment of the Muslim French public, commensurate with his profile.

The deportation order was first announced by Darmanin on Twitter in late July 2022: "This preacher has for years maintained a discourse that is hateful to French values, contrary to our principles of secularism and equality between men and women. He will be expelled from French territory."[64] Although Iquioussen was not charged with, much less convicted of, any specific crime, the minister of the interior argued that Iquioussen posed a "grave danger to public order" that legitimized his expulsion. Iquioussen fled France of his own accord before the deportation order could be executed, living for some months in exile in Belgium, before finally being deported to Morocco in January 2023. In the meantime, his deportation order was stayed by an appeals court, then eventually validated by the Conseil d'État, the highest French administrative court. Iquioussen is not the only Muslim religious leader to have been deported on the basis of the alleged threat posed to "public order," but he is by far the most prominent.[65]

I am not concerned here with relitigating the politics of Iquioussen's four decades of speeches and sermons. Other scholars have made close study of his rhetoric.[66] Instead, I am interested in understanding how his case contributes to the concept of "public order" in French law, and the relationship between this idea of public order and the oft-proclaimed Republican values of secularism and male-female equality. Iquioussen's case intensifies a shift to an "immaterial" understanding of public order that allows the state to legislate and execute orders on the basis of a supposedly shared common morality, grounded in specific understandings of secularism and male-female equality. This fits into my broader argument that state governance of Islam in France has shifted from a focus on secularism in the 1990s and 2000s to a focus on immaterial public order since the 2010s. At the same time, this nebulous and "immaterial" public order has bearing on very material embodied practices (like different forms of modest dress) and facilitates very material action by the state, such as the deportations of Iquioussen and other religious leaders.

French law makes systematic reference to the maintenance of "public order" as grounds for an exception to numerous laws guaranteeing civil liberties, including the freedom of conscience as outlined in the law of 1905. The first article of the law of 1905 on secularism reads, "The Republic guarantees freedom of conscience. It guarantees the free exercise of religion under the sole restrictions decreed below, in the interest of public order."[67] Article 25 of the same law states that religious organizations "remain placed under the surveillance of the authorities in the interest of public order."[68] Historically, this has been understood to refer to a "material public order": conditions of social peace, the absence of violence or property damage. In recent years, however, there have been numerous turns to reasoning on the basis of an "immaterial public order," or sometimes "moral public order," referring to a specific conception of human dignity and social values.[69] It is this moral order, rather than any material condition of order or safety, that many expressions of Islam have been taken to threaten, ranging from Iquioussen's speeches to the wearing of niqabs, as we saw in the previous section. Public order is the main legal constraint on the freedom of conscience and religious practice. It is therefore unsurprising that government officials turn to this concept, going beyond the previously standard jurisprudence of secularism, when they seek to regulate religious speech and behavior.

Public order has proved useful as a concept to regulate religious practice in the present in part because it has always been inscribed in the law as the principal limiting factor on individual liberties, including religious freedom. It has also systematically been invoked in cases to do with perceived Muslim difference as pertaining to gender and family structure, dating back to the colonial period.[70] However, until recently, immaterial public order had waned in prominence. Nevertheless, the French Civil Code makes reference to public order in nearly every section. It is a cardinal underlying principle of French law. Indeed, France exported this legal category to countries under its colonial influence, where it has had surprising afterlives. For example, Mona Oraby demonstrates how public order is used in Egypt, to legislate on the basis of a presumed Islamic common morality in order to sanction cases of religious conversion to Christianity.[71] Not coincidentally, this deployment of public order as common morality is not so different from the French version: in both cases, jurists draw on the criteria of public order together with a specific imagination of national values to manage religious difference.[72]

As legal scholar Marie-Odile Peyroux-Sissoko has argued, public order is deployed by French state actors in response to perceived crises.⁷³ In particular, the turn to the "immaterial" sense of public order, or the legislation of "good morals" (*bonnes moeurs*), is a response, Peyroux-Sissoko argues, to a social or political experience of threat. In the case of the ban on the face veil, for example, the threat in question is not a material threat posed by fully covered women, although the specter of such a material threat was invoked throughout the Gerin Commission hearings. Rather, it is the immaterial threat that is posed to Republican values by the very presence of veiled women on French territory, or by Iquioussen's gender-hierarchical rhetoric, that elicits the response in terms of public order. It seems to be no coincidence, however, that these immaterial threats come always and only from Muslims, not from traditional French Catholics and their own gender-hierarchical views of marriage, for example.⁷⁴

The rhetoric of threat and the response in terms of public order is repeated in French government sources, particularly with reference to women's modest dress. For example, the 2017 parliamentary report "on secularism and male-female equality" overseen by Senator Chantal Jouanno, raises the threat to women's rights ostensibly posed by the burkini. The report notes that in the series of burkini bans at public beaches in 2016, the French courts did not find the burkini to pose a threat to public order. But the Jouanno report then contests these decisions, arguing that the courts were using the "narrow" conception of merely material public order, and thereby finding that the burkini posed no threat to social peace. Instead, the report argues, they could have used the broader, immaterial conception of public order, "taking into consideration the notion of an attack on the dignity of the human person."⁷⁵ The implication here is clear: had the court drawn on immaterial public order and its underlying notion of human dignity, the burkini bans could have been upheld. From banning the burkini, which after all is only a full-coverage outfit with a hood, it is but one small step to a ban on women's head covering generally. The Jouanno report retreats from this shocking conclusion, and yet it is clearly the end point of the report's line of reasoning, which amplifies the "reconfiguration" of public order to underscore its immaterial—that is to say, moral—dimension.⁷⁶ If references to "public order" throughout French law are taken to refer equally to an immaterial moral notion of human dignity and gender parity as conceptualized by French lawmakers, the way is paved for significant restrictions on individual liberties in the name of the preservation of a majoritarian view of common morality.

With the passage of the separatism law in 2021, discussed in detail in chapter 4, the reach of public order has only broadened. For example, the newly established Special Committee to Fight Radical Islamism and Communalist Withdrawal (CLIR) can now use public order as a reason to shut down a private school, or to prevent one from opening in the first place. Before, as the press release announcing the CLIR admits, the government was forced to use "artifices such as violation of fire security regulations or sanitary regulations" to force the closure of such establishments.[77] Recourse to public order streamlines this process for the state and brings it under a coherent ideological regulation rather than a trumped-up excuse related to health or fire security protocols. Public order was also introduced into the law regulating community organizations, as an element of the "Republican contract" that all such organizations are now required to sign. As we saw in chapter 4 with the demand for repayment of state subsidies from the nonconfessional environmental organization Alternatiba Poitiers based on their hosting of a nonviolent civil disobedience training, this provision for public order has the potential to be used to police civil society generally. While Muslims are the primary target of these state measures and are most impacted by the recourse to public order, these measures also signal a broader orientation toward community organizations and civil society. Policing Muslims is also about policing the polity at large.[78] The state is able to use "counterterror" measures for sundry purposes in various moments of "crisis."

FROM SECULARISM TO PUBLIC ORDER, AND BACK AGAIN?

It might seem that public order is merely an intensification of secular governance under another name. And indeed, secularism is not going anywhere as a regulatory framework for Islam in France. However, there is an unstable relationship between these two concepts, linked to the instability of secularism itself.[79] Sometimes they operate in tandem, other times in tension. Secularism is a values framework with multiple points of entry and discursive patterns, including the claims of French Muslim social actors. By contrast, public order is by definition monopolized by state power and the elites who represent it. Where secularism putatively may constrain the state, as in the laws on religious neutrality, public order empowers it unilaterally. As we saw with the Muslim activists who claim secularism as an inheritance and a protective principle, secularism is not always and only deployed against Islam. At the same time, the broader framework of secularism, which incorporates public order as part of the *police des cultes*, places religions under state control. This has resulted in what I call "surveillance secularism," where the rhetoric of secularism plays a key role in the counterterror apparatus that surveils Muslims.[80]

However, this apparatus of surveillance also exceeds the *legal* boundaries of secularism in multiple ways. It does so through its reliance on immaterial public order and le vivre ensemble to regulate Muslim expression and discourse according to supposedly French *moral* standards. These standards include a particular conception of human dignity that revives older legal language of *bonnes moeurs* (good morals). Bonnes moeurs is redeployed here to characterize a French moral community in which the very idea of coexistence (*le vivre ensemble*) is predicated upon the erasure of certain forms of religious difference, and this in "private" spaces like workplaces, community organizations, and the open street, as much as "public" ones like schools, state offices, and even municipal pools. This idea of coexistence as a French moral concept corresponds to the surveillance of ideas and practices of Muslim community and collectivity that we saw in chapter 4. As we have seen throughout this book, the multivalent concept of moral community is central to French Muslim social activism—both as a contested aspirational ideal and as a set of regulatory frameworks that condition the very existence of Muslim social life in France.

CONCLUSION

Social Ethics and the Fragilization of the Collective

In a video posted to Instagram in May 2023, Muslim French feminist and anti-racist activist Fatima Bent observed that "racism and Islamophobia fragilize our communities. That is to say, these forms of violence also work to break the bonds of solidarity."[1] Bent was speaking of the "racist recuperation" of Muslim women's lived experiences of patriarchy by political forces that seek to instrumentalize these experiences in order to reiterate damaging colonialist narratives of Muslim women's oppression and Muslim men's barbarism. In parallel ways, the multiple forms of state surveillance and management of Muslim collective life that we saw in part II of this book combine to imperil the culture of fraternal critique that we explored in part I. The more that their communities are under attack and scrutiny by government and media elites, the harder it becomes for engaged Muslims to leverage intracommunal argument and debate as forms of solidarity and belonging. For Women in the Mosque, struggling to pray in the main hall at the Mosquée de Paris, or for the young students in the grandes écoles, working to harmonize elite professional ambitions with religious devotion and committed activism, policies like the separatism law straiten their possibilities of expression. These policies put them in danger of being seen as "traitors" to their communities, part of the "racist recuperation" of intra-Muslim critique that Bent referenced.

And yet, despite all of this, fraternal critique has not been silenced in French Muslim contexts. Indeed, even as the state consolidates its efforts to manage Muslims through select "leaders," community debate remains spirited and remains an expression of kinship and solidarity. In response to the state's gathering of privileged interlocutors through the Forum on French Islam (FORIF), in February 2023, prominent French Muslim activist Marwan Muhammad posted on Facebook a message piercingly addressed to the attendees: "You don't know what you are doing." Not only, he argued, was participation in the gathering politically naive, but it was both a strategic and a religious misstep, capitulating to the "de-Islamization of Muslims" and aligning with the powerful against the vulnerable, contrary to the values of Islam. "Islam as we have known it," Muhammad warned, "living, inspiring, dynamic, oriented toward the common good, carrying the values of mutual aid, enthusiasm, and fraternity, will not exist anymore. All that will be left are the memories of what we have lived, plus a few selfies you took with a president who judges our sisters' scarves to be 'contrary to the civility of our country' and an interior minister who finds the far right to be 'too soft' on us."[2] In short, he argued, the participants in FORIF are directly facilitating the racist and Islamophobic "fragilization of our communities" that Bent spoke about, participating in nothing less than the wholesale dismantling of the vibrant Muslim culture of France. Intellectuals and activists like Bent and Muhammad are sounding the alarm that French Muslims are fighting for their very collective existence.

Muhammad's post circulated on social media and WhatsApp. In response, a senior religious figure who had participated in the FORIF gathering wrote a message dismissing Muhammad's post as an "insult" and a misunderstanding of the dynamics of the event. Muhammad replied publicly on his Facebook page, with a four thousand-word point-by-point takedown of the religious figure's critique. (Muhammad left the FORIF attendee unnamed.) "I don't know what you said to the people who closed so many mosques under improper pretexts," Muhammad wrote to him, "or to the people who engineered a manhunt for Hassan Iquioussen as though he were public enemy number one.... I don't know what you said to them. But I know what I said to them. And I know the price that comes with it: knowing how to differentiate between an 'insult' and a *fraternal critique*."[3] Muhammad's "fraternal critique" of his interlocutor pulled no punches. It was a searing indictment of the dangers of collaboration with government authorities who have their own clearly articulated agenda for the management of Islam in France. Even a little bit of research into initiatives like FORIF, Muhammad argued, "would permit one to realize that the target is not 'extremism,' (whatever that means), but the Muslim community in its entirety, and in particular the average Muslims [*les musulmans lambda*], these millions of families who simply practice their religion, who try to fast, to pray, to educate their children, and to act in accordance with the Good, as best they can. In other words, the target is you. It's us. All of us." My analysis of French law, policy, and public discourse in chapters 4 and 5 aligns with Muhammad's claim here. It is *les musulmans lambda*, the average Muslims,[4] who are targeted by statements like the Charter of Principles for French Islam and policies like the separatism law, written and implemented with the cooperation of certain Muslim elites. Engaged Muslim activists know this, and like Muhammad, many others are engaging in vociferous fraternal critique of these efforts, which they perceive as endangering the very survival of their communities. Importantly, their critique is a marker of the maintenance, not the severing, of a bond of relationship and brotherhood with those they criticize. The culture of fraternal critique that we saw in part I of this book is alive and well, if embattled, and it is engaging directly with the patterns of managing moral community that we explored in part II.

FRATERNITÉ AS A THREAT AND AN OFFERING

I wrote *Fraternal Critique* out of a desire to fully account for the vibrant, living Muslim ethical culture that I experienced during my years in France. This must include an accounting of the political factors that, as Muhammad and Bent argue, seek to weaken and ultimately erase it. We cannot understand Muslim collective life in France, and the ethical project of shaping a collective subject that runs through this book, without understanding the forces that seek to mold it in their image in the name of a racialized project of Republican identity and public order. Similarly, we cannot understand Muslim collective life and discourse in France without grasping the forces that threaten it—not just the threat posed to individual Muslim figures like Hassan Iquioussen or other imams, but the threat posed to the fabric of French Muslim collective life, to Muslims' very ability to cultivate fraternité on their own terms. One of the lessons of this book is that the national value of fraternité is not available equally to all in the national imagination. Muslims, in particular, are supposed to exist not as a collective but as atomized individuals, bereft of thick group commitments or community ties. As we have seen, the forms of kinship and community that Muslims build are expressed through the language of fraternité, language that the Republic tries but ultimately fails to claim a monopoly on. These forms of kinship are not seen by the state as valuable resources for reinforcing broader axes of solidarity and mutual aid. On the contrary, they are seen as obstacles and threats. *Fraternal Critique* contends that this is far from true. Instead, Muslim practices of brotherly and sisterly kinship, including the specific practices of fraternal and sororal critique, are offerings to the wider communities and societies that Muslims call home. They are theoretical and ethical offerings that have applicability outside of the specific French Muslim context in which they emerged.

When I began writing this book, I thought the main argument would be that French Muslims are invested in social ethics, in the project of cultivating a collective ethical subject, as opposed to focusing on the cultivation of individual moral selves. We can still see this cultivation of the collective subject from the first pages of the book, with the story of Dounia, for example, who prioritized volunteering with Muslim youth over her own more traditional religious education. This line of argument, while accurate, was perhaps too invested in speaking back to a particular tendency within ethnographies of religion to focus on subject formation in a Foucauldian frame. As I wrote and rewrote the book, the concern with social ethics receded somewhat from view, and in its place came a concern with critique, debate, and restless discontent that had previously been the focus of only one chapter. However, *Fraternal Critique* remains a book about social ethics, a book about how people find ways to live together in kinship and right relationship despite their profound disagreements and exasperation with one another, and sometimes with themselves as well. For fraternal critique can also be an auto-critique: a complaint of collective moral shortcomings that implicates the self as well.

"MUSLIMS OF THE PRESENT"

This complaint was expressed sharply by one of my teachers in Islamic sciences, during a free-flowing class discussion at a small institute in a southern suburb of Paris. Mounir, the instructor, framed his exasperation with "Muslims in France today" in a temporal framework of future, past, and present:

> Today's French Muslim is in a situation that is full of paradoxes. He doesn't know which way he is headed in this country, and he doesn't know where he has come from. At the same time, he is either a Muslim

of the future or a Muslim of the past. That is, either he is waiting for some future moment to really live his faith, or he is nostalgic for some golden age of the Islamic past.

But where are the *Muslims of the present*? That's what our community needs—Muslims of *now*.

This sense of urgency to become "Muslims of the present" motivated many of my interlocutors to found grassroots community organizations, to seek out new forums for theological debate, to develop entrepreneurial projects and professional networks, and to develop new cultural forms. All of these ventures could be understood as social ethics—projects of seeking to form and transform the collective subject.

Islam has a robust tradition of pious social justice activism. But what I see in this book as social ethics is not simply Muslims' charitable activities or mobilizations for social justice. Amira Mittermaier has elaborated how pious charity can be a *nonhumanitarian* ethics, in other words, an ethic of the giver's relationship to God, rather than an act of compassion for the poor. She describes pious charity as a triadic gifting, in which God "is an active player who transforms the relationship between giver and recipient."[5] In the sphere of Muslim French social ethics, there is a similar triadic relationship between the self, God, and the community. That is, many French Muslims feel accountable to God for what they have done or said on behalf of their brothers and sisters. Their projects of community formation and transformation are not simply humanitarian efforts at collective uplift. They are expressions of a sense of divine responsibility. Mounir's call for "Muslims of now" attempted to pull his listeners out of their personal circumstances and address what he saw as a moral urgency for all of them: the collective state of "today's French Muslim." Mounir's ethics of the present pointed to a divine obligation of collective formation.

But if Mounir and many others like him are engaged in social ethics from the perspective of divine obligation, we have seen that the French state, too, is engaged in a project of attempting to form and transform the collective Muslim subject. There are both bottom-up and top-down social ethics at work. The politics of "Enlightenment Islam" and public order operate with a thick vision of moral community. State actors draw on this vision of moral community or moral order as the grounding substrate of, as well as the limit on, freedoms of expression and association. As the two complementary parts of this book have shown, the idea and ideal of moral community is shaped both by those who aspire to it and by those who would constrain it.

Fraternal critique has been a vibrant and vital French social practice throughout the 2010s and into the 2020s. I don't know if it will be able to continue in the same way in the face of the fragilization enacted by the politics of public order. But if we zoom back out to think about social ethics writ large, there are other ethical formations, such as Mounir's call for "Muslims of the present," that may take up this role. The question that remains, not only for French Muslims but for all French people, and for those of us beyond France, is: What forms of solidarity are possible and necessary in the face of the increasing consolidation of claims of moral authority and practices of regulatory power in the hands of state elites? Fraternal critique has been one compelling answer to this question. I hope it can be an offering and an inspiration to others who need to find their own.

ACKNOWLEDGMENTS

I begin in the name of God, the everlastingly Compassionate, the infinitely Caring.

Over the course of the circuitous journey that culminated in this book, I have accumulated debts and ties of gratitude too numerous and too profound to fully account for here. This project's original and most enduring debt is to the many unnamable people who, out of their generosity, sincerity, and abiding belief in seeking knowledge, shared their time, their thoughts, their homes, their disappointments, their aspirations, and their lives with me in France. I first walked into a French mosque—in this case a set of makeshift modular trailers in the parking lot of a suburban commercial plaza—as a naive and nervous undergraduate in 2005. Through what I can only attribute to divine grace, I was met by open-hearted people who would become teachers, mentors, guides, and friends. They would introduce me to patterns of living—orientations to the transcendent, ways of pursuing justice, relationships to an inherited past and an imagined future—that would change the course of my intellectual and personal existence. Among many other things, these encounters set me on the path of ethnography as a way of seeking responses to my persistent "big questions." Many of my teachers, friends, and acquaintances from France do not appear as characters in this book, even pseudonymously. Even so, each of their perspectives informed and shaped it—and shaped me. To all those who entrusted me with their words and experiences over the years, who took me under their wing, who pushed, challenged, and questioned me, and who made my life in France so full, unpredictable, and fun—*jazak Allah khairan*; *merci du fond du coeur*. You have my eternal gratitude and respect.

At Harvard University, I was fortunate to have teachers, advisors, and mentors who gave me the confidence to pursue doctoral research, the tools to make sense of my questions and to pose new ones, and the guidance to wrangle my scattered thoughts and writings into a substantive piece of scholarship. Leila Ahmed, Steven Caton, Diana Eck, Khaled El-Rouayheb, Marla Frederick, Amy Hollywood, Mark D. Jordan, Ousmane Kane, Smita Lahiri, Anne Monius, Afsaneh Najmabadi, Ahmed Ragab, Ronald Thiemann, and, above all, Malika Zeghal each shaped me in a particular way as a scholar, a teacher, and a human being. Erwan Dianteill extended a gracious welcome at the Centre d'Anthropologie Culturelle at what was then Paris Descartes–Sorbonne, during one of my longer stays in France. During my later years at Harvard, I was blessed to learn from Courtney Lamberth's generous mentorship and warm company.

At Willamette University, Sally Markowitz and Randall Havas taught me how to write as a scholar and gave me the scaffolding for deeper intellectual inquiry. Karen Wood opened my mind to the academic study of religion and ethics, and helped me begin to chart a path forward in the field. Isabelle Jaffe, as well as so many other patient teachers and several brave host families, first helped me carve out a home in France.

My peers, cohort-mates, and comrades at Harvard made graduate study not only bearable, but a season of creativity, solidarity, and joy. Liz Angowski, Youssef Ben Ismail, Deirdre DeBruyn Rubio, Mary Elston, Greg Halaby, Amy Howe, Nancy Khalil, Bethany Kibler, Michael Lesley, Ernie Mitchell, Deonnie Moodie, Arjun Nair, Jasmine Samara, Adam Stern, Travis Stevens, Laura Thompson, Lispeth Tibbits-Nutt, Jay Williams, Kimberly Wortmann, Klaus Yoder, Sunny Yudkoff, and Pegah Zohouri Haghian, along with so many others, were teachers to me as well as friends. I learned from their incisive comments on my work in progress, from our innumerable conversations in classes, cafés, and hallways, and from their own brilliant research. Olivia Moseley, James Stanton, and other dear friends made Somerville home for so many years. In Paris and beyond, Juliette Galonnier, Carol Ferrara, and Alexandra Steinlight have been effervescent and thoughtful conversation partners. I treasure and miss all of these now far-flung loved ones.

In the Religion Department at Vassar College, I have been blessed with wise, patient, and deeply humane colleagues, which I never take for granted. Marc M. Epstein, Jonathon Kahn, Rick Jarow, Wendy Post, Ági Vetö, Michael Walsh, Christopher White, Klaus Yoder, and recently Nell Hawley have infused Blodgett Hall with camaraderie and a sense of humor. Across campus, Saba Ali, Annie Brancky, Sam Cavagnolo, Katie Hite, Maria Höhn, Candice Lowe Swift, Taneisha Means, Mariam Rashid, Louis Römer, China Sajadian, Joshua Schreier, Samuel Speers, Jasmine Syedullah, Kimberly Williams Brown, and other brilliant colleagues have gifted me with their advice, their mentorship, their companionship, and their collaborative spirit. The programs in Africana Studies, International Studies, Migration & Displacement Studies, and Women, Feminist, & Queer Studies have been generative spaces for transdisciplinary collaboration with dynamic colleagues and students. Special love and gratitude go to Annie Brancky, Taneisha Means, and Kimberly Williams Brown, for sharing our journeys and our classrooms through these past tumultuous years. Over countless dinners and around many backyard campfires, Louis and Johanna Römer have been true comrades and intellectual influences on this book.

At Vassar and at Harvard, it has been a joy to work with curious and challenging undergraduates. Whenever I sit down to write, I have students past and present in mind as my ideal readers. I continue to learn from my students each and every semester, in stimulating ways. In particular, students in seminars where we read excerpts from this book contributed fresh ideas and raised important new questions for me. Outside the seminar room, Mohtad Allawala, Meghan Cook, Tess Foley-Cox, Huda Rahman, Sophia Slater, and Megan Wang have been top-notch research assistants, from the beginning to the very end of this process.

Beyond any institutional container, this book (and all the research that preceded it) has been sustained and enriched by conversations with fellow scholars from multiple fields of study, at conferences and workshops, in print, over Zoom, and in less formal settings. I am indebted to insights, questions, and critiques from Iman AbdoulKarim, Zaid Adhami, Zahra Ayubi, Kirsten Beck, Elisabeth Becker Topkara, Liz Bucar, Jan Felix Engelhardt, Rachel Friedman, Kambiz GhanneaBassiri, Todd Green, Juliane Hammer, Aysha Hidayatullah, Justine Howe, Roshan A. Jahangeer, Sajida Jalalzai, Sohaib Khan, Thomas A. Lewis, Charles Mathewes, Nermeen Mouftah, Martin Nguyen, Johanna Römer, Noah Salomon, Gülay Turkmen, Saadia Yacoob, Xiaobo Yuan, and numerous others. I owe particular gratitude to the far-flung members of JAM-2 for their virtual support over all these years.

Among those already listed above, several people have been generous enough to read and comment on draft chapters of this book over the years: Zaid Adhami, Kirsten Beck, Carol Ferrara, Rachel Friedman, Amy Hollywood, Huda Rahman, Laura Thompson, and Michael Walsh offered essential feedback and encouragement, often at moments when I wondered whether this work would ever see the light of day. A few went even further, and bravely read a full draft manuscript in the midst of busy lives and many other pressing priorities: Juliane Hammer, Louis Römer, and Noah Salomon improved and sharpened this book in many ways, and I only wish I could have done justice to every one of their comments. And then there are those who have been steadfastly reading and writing alongside me the whole time. Nancy Khalil and Jasmine Samara are true sister-writers, tireless readers of sloppy first drafts and final edits, steadfast encouragers, role models, and inspirations. Their insights and influence run throughout this book. I was lucky enough to have Kali Handelman come into my writing life at just the right moment. Her clarity, acumen, good humor, and confidence in this project pulled it through some especially challenging times, and helped to shape voluminous research and amorphous writing into something like a *book*.

I have been honored to share parts of this project with colleagues and students at several institutions. Audiences at Harvard University (especially the Middle East Beyond Borders Workshop), Middlebury College, Northeastern University, Stanford University (with particular thanks to Ari Y. Kelman and the Religion & Education Workshop), the University of Arkansas, University College London, the University of Virginia, and many successive meetings of the American Academy of Religion, the Council for European Studies, the American Anthropological Association, and the Society for the Study of Muslim Ethics have posed thoughtful questions, made surprising observations, and influenced the direction of this project. I only wish I could thank each insightful commentor and generous host by name.

I have had the immense privilege of material support for this project from grants and fellowships, including the Fulbright Fellowship, the International Dissertation Research Fellowship from the Social Science Research Council, the Lurcy Fellowship, the Council for European Studies Graduate Fellowship, the Weatherhead Center for International Affairs Dissertation Fellowship, the Jens Aubrey Westengard Fellowship, the Loeb Fellowship in Religion, summer grants from the Center for the Study of Islam in the Contemporary World and the Center for the Study of Religion and the City, and several grants from the Vassar College Faculty Research Committee, including from the Elinor Nims Brink Fund and the Jane Rosenthal Heimerdinger Fund. Early research in France was funded by a Sheldon Fellowship and a Harvard Graduate School of Arts and Sciences Pre-Dissertation Research Fellowship.

Portions of this book have been revised from earlier published work. Sections of chapter 3 are adapted from "The Constraints of Choice: Secular Sensibilities, Pious Critique, and the Islamic Ethic of Sisterhood in France," *Sociology of Islam* 7, no. 4 (2019): 226–44. This article was part of a special issue in memory of the inimitable Saba Mahmood, who left such an impact on my work and on multiple fields of study, generously organized and edited by

Sultan Doughan and Jean-Michel Landry. Brief passages from the introduction and chapter 1 appeared in "The Inheritances of Immigration," *Political Theology* 23, no. 7 (2022): 706–10, my contribution to a lively roundtable on the roots of Islamic piety, capably curated by Aaron Rock-Singer.

This book, and I as a first-time author, have found an unparalleled home at the University of Chicago Press. Editor Kyle Wagner and the series editors of Class 200, Kathryn Lofton and John Lardas Modern, have been full of sharp feedback, good counsel, and patience. Kyle understood core elements of this project early on, and shepherded it through several iterations. Through this process, I had the marvelous good fortune to learn from two rounds of generous and perceptive anonymous reviewers. They pushed me to improve this book and helped me to see it in a new light, even toward the end of a long road. Kristin Rawlings and Elizabeth Ellingboe have been keen stewards of the manuscript through production. Charles Dibble provided attentive copyediting, and Varsha Venkatasubramanian prepared the index.

Very few books would be written without the contributions and labor, so often invisible and insufficiently acknowledged, of those sharing the care work that helps carve out time and space to research and write. From Somerville to Montreuil to New Paltz, a long series of day care providers, babysitters, and educators, as well as friends and family, have created safe and loving spaces for my children, helping to raise them in community. I am grateful to each of them.

My own first teachers were my family, who have been challenging and inspiring me since childhood. I was blessed to be born into a wide family of intellectuals—readers, debaters, and writers, even if most of them never sat in a college classroom. My parents, John and Deborah, taught me from the beginning to ask difficult questions, persevere with determination, and reflect deeply about ethics, religion, and spirituality. Even now in his absence, my father continues to teach me and shape my thinking. My *belle-mère*, Maureen, has nurtured me with friendship and love, and has been a role model of creative integrity, independence, and wisdom. Ky, Jenna, Christian, Todd, Erika, and all the rest of our family have been a ballast to return to over the years.

Finally, Klaus Yoder has lived with this project for as long as I have, and with far, far greater patience and compassion. Not only has he read nearly every page in numerous versions, rehashed every line of argument and piece of evidence, but he has also worked alongside me to build a life that endeavors to express the best of the aspirations to community, solidarity, and kinship that animate this book. He has—just as promised—been my closest friend and my steadfast partner, across continents and languages, through precarious days, sleepless nights, and joyful times alike. Together, we get to watch these irrepressible bright souls, Stella and Felix, grow into themselves and into the world. Klaus, Stella, and Felix teach me every day how to live—and how to live well. This book is for the three of them.

NOTES

INTRODUCTION

1. All given names used in this book are pseudonyms, and identifying details have been changed.
2. This chapter is derived in part from an article published as "The Inheritances of Immigration," in *Political Theology* 23, no. 7 (2022): 706–10. © Taylor & Francis, https://doi.org/10.1080/1462317X.2022.2092335.
3. Twentieth-century migrants to France from its colonies or former colonies on the African continent (many of whom were Muslim) were largely employed in low-wage jobs. Faced with systemic racial discrimination and socioeconomic disenfranchisement, the children of these migrants have a much higher than average rate of unemployment and underemployment. Nevertheless, a significant number of the descendants (or "inheritors") of these migrants, raised in working-class or poor households, have pursued university degrees and more secure and remunerative professional careers. This mobility requires negotiating not only the discrimination of higher education and the job market, but also the racial politics of class and capitalism in postcolonial France, including the culture of "color-blindness." Shirin Shahrokni, *Higher Education and Social Mobility in France: Challenges and Possibilities* (New York: Routledge, 2021).
4. As Jennifer Fredette has observed, French Muslims have highly divergent life experiences, political orientations, and views on religion and social life, which she argues are broadly characterized by "dissensus." Those community activists who are deeply invested in shaping the Muslim community, like Dounia and Hamza, are only one subset of French Muslims generally. Jennifer Fredette, "Social Movements and the State's Construction of Identity: The Case of Muslims in France," *Studies in Law, Politics and Society* 54 (2011): 45–76.
5. These works range from Gilles Kepel, *Terreur dans l'Hexagone* (Paris: Gallimard, 2017), a sociological analysis of French terrorism as rooted in the culture of the disenfranchised banlieues, to Michel Houllebecq, *Soumission* (Paris: J'ai Lu, 2015), a controversial novel imagining an Islamist political takeover of the Republic. More polemical works include Renaud Camus's *Le grand remplacement* (Plieux: Chez l'auteur, 2010), Éric Zemmour's

Le suicide français (Paris: Albin Michel, 2014), and Mohammed Sifaoui's *Taqiyya* (Paris: Éditions de l'Observatoire, 2019), all of which allege a pernicious, mass-movement Muslim takeover of France.

6. Jim Wolfreys, *Republic of Islamophobia: The Rise of Respectable Racism in France* (New York: Oxford University Press, 2018); Nacira Guénif-Souilamas, "The Other French Exception: Virtuous Racism and the War of the Sexes in Postcolonial France," *French Politics, Culture, and Society* 24, no. 3 (2006), 23–41.

7. Mame-Fatou Niang, "Des particularités françaises de la négrophobie," in *Racismes de France*, ed. Omar Slaouti and Olivier Le Cour Grandmaison (Paris: La Découverte, 2020), 192.

8. Abdellali Hajjat and Marwan Muhammad, *Islamophobie: Comment les élites françaises fabriquent le "problème musulman"* (Paris: La Découverte, 2013).

9. Anne Norton, *On the Muslim Question* (Princeton, NJ: Princeton University Press, 2013).

10. Tareq Oubrou, "Le musulman ne doit pas s'exposer," *Le Point*, June 13, 2019.

11. An incident during which one of my interlocutors used this term is described in detail in chapter 1. Another reference to the term is discussed in the conclusion.

12. Chantal Mouffe, *The Return of the Political* (New York: Verso, 1993), 7.

13. Mouffe, *The Return of the Political*, 8.

14. Fraternal critique bears obvious resonances with other Islamic discursive practices such as *nasiha* (advice), as analyzed by Talal Asad. In Asad's terms, "*nasiha* reflects the principle that a well-regulated polity depends on its members being virtuous individuals who are partly responsible for one another's moral condition—and therefore in part on continuous moral criticism." Asad, *Genealogies of Religion: Discipline and Reasons of Power in Christianity and Islam* (Baltimore, MD: Johns Hopkins University Press, 1993): 233. As Noah Salomon and Jeremy Walton elaborate, Asad's analysis of *nasiha* simultaneously "succeeds in highlighting the disciplines of power that undergird liberalism in all its contexts, even those Western ones in which it maintains an ersatz naturalness," and also "explores the constitutive practices and political possibilities of other, nonliberal modes of criticism." Noah Salomon and Jeremy Walton, "Religious Criticism, Secular Critique, and the 'Critical Study of Religion': Lessons from the Study of Islam," in *The Cambridge Companion to Religious Studies*, ed. Robert Orsi (Cambridge: Cambridge University Press, 2011), 412. For other pertinent examples of critique as an Islamic discursive practice, see Noah Salomon, *For Love of the Prophet: An Ethnography of Sudan's Islamic State* (Princeton, NJ: Princeton University Press, 2016); Yasmin Moll, "Subtitling Islam: Translation, Mediation, Critique," *Public Culture* 29, no. 2 (2017): 333–61; Irfan Ahmad, *Religion as Critique: Islamic Critical Thinking from Mecca to the Marketplace* (Chapel Hill: University of North Carolina Press, 2017).

15. Zareena Grewal, "Destabilizing Orthodoxy, De-territorializing the Anthropology of Islam," *Journal of the American Academy of Religion* 84, no. 1 (2016): 45.

16. Ahmad, *Religion as Critique*; Talal Asad, Wendy Brown, Judith Butler, and Saba Mahmood, *Is Critique Secular? Blasphemy, Injury, and Free Speech* (Stanford, CA: Townsend Papers in the Humanities, 2009); Salomon and Walton, "Religious Criticism."

17. In an analogous way, Julie Kleinman describes the "alternative forms of meaningful integration" developed by West African migrants hanging out in the Gare du Nord train

station in Paris. While they are quite differently situated in terms of class and migration history than my mostly middle-class and French-born interlocutors, the "adventurers" of the Gare du Nord likewise forge ways of belonging in French society and connecting across lines of difference that "come much closer than French institutions at actualizing the promise of mutual belonging encapsulated in *living-together*." Julie Kleinman, *Adventure Capital: Migration and the Making of an African Hub in Paris* (Berkeley: University of California Press, 2019), 7.

18. Abdelwahab Boudhiba, "Le message de l'Islam," *Diogène* 205, no. 1 (2017): 131.
19. Edgar Morin, *La fraternité, pourquoi?* (Paris: Actes Sud, 2019), 57. This and all other translations from the French are mine, unless otherwise noted.
20. Ruth Mas argues that it is "precisely the intellectual act of separating it from criticism [that] lends critique its force as a tool of modernity. It does so by putting critique forward as the impartial and refined alternative to a churlish exercise of criticism." Ruth Mas, "Why Critique?," *Method & Theory in the Study of Religion* 24, no. 4/5 (2012): 390. As we will see in chapter 1, the concept of "fraternal critique" does not make this idealized differentiation with criticism. Instead, it comes out of a broader "ethics of discontent" that includes dissatisfaction, disagreement, and what some of my interlocutors called "engaged pessimism." Critique should therefore not be understood in the Kantian sense of "that philosophical exercise by which the limits of knowledge are discerned" but instead in the sense of "a purposeful craft" of discernment and judgment that can be expressed in multiple registers. Mas, "Why Critique?," 389-90.
21. Moncef Zenati, *La fraternité humaine en islam* (Aubervilliers: Maison d'Ennour, 2008).
22. Abdennour Bidar, *Plaidoyer pour la fraternité* (Paris: Albin Michel, 2015), 13.
23. Bidar, *Plaidoyer pour la fraternité*, 12.
24. Seydi Diamil Niane, *Moi, musulman, je n'ai pas à me justifier* (Paris: Groupe Eyrolles, 2017), 91–99. Drawing on Aimé Césaire, Frantz Fanon, and Amadou Hampâté Bâ, Niane connects Césaire's anticolonial "humanism made to the measure of the world" with the Sufi concept of unicity and a divine anthropology that sees humanity through the "creative breath" (*souffle créateur*). Aimé Cesaire, *Discourse on Colonialism*, trans. Joan Pinkham (New York: Monthly Review Press, 2000 [1950]), 73. Niane, *Moi, musulman*, 93.
25. Chandra Mohanty, *Feminism without Borders: Decolonizing Theory, Practicing Solidarity* (Durham, NC: Duke University Press, 2003); Elora Shehabuddin, *Sisters in the Mirror: A History of Muslim Women and the Global Politics of Feminism* (Berkeley: University of California Press, 2021).
26. Shenila Khoja-Moolji describes how religious community "is not a given, but an ethical relation that is maintained daily and intergenerationally through everyday acts of care." In the French context that my book comes out of, these "everyday acts of care" were both material practices of labor and sociality, as Khoja-Moolji describes, and simultaneously agonistic practices of discourse. *Rebuilding Community: Displaced Women and the Making of a Shia Ismaili Muslim Sociality* (New York: Oxford University Press, 2023), 9–10.
27. I follow Joan Wallach Scott in translating *laïcité* as secularism without attributing any special untranslatability to the French term. Scott, *The Politics of the Veil* (Princeton, NJ: Princeton University Press, 2007). I agree with Scott that to leave laïcité untranslated

contributes to the mythology of French exceptionality of secularism. While Anglo-American traditions of secularism have typically prioritized freedom *for* religious expression and French traditions of secularism have typically prioritized the state as a sphere free *from* religion, both forms of secularism manage the boundary between "good" and "bad" religion. On the contiguity of French and other North Atlantic traditions of secularism, see Valentine Zuber, "La laïcité française, une exception historique, des principes partagés," *Revue du droit des religions* 7 (2019): 193–205; and Joan Wallach Scott, *Sex and Secularism* (Princeton, NJ: Princeton University Press, 2018).

28. A later ruling denied the day care the status of "business of conviction," while upholding the permissibility of firing an employee for her religious expression, on the grounds that a day care, as a business with a public mission, could require "neutrality" of its representatives. For a detailed legal analysis of the *Baby Loup* case, see Stéphanie Hennette-Vauchez and Vincent Valentin, *L'affaire Baby Loup ou la nouvelle laïcité* (Paris: Lextenso, 2014) and Juliette Brunie, "Affaire Baby Loup: L'admission du principe de neutralité dans les entreprises privées 'ordinaires,'" *Revue juridique de l'Ouest*, no. 1 (2015): 75–84.

29. La Poste, "Tarifs d'envoi de documents culturels," https://www.laposte.fr/tarifs-livres-brochures.

30. Ahmed Boubeker, "Les mondes de l'immigration des héritiers," *Multitudes* 49, no. 2 (2012): 108.

31. Fareen Parvez, *Politicizing Islam: The Islamic Revival in France and India* (Oxford: Oxford University Press, 2017); Olivier Esteves, "France, You Love It but Leave It: The Silent Flight of French Muslims," *Modern and Contemporary France* 31, no. 2 (2023): 243–57; Karel Arnaut et al., "Leaving Europe: New Crises, Entrenched Inequalities and Alternative Routes of Social Mobility," *Journal of Immigrant and Refugee Studies* 18, no. 3 (2020): 261–69.

32. John Bowen, *Can Islam Be French? Pluralism and Pragmatism in a Secularist State* (Princeton, NJ: Princeton University Press, 2010).

33. John Bowen, *Why the French Don't Like Headscarves: Islam, the State, and Public Space* (Princeton, NJ: Princeton University Press, 2006); Jonathan Laurence and Justin Vaisse, *Integrating Islam: Political and Religious Challenges in Contemporary France* (Washington, DC: Brookings Institution Press, 2006); Scott, *Politics of the Veil*.

34. Naomi Davidson, *Only Muslim: Embodying Islam in Twentieth-Century France* (Ithaca, NY: Cornell University Press, 2012); Mayanthi Fernando, *The Republic Unsettled: Muslim French and the Contradictions of Secularism* (Durham, NC: Duke University Press, 2014); Frank Peter, *Islam and the Governing of Muslims in France: Secularism without Religion* (London: Bloomsbury Academic, 2021).

35. Jean Beaman, *Citizen Outsider: Children of North African Immigrants in France* (Berkeley: University of California Press, 2017).

36. Fernando, *The Republic Unsettled*.

37. Paul Silverstein, *Postcolonial France: Race, Islam, and the Future of the Republic* (London: Pluto Press, 2018).

38. Silverstein, *Postcolonial France*, 10.

39. Mayanthi Fernando shows how Muslim French (in her locution) do not simply argue for the compatibility of Islam and Frenchness, but instead "make the more radical claim

that Muslim *is* French. French Muslim thus problematize any neat separation between public and private, politics and religion, and universal and particular, a separation that secular-republican citizenship both demands and consistently contravenes." Fernando, *The Republic Unsettled*, 62. In my own fieldwork a decade later, I did not find French Muslims to be invested in "making the claim" that Muslim is French so much as I found them to be taking this confluence for granted.

40. Vincent Valentin, "L'effacement de la laïcité libérale en France," *Canadian Journal of Law and Society* 36, no. 2 (2021): 303–21.
41. "Gérald Darmanin veut dissoudre une maison d'édition 'légitimant le djihad,'" *Le Figaro*, September 17, 2021, https://www.lefigaro.fr/flash-actu/gerald-darmanin-veut-dissoudre-une-maison-d-edition-legitimant-le-djihad-20210917.
42. Hichem Benaissa, "Depuis quand l'islam est un problème en France?," interview by Jalal Kahliouli, *Bondy Blog*, February 18, 2021.
43. Nadia Marzouki, *Islam: An American Religion* (New York: Columbia University Press: 2017).
44. Kim Willsher, "Samuel Paty's Murder: How a Teenager's Lie Sparked a Tragic Chain of Events," *The Guardian*, March 8, 2021.
45. Sonia Mabrouk, "Interview de M. Gérald Darmanin, ministre de l'intérieur, sur l'attentat de Conflans-Sainte-Honorine et la lutte contre l'islamisme radical," *Europe 1*, October 19, 2020.
46. Mathilde Durand, "'Ce qu'on appelle l'islamo-gauchisme fait des ravages,' dénonce Jean-Michel Blanquer," *Europe 1*, October 22, 2020.
47. Patrick Simon, "Le tigre de papier communautaire," in *Communautarisme?*, ed. Marwan Muhammad and Julien Talpin (Paris: Presses Universitaires de France, 2018), 41–54.
48. Marwan Muhammad and Julien Talpin, eds., *Communautarisme?* (Paris: Presses Universitaires de France: 2018).
49. Eric Maurin, *Le ghetto français: Enquête sur le séparatisme social* (Paris: Seuil, 2004); Loïc Wacquant, "A Janus-Faced Institution of Ethnoracial Closure: A Sociological Specification of the Ghetto," in *The Ghetto: Contemporary Global Issues and Controversies*, ed. Ray Hutchison and Bruce D. Haynes. (Boulder, CO: Westview Press, 2012), 15–20.
50. This runs parallel in certain ways to Cemil Aydin's argument about the concept of the "Muslim world." According to Aydin, "starting in the late nineteenth century, pan-Islamists and Islamophobes have used the assumption, ideal, and threat of Muslim unity to advance political agendas. Together, and in tension, they created the Muslim world for their own strategic purposes and positioned it in everlasting conflict with the West." Cemil Aydin, *The Idea of the Muslim World: A Global Intellectual History* (Cambridge, MA: Harvard University Press, 2017), 5. Like Aydin argues here, I understand the concept of "Muslim community" to be shaped by its proponents and detractors alike, in a context of empire and the racialization of Muslimness. However, unlike the idea of the "Muslim world," my interlocutors' understanding of Muslim community was spiritual rather than geopolitical, a local, deterritorialized practice rather than an internationalist essentialized claim. Aydin distinguishes between the geopolitical idea of the Muslim world and the theological idea of the *umma*, or global Muslim community. The ideal of community pursued by socially engaged French Muslims is related to the idea of the

umma, while the conception of Muslim community expressed by French political elites is related to the racialized fear of Muslim solidarity that Aydin identifies in the concept of the "Muslim world."
51. Olivier Roy, "La peur d'une communauté qui n'existe pas," *Le Monde*, January 9, 2015.
52. Elayne Oliphant, *The Privilege of Being Banal: Art, Secularism, and Catholicism in Paris* (Chicago: University of Chicago Press, 2021), 7.
53. Institut nationale de la statistique et des études économiques (INSEE), "Populations légales 2020" (December 2022), https://www.insee.fr/fr/statistiques/6683037.
54. Historian Tyler Stovall has argued that, in contrast to more recent narratives of the passage from class to race as the primary axis of difference in the banlieues, these urban spaces have been sites of the *confluence* of class and racial difference going back to the nineteenth century. Stovall, "From Red Belt to Black Belt: Race, Class, and Urban Marginality in Twentieth-Century Paris," in *The Color of Liberty: Histories of Race in France*, ed. Tyler Stovall and Sue Peabody (Durham, NC: Duke University Press: 2001), 351–70.
55. Mustafa Dikeç, *Badlands of the Republic: Space, Politics, and Urban Policy* (Malden, MA: Blackwell, 2007); Theresa Enright, *The Making of Grand Paris: Metropolitan Urbanism in the Twenty-First Century* (Cambridge, MA: MIT Press, 2016).
56. Kleinman, *Adventure Capital*, 6.
57. Kleinman, *Adventure Capital*, 6.
58. Davidson, *Only Muslim*.
59. Tahar Ben Jelloun, *Hospitalité française* (Paris: Seuil, 1984), 15.
60. Nedjib Sidi Moussa, *La fabrique du Musulman* (Paris: Libertalia, 2017); Ferruh Yilmaz, *How the Workers Became Muslims: Immigration, Culture, and Hegemonic Transformation in Europe* (Ann Arbor: University of Michigan Press, 2016).
61. Beaman, *Citizen Outsider*.
62. Sahar Aziz, *The Racial Muslim: When Racism Quashes Religious Freedom* (Berkeley: University of California Press: 2021). On Islamophobia as a form of racism in France, see, for example, Juliette Galonnier, "Discrimination religieuse ou discrimination raciale?," *Hommes & Migrations* 1324 (2019): 29–37; Jean Beaman, "France's Ahmeds and Muslim Others: The Entanglement of Racism and Islamophobia," *French Cultural Studies* 32, no. 3 (2021): 269–79.
63. Fatima El-Tayeb, *European Others: Queering Ethnicity in Postnational Europe* (Minneapolis: University of Minnesota Press), xv. In the words of Mame-Fatou Niang and Julien Suaudeau, "The mythology of imported racism is a means of repression that also serves as a form of negationism: racism is a product that originated in Europe, from where it was exported by the colonial powers as they expanded their territories," "21st-century Universalism Will Be Anti-Racist, or It Won't Be at All" (October 2020), https://www.rosalux.eu/en/article/1812.21st-century-universalism-will-be-anti-racist-or-it-won-t-be-at-all.html.
64. Sadri Khiari, *La contre-révolution coloniale en France: De de Gaulle à Sarkozy* (Paris: La Fabrique, 2009), 26.
65. Sylvia Chan-Malik analyzes Islam as a "racial-religious form" in the US context, writing that "to name Islam as both a racial and religious form—a racial-religious form—in the United States is to note how not only Muslim bodies but also Islamic beliefs and

practices are marked by abject monstrosity." Chan-Malik, *Being Muslim: A Cultural History of Women of Color in American Islam* (New York: New York University Press, 2018): 21. On race in France as a "condition" rather than an identity, a caste, or a community, see Pap Ndiaye, *La condition noire: Essai sur une minorité française* (Paris: Calmann-Levy, 2008); and Mathilde Cohen and Sarah Mazouz, "A White Republic? Whites and Whiteness in France," *French Politics, Culture, and Society* 39, no. 2 (2021): 1–25. On race-blindness in France, see, for example, Sarah Mazouz, *Race* (Paris: Anamosa, 2020); Angéline Escafré-Dublet et al., "Fighting Discrimination in a Hostile Political Environment: The Case of 'Colour-Blind' France," *Ethnic and Racial Studies* 46, no. 4 (2023): 667–85; Trica Danielle Keaton, *You Know You're Black in France When . . . : The Fact of Everyday Antiblackness* (Cambridge, MA: MIT Press, 2023).

66. Muriam Haleh Davis, *Markets of Civilization: Islam and Racial Capitalism in Algeria* (Durham, NC: Duke University Press, 2022), 6. See also Davidson, *Only Muslim*, 4.

67. The adjective *racisé*, used to describe people who are ascribed a form of racialized difference and may experience racist discrimination, is roughly equivalent to the American phrase "person of color." This term gained currency fairly rapidly during the 2010s, as documented by Google Ngram Viewer. While I did not hear this term at all in my early fieldwork in the late 2000s, by 2014 it was in circulation among university students and some young professionals. The term, like all discourse on race and racialization, remains controversial in France.

68. On "Californian Muslims" and the wider trans-Atlantic attention among French Muslims, see Kirsten Wesselhoeft, "Muslim Ethics and the Ethnographic Imagination," *Journal of Religious Ethics* 51, no. 1 (2023): 108–20.

69. I borrow Amina Wadud's terminology of "transition" to describe religious conversion as an extended ongoing process of becoming. Amina Wadud, *Inside the Gender Jihad: Women's Reform in Islam* (Oxford: Oneworld, 2006).

70. In 2015, the French Ministry of the Interior launched a wide-ranging and expensive new counterinsurgency initiative, promoted through a government website called "Stop Djihadisme" (now defunct). A widely circulated infographic listed "initial warning signs" of supposed radicalization, including sartorial changes, cultural changes, changes in social habits, and dietary changes (symbolized by a baguette with an X through it). Ishaan Tharoor, "Chart: Are You a Jihadist? The French Government Made This Checklist," *Washington Post*, January 29, 2015.

71. Donatella Della Porta et al., *Discursive Turns and Critical Junctures: Debating Citizenship after the Charlie Hebdo Attacks* (Oxford: Oxford University Press, 2020).

CHAPTER 1

1. This is a pseudonym for the town.
2. Jeanette Jouili, *Pious Practice and Secular Constraints: Women in the Islamic Revival in Europe* (Stanford, CA: Stanford University Press, 2015).

3. Brannon Ingram, *Revival from Below: The Deoband Movement and Global Islam* (Berkeley: University of California Press, 2018).
4. Saba Mahmood, *Politics of Piety: The Islamic Revival and the Feminist Subject* (Princeton, NJ: Princeton University Press, 2005); Lara Deeb, *An Enchanted Modern: Gender and Public Piety in Shi'i Lebanon* (Princeton, NJ: Princeton University Press, 2004); Adeline Masquelier, *Women and Islamic Revival in a West African Town* (Bloomington: Indiana University Press, 2009).
5. The UOIF is now known as Musulmans de France (MF).
6. John Bowen, *Can Islam Be French?*, 24.
7. Françoise Duthu, *Le maire et la mosquée: Islam et laïcité en Île-de-France* (Paris: Harmattan, 2009), 28.
8. Nicolas Sarkozy, speech given on March 29, 2003, at Mosquée Tariq Ibn Zyad, Les Mureaux, France.
9. Duthu, *Le maire et la mosquée*, 25; Anne-Laure Zwilling, "A Century of Mosques in France: Building Religious Pluralism," *International Review of Sociology* 25, no. 2 (2015): 333. Hervé Viellard-Baron, "L'Islam en France: Dynamiques, fragmentation et perspectives," *L'Information Géographique* 80, no. 1 (2016): 22–53.
10. Ahmed Eid, *Unmosqued: The Movie* (Eid Films, 2014).
11. Institut Français d'Opinion Publique, "Le pessimisme des Français en question," *IFOP Focus*, no. 101 (January 2014). See also Hervé Le Bras, *Se sentir mal dans une France qui va bien: La société paradoxale* (Paris: Editions de l'Aube, 2019) and Marcel Gauchet, *Comprendre le malheur français* (Paris: Stock, 2016).
12. Jouili, *Pious Practice and Secular Constraints*.
13. The CFCM was for many years supposed to be the major representative institution for French Muslims. Founded at the behest of then interior minister Nicolas Sarkozy in 2003, the CFCM was the site of interaction between Muslim leaders and the French state until the end of 2021, when Interior Minister Gérald Darmanin declared that the CFCM "in terms of the authorities, does not exist anymore." President Emmanuel Macron inaugurated the new Forum for Islam of France (FORIF) in early 2022. Bernadette Sauvaget, "2003–2022: Fin de service pour le Conseil français du culte musulman," *Libération*, January 20, 2022, https://www.liberation.fr/societe/religions/2003-2022-fin-de-service-pour-le-conseil-francais-du-culte-musulman-20220120_VTPKMX7E3NBNHK6G4QY7D7U6T4/. On the CFCM, see, for example, Franck Fregosi, "De quoi le gouvernement de l'islam en France est-il le nom?," *Confluences Méditerannée* 106, no. 3 (2018): 35–51.
14. Le Bras, *Se sentir mal dans une France qui va bien*.
15. Paul Yonnet, *Voyage au centre du malaise français: L'antiracisme et le roman national* (Paris: Éditions Gallimard, 1993); Jean-Marie Domenach, *Regarder la France: Essai sur le malaise français* (Paris: FeniXX, 1997); Michèle Tribalat, *Dreux, voyage au coeur du malaise français* (Paris: Éditions La Découverte, 1999).
16. Pierre Rosanvallon et al., "Tribune: Quelle crise des banlieues?," *Libération*, November 21, 2005, https://www.liberation.fr/tribune/2005/11/21/quelle-crise-des-banlieues_539661/.
17. Sylvain Brouard and Vincent Tiberj, *As French as Everyone Else? A Survey of French*

NOTES TO PAGES 46–54　　　　　　　　　　　　　　　　　　　　　　　　　　183

　　　Citizens of Maghrebin, African, and Turkish Origin (Philadelphia, PA: Temple University Press, 2011).
18. Marwan Muhammad, *Foul Express* ([Mérignac]: Éditions Sentinelles, 2014), 123.
19. On Muhammad's personal trajectory, see also Marwan Muhammad, *Nous (Aussi) Sommes La Nation* (Paris: La Découverte, 2017), 9–58.
20. Nabil Ennasri, *Les 7 défis capitaux: Essai à destination de la communauté musulmane* (Self-published, 2014).
21. Mohammad Kamali, "The Scope of Diversity and 'Ikhtilaf' (Juristic Disagreement) in the Shari'ah," *Islamic Studies* 37, no. 3 (1998): 315–37; Youcef Soufi, *The Rise of Critical Islam: 10th–13th-Century Legal Debate* (New York: Oxford University Press, 2023). I regret that I encountered Dr. Soufi's important work on ikhtilaf and critique too late in the process of revising this manuscript to engage it in the substance it deserves.
22. Taha al-Jabir Al-'Alwani, *The Ethics of Disagreement in Islam*, trans. AbdulWahid Hamid (Herndon, VA: International Institute of Islamic Thought, 2011), 1–2.
23. Ahmed Fekry Ibrahim, *Pragmatism in Islamic Law: A Social and Intellectual History* (Syracuse, NY: Syracuse University Press, 2015). While Sunni legal pluralism is sometimes framed as a modernist approach to Islamic law, coming partly in response to codification, Ibrahim argues that it is a long-standing feature of Islamic legal practice.
24. Robert Hefner, ed. *Shari'a Law and Modern Muslim Ethics* (Bloomington: Indiana University Press, 2016).
25. Taha al-Jabir Al-'Alwani, *Islam, conflit d'opinions: Pour une éthique du désaccord*, trans. Ilham Benmahdjoub (Paris: Al Qalam, 2010). Al-'Alwani was a founding member and president of the International Institute of Islamic Thought in Herndon, VA, which for a time had connections and partners in Paris.
26. Here the professor invokes another widely known hadith that frames ikhtilaf as a divine mercy.
27. Whether it is licit for women to lead mixed-gender prayers is a topic of some debate. On these conversations in the North American context, see Juliane Hammer, *More than a Prayer: American Muslim Women, Religious Authority, and Activism* (Austin: University of Texas Press, 2012); Meena Sharify-Funk and Munira Haddad, "Where Do Women 'Stand' in Islam? Negotiating Contemporary Muslim Prayer Leadership in North America," *Feminist Review* 102, no. 1 (2012): 41–61; Ahmed Elewa and Laury Silvers, "'I *Am* One of the People': A Survey and Analysis of Legal Arguments on Women-Led Prayer in Islam." *Journal of Law and Religion* 26, no. 1 (2012): 141–71.
28. Amina Jamal, *Jamaat-e-Islami Women in Pakistan: Vanguard of a New Modernity?* (Syracuse, NY: Syracuse University Press, 2013); Aaron Rock-Singer, "The Sunni Islamic Revival," in *The Oxford Handbook of the Sociology of the Middle East*, ed. Armando Salvatore, Sari Hanafi, and Kieko Obuse (Oxford: Oxford University Press, 2020): 395–409.
29. Justine Howe, *Suburban Islam* (New York: Oxford University Press, 2018).
30. Catherine Wihtol de Wenden and Rémy Leveau, *La beurgeoisie: Les trois âges de la vie associative issue de l'immigration* (Paris: CNRS, 2001), 83.
31. In French, "Miroir d'Eau." This is a pseudonym from the organization drawn from their discursive repertoire. With a very few exceptions (such as the internationally known

CCIF), all community organizations mentioned in this book are referred to by pseudonyms, to protect the identities of their members.
32. Brouard and Tiberj, *As French as Everyone Else?*; Laurence and Vaisse, *Integrating Islam*.
33. The video can be viewed here: https://www.youtube.com/watch?v=iZ8T-pQrwcI (last accessed May 24, 2023).
34. "Nous sommes les indigènes de la République" (January 2005), https://indigenes-republique.fr/le-p-i-r/appel-des-indigenes-de-la-republique/. On the Parti des Indigènes de la République, see Houria Bouteldja and Sadri Khiari, eds., *Nous sommes les indigènes de la République* (Paris: Éditions Amsterdam, 2012) and Olivia C. Harrison, *Natives against Nativism: Antiracism and Indigenous Critique in Postcolonial France* (Minneapolis: University of Minnesota Press, 2023), as well as Silverstein, *Postcolonial France*.
35. Fredette, "Social Movements and the State's Construction of Identity."
36. Margot Dazey, "Polite Responses to Stigmatization: Ethics of Exemplarity among French Muslim Elites," *Ethnic and Racial Studies* 46, no. 4 (2023): 686–706.
37. Éditions du Grand Remplacement, *Téléramadan*, issue 1 (Paris, 2016): 3.
38. Samuli Schielke, "Second Thoughts about the Anthropology of Islam, or How to Make Sense of Grand Schemes in Everyday Life," *Zentrum Moderner Orient Research Papers*, no. 2 (2010): 2.
39. As Lara Deeb pointed out, this imbalance is a result of how influential work such as Mahmood's has been *read*, rather than an implication of the work itself. Deeb, "Thinking Piety and the Everyday Together: A Response to Fadil and Fernando," *Hau: Journal of Ethnographic Theory* 5, no. 2 (2015): 93–96.

CHAPTER 2

1. On Muslim epistemic and material survival, see Maryam Kashani, *Medina by the Bay: Scenes of Muslim Study and Survival* (Durham, NC: Duke University Press, 2023). On stagnant social mobility in France, see INSEE, "Mobilité sociale" (March 2020), https://www.insee.fr/fr/statistiques/4797592.
2. Davis, *Markets of Civilization*, 3.
3. For other work on racial capitalism in French colonial contexts, see notably Françoise Vergès, *The Wombs of Women: Race, Capital, and Feminism*, trans. Kaiama L. Glover (Durham, NC: Duke University Press, 2020).
4. Shahrokni, *Higher Education and Social Mobility in France*.
5. Nadia Fadil also attends to the way that some young European Muslims identify and pay tribute to their parents' Islam. Fadil describes how her interlocutors, second-generation Maghrebi Belgians, "explicitly demarcated themselves from the turn to religious orthodoxy through an active reference to the 'Islam of the parents.'" Nadia Fadil, "Recalling the 'Islam of the Parents': Liberal and Secular Muslims Redefining the Contours of Religious Authenticity," *Identities* 24, no. 1 (2017): 85. I observed this identification with

the "Islam of the parents" (or grandparents) not only among French Muslims who, like Fadil's Belgian interlocutors, sought alternatives to "modernist" or "revivalist" modes of Islamic piety, but also among French Muslims who identified with these modes of piety, which is often presumed to contrast with the Islamic practice of older generations.

6. Abdelmalek Sayad, *The Suffering of the Immigrant*, trans. David Macey (Malden, MA: Polity Press, 2004), 89.
7. Pierre Bourdieu and Jean-Claude Passeron, *The Inheritors: French Students and Their Relation to Culture*, trans. Richard Nice (Chicago: University of Chicago Press, 1979).
8. Boubeker, "Les mondes de l'immigration des héritiers," 101.
9. On the March for Equality and against Racism, see Abdellali Hajjat, *The Wretched of France: The 1983 March for Equality and against Racism*, trans. Andrew Brown (Bloomington: Indiana University Press, 2022).
10. Lara Deeb and Mona Harb, *Leisurely Islam: Negotiating Geography and Morality in Shi'ite South Beirut* (Princeton, NJ: Princeton University Press, 2013).
11. Su'ad Abdul Khabeer, "Hip Hop Matters: Race, Space, and Islam in Chicago," *City and Society* 30, no. 2 (2018): 141–64.
12. Zareena Grewal, *Islam Is a Foreign Country: American Muslims and the Global Crisis of Authority* (New York: New York University Press, 2014), 85.
13. Enright, *The Making of Grand Paris*, 15.
14. "Une ville durable et inventive," Société du Grand Paris, April 9, 2014. https://www.societedugrandparis.fr/projet/le-grand-paris/ville-durable-inventive.
15. Enright, *The Making of Grand Paris*, 8.
16. Éric Hazan, *Paris sous tension* (Paris: La Fabrique, 2011), 115.
17. Médine, "Grand Paris" (2017). This hook is consonant with what Jeanette Jouili has analyzed as Médine's simultaneous trenchant critique and enduring optimism, his insistence that "for him, being French means 'being a revolutionary.'" Jouili, "Rapping the Republic: Utopia, Critique, and Muslim Role Models in Secular France," *French Politics, Culture, and Society* 31, no. 2 (2013): 58–80.
18. Gilles Kepel, *Les banlieues de l'Islam: Naissance d'une religion en France* (Paris: Éditions du Seuil, 1987).
19. The *classes préparatoires*, commonly called *prépas*, consist of two years of extremely intensive study in between passage of the baccalaureate exam and application to one of the grandes écoles.
20. Cécile Bonneau et al., "Grandes écoles: Des politiques 'd'ouverture sociale' en echec," *Éducation et formations*, no. 103 (2022): 156–74.
21. Kaoutar Harchi, "Le concept de transfuge est un concept blanc," interview by Joseph Andras, *Frustration*, February 28, 2023, https://www.frustrationmagazine.fr/entretien-harchi-andras-i/; emphasis in original.
22. Kaoutar Harchi, *Comme Nous Existons* (Paris: Actes Sud, 2021). On social mobility in Harchi's memoir as well as other contemporary texts, see Morgane Cadieu, *On Both Sides of the Tracks: Social Mobility in Contemporary French Literature* (Chicago: University of Chicago Press, 2024).
23. Abdelmalek Sayad, *L'immigration ou les paradoxes de l'altérité*, vol. 3, *La fabrication des identités culturelles* (Paris: Raisons d'Agir, 2014), 186–87.

24. See, for example, Marie-Anne Valfort, "La religion, facteur de discrimination à l'embauche en France," *Revue Économique* 68, no. 5 (2017): 895–907, and Yaël Brinbaum and Jean-Luc Primon, "Parcours scolaires et sentiment d'injustice et de discrimination chez les descendants d'immigrés," *Économie et Statistique* 464, no. 1 (2013): 215–43, and more broadly the large-scale survey data in Cris Beauchemin, Christelle Hamel, and Patrick Simon, *Trajétoires et origines: Enquête sur la diversité des populations en France* (Paris: Ined éditions, 2015).
25. Musulmans de France (MF) was formerly known as the UOIF.
26. Gilles Kepel, *Quatre-vingt-treize* (Paris: Gallimard, 2012), 81.
27. Annabelle Allouch, *Les nouvelles portes des grandes écoles* (Paris: Presses Universitaires de France, 2022).
28. Natasha Warikoo, *The Diversity Bargain, and Other Dilemmas of Race, Admissions, and Meritocracy at Elite Universities* (Chicago: University of Chicago Press, 2016).
29. Leila Babès, *L'Islam positif: La religion des jeunes musulmans de France* (Paris: Éditions de l'Atelier, 1997); Farhad Khosrokhavar, *L'Islam des jeunes* (Paris: Flammarion, 1997).
30. On Muslim entrepreneurialism in France, see Hicham Benaissa, "Islam et capitalisme: Les entrepreneurs musulmans en France," *Entreprises et Histoire*, no. 81 (2015): 111–25; Hanane Karimi, "The Hijab and Work: Female Entrepreneurship in Response to Islamophobia," *International Journal of Politics, Culture, and Society* 31, no. 4 (2018): 421–35.
31. Kirsten Wesselhoeft, "'On the Front Lines of the Classroom': Moral Education and Muslim Students in French State Schools," *Oxford Review of Education* 43, no. 5 (2017): 626–41.

CHAPTER 3

1. In her ethnographic reading of *L'Étoile Brillante*, Jeannette Jouili has observed that the production contributed to cultivating a modern Muslim subject through a pedagogy of punctuality and attentive listening, fusing middle-class cultured dispositions with Islamic virtues. As part of a burgeoning "halal arts" scene of the 2010s, Jouili argued that *L'Étoile Brillante* was part of an "emerging counter-public" that aimed to "refine skills, habits and dispositions through exposure to the arts," generating "new types of listeners and spectators rather than merely debaters." Jeanette Jouili, "Refining the Umma in the Shadow of the Republic: Performing Arts and New Islamic Audio-Visual Landscapes in France." *Anthropological Quarterly* 87, no. 4 (2014): 1079–104.
2. Amel Boubekeur, "Post-Islamist Culture: A New Form of Mobilization?," *History of Religions* 47, no. 1 (2007): 75–94.
3. More loosely, *mixité* can refer to any kind of heterogenous social interaction.
4. On mixité, see Kirsten Wesselhoeft, "Mixité, Gender Difference and the Politics of Islam in France after the Headscarf Ban," in Justine Howe, ed. *The Routledge Handbook of Islam and Gender* (New York: Routledge, 2021), 146–60.

5. Scott, *Sex and Secularism*, 31.
6. Scott, *Sex and Secularism*, 32.
7. Éric Fassin, "La démocratie sexuelle et le conflit des civilisations," *Multitudes* 26, no. 3 (2006): 123–31; Nacira Guénif-Souilamas and Éric Macé, *Les féministes et le garçon arabe* (Paris: Éditions de l'Aube, 2004).
8. For example, see the 2016 Jouanno Report, discussed in chapter 5.
9. Nadia Fadil, "Performing the Salat [Islamic Prayers] at Work: Secular and Pious Muslims Negotiating the Contours of the Public in Belgium," *Ethnicities* 13, no. 6. (2013): 731.
10. Chloé Delaume, ed., *Sororité* (Paris: Points, 2021), 9.
11. Delaume, *Sororité*, 13.
12. Fatima Ouassak, "Protégeons nos enfants, ensemble!," in *Sororité*, ed. Chloé Delaume (Paris: Syllepse, 2021), 154.
13. Mwasi, *AfroFem* (Paris: Syllepse, 2018).
14. Chan-Malik, *Being Muslim*, 33–34.
15. Chan-Malik, *Being Muslim*, 34.
16. Chan-Malik, *Being Muslim*, 5.
17. Chan-Malik, *Being Muslim*, 16.
18. Christine Delphy, "La non-mixité: Une nécessité politique," *LMSI: Les mots sont importants*, November 24, 2017, https://lmsi.net/La-non-mixite-une-necessite; Christine Delphy, *Un universalisme si particulier: Féminisme et exception française (1980–2010)* (Paris: Syllepse, 2010).
19. Delphy, "La non-mixité."
20. Davidson, *Only Muslim*, 47.
21. Davidson, *Only Muslim*, 61.
22. Les Femmes dans la Mosquée, "Lettre ouverte au Recteur de la Mosquée de Paris," Oumma.com, November 28, 2013, https://oumma.com/lettre-ouverte-au-recteur-de-la-mosquee-de-paris/.
23. Olfa Khamira, "La decision de la Grande Mosquée de Paris de séparer les femmes et les hommes pendant la prière fait polemique," *Huffington Post*, December 24, 2013.
24. Stéphane Kovacs, "Guerre des sexes à la Mosquée de Paris," *Le Figaro*, December 26, 2013.
25. Khamira, "La decision de la Grande Mosquée de Paris."
26. Aisha Manoubia (1199–1267) was a prominent Tunisian Sufi scholar. Aisha As-Sadiq is an appellation of one of the wives of the Prophet Muhammad. (Aicha is a French spelling of Aisha.)
27. Aicha and Selma, "Deux femmes dans la mosquée," Facebook, January 19, 2014.
28. Ndella Paye, "'Les femmes dans la mosquée' pour les droits des femmes," PSM En Ligne, https://www.psm-enligne.org/societe/articles-societe/2548-qles-femmes-dans-la-mosqueeq-pour-les-droits-des-femmes.
29. Elles & Dyn, "Nous connaître," ellesetdyn.com (site discontinued).
30. Howe, *Suburban Islam*, 11.
31. Saba Mahmood, *Religious Difference in a Secular Age: A Minority Report* (Princeton, NJ: Princeton University Press, 2016), 212.
32. Saba Mahmood, "Can Secularism Be Other-wise?," in *Varieties of Secularism in a Secular*

Age, ed. Michael Warner, Jonathan VanAntwerpen, and Craig J. Calhoun (Cambridge, MA: Harvard University Press, 2010), 294.
33. Emmanuel Macron, interview with Jean-Jacques Bourdin and Edwy Plenel, 2018, https://www.bfmtv.com/politique/retrouvez-l-integralite-de-l-interview-d-emmanuel-macron-sur-bfmtv-rmc-mediapart_VN-201804160086.html.
34. Fabrice Lhomme and Gérard Davet, *Un président ne devrait pas dire ça...* (Paris: Stock, 2016); my emphasis.
35. Charles Taylor, *A Secular Age* (Cambridge, MA: Harvard University Press, 2016), 42.
36. Malika Zeghal, "Competing Ways of Life: Islamism, Secularism, and Public Order in the Tunisian Transition." *Constellations* 20, no. 2 (2013): 254–74.
37. Saba Mahmood, *Politics of Piety: The Islamic Revival and the Feminist Subject* (Princeton, NJ: Princeton University Press, 2005), 335–44.
38. Mahmood, *Politics of Piety*, 37.
39. Mahmood, *Politics of Piety*, 23.
40. Ahmed Boubeker, "Les mondes de l'immigration des héritiers," *Multitudes* 49, no. 2 (2012): 100–110; Jouili, *Pious Practice and Secular Constraints*.
41. Jouili, *Pious Practice and Secular Constraints*, 51.
42. On distancing from feminism, see also Jouili, *Pious Practice and Secular Constraints*, 93–120.
43. Mayanthi Fernando notes the prominence of the same Qur'anic citation in conversations on this topic during her fieldwork. Fernando, *The Republic Unsettled*, 150.
44. As others have noted, this line of argument is a prominent feature of modernist Islam. Dale Eickelman and James Piscatori, *Muslim Politics* (Princeton, NJ: Princeton University Press, 2004 [1996]); Deeb, *An Enchanted Modern*; Fernando, *The Republic Unsettled*.
45. Mahmood, *Politics of Piety*, 342–43.
46. Kirsten Wesselhoeft, "On the 'Front Lines' of the Classroom: Moral Education and Muslim Students in French State Schools," *Oxford Review of Education* 43, no. 5 (2017): 626–41.

CHAPTER 4

1. The word *communautarisme* is sometimes also translated into English as "communitarianism." Like others, I distinguish between "communalism," the distinctively French construct of public discourse, and "communitarianism," the political philosophy popularized by figures like Michael Sandel, which opposes the atomism of liberal political theory.
2. In addition to the CCIF, the Minister of the Interior forcibly dissolved other prominent actors in anti-racist organizing, notably including the Coordination against Racism and Islamophobia (CRI) and the Black African Defense League (LDNA) in late 2021. For an analysis of the closure of the CCIF, see Ibrahim Bechrouri, "'L'esprit de

défense': Separatism, Counterinsurgency, and the Dissolution of the Collective Against Islamophobia in France," *Modern and Contemporary France* 31, no. 2 (2023): 199–218.
3. Deva Woodly, *Reckoning: Black Lives Matter and the Democratic Necessity of Social Movements* (New York: Oxford University Press, 2022), 17.
4. Roshan A. Jahangeer, "Good Islam, Bad Islam? France's Republican Principles, Anti-Veiling, and the 'New Secularism,'" in *Islamophobia and/in Post-Secular States*, ed. Sharmin Sadequee (Edmonton: University of Alberta Press, forthcoming).
5. Francesco Ragazzi, "Policed Multiculturalism? The Impact of Counter-Terrorism and Counter-Radicalisation and the 'End' of Multiculturalism," in *Counter-Radicalisation: Critical Perspectives*, ed. Christopher Baker-Beall, Charlotte Heath-Kelly, and Lee Jarvis (New York: Routledge, 2014), 156–74.
6. Article 2 of this law reads, "The Republic neither recognizes, salaries, nor subsidizes any religion [*culte*]." "Loi du 9 décembre 1905 concernant la separation des Eglises et de l' Etat," https://www.legifrance.gouv.fr/loda/id/LEGITEXT000006070169.
7. Mayanthi Fernando has noted the pitfalls of this "politics of recognition" and has shown how Muslim actors increasingly demand the indifference of the state (or express indifference to the state), rather than demanding the recognition of their difference, which only serves to further secure state sovereignty. Mayanthi Fernando, "State Sovereignty and the Politics of Indifference," *Public Culture* 31, no. 2 (2019): 261–73.
8. Éric Marlière observes that these terrorist attacks have been not only physically but symbolically violent, targeting "the symbols that constitute 'French identity' in the twenty-first century: the satirical press, the Republican school, and the Catholic Church." Marlière, *La fabrique sociale de la radicalisation: Une contre-enquête sociologique* (Boulogne-Billancourt: Berger-Levrault, 2021), 12. (Attacks on the Catholic Church include the murder of a priest in 2016 and the 2020 killing of three worshippers at the Notre Dame Basilica in Nice.)
9. Loi du 30 octobre 2017 renforçant la sécurité intérieure et la lutte contre le terrorisme. On the "state of emergency," see Stéphanie Hennette-Vauchez, "The State of Emergency in France: Days without End?," *European Constitutional Law Review* 14, no. 4 (2018): 700–720.
10. Nathalie Guibert, Cédic Pietralunga, and Nicolas Chapuis, "Les militaires de 'Sentinelle' seront mobilisés pour l'acte XIX des 'gilets jaunes,'" *Le Monde*, March 20, 2019, https://www.lemonde.fr/police-justice/article/2019/03/20/les-militaires-de-sentinelle-seront-mobilises-pour-l-acte-xix-des-gilets-jaunes_5438862_1653578.html.
11. Mohammed and Talpin, *Communautarisme?*, 5.
12. Simon, "Le tigre de papier communautaire."
13. Fabrice Dhume, "L'émergence d'une figure obsessionnelle: Comment le 'communautarisme' a envahi les discours médiatico-politiques français," *Revue Asylon(s)* 8 (2010), http://reseau-terra.eu/article945.html.
14. As Muriam Haleh Davis has observed, "Islamo-leftism" is eerily reminiscent of "Judeo-Bolshevism," invoking earlier anti-Semitic ideas about a global leftist Jewish conspiracy. Muriam Haleh Davis, "Racial Capitalism and the Campaign against 'Islamo-gauchisme' in France," *Jadaliyya*, August 14, 2018. In this case, the foreign ties of Islamo-leftism are not to Russia, as they were with "Judeo-Bolshevism," but to the United States. The

government's insistence on statements of loyalty to national cohesion, obsession with forms of collectivism that stand outside the nation, and claims that some groups possess an immutable genealogical inheritability of difference, all resonate with the racializing ideology of anti-Semitism. Historian David Nirenberg has noted the operation of "judaizing"—the ascription of Jewishness to all sorts of unrelated and even opposing things and people—as part of a conspiracy theory that waxes and wanes throughout Western modernity, and certainly in France. David Nirenberg, *Anti-Judaism: The Western Tradition* (New York: Norton, 2013). A parallel "Islamizing" logic underpins the rhetoric of "Islamo-leftism." This rhetoric simultaneously construes Muslims as part of a left-wing conspiracy for cultural power, on the one hand, and attempts to taint leftist critique with the taboo of Muslimness, on the other. For a genealogy of "Islamo-leftism" as a metanarrative rooted in French resistance to Algerian decolonization, see Ibrahim Bechrouri, "From 'Red and Green Decay' to 'Islamo-Leftism': The Counterinsurgency Fantasies of the French Elite," *Contemporary French and Francophone Studies* 27, no. 2 (2023): 240–51.
15. "Islamophobie: Débats houleux à l'Assemblée Nationale," FranceInfo, October 29, 2019, https://www.francetvinfo.fr/politique/gouvernement-d-edouard-philippe/islamophobie-debats-houleux-a-l-assemblee-nationale_3680983.html; my emphasis.
16. Emmanuel Macron, "Protéger les libertés en luttant contre le séparatisme islamiste," press conference in Mulhouse, February 18, 2020.
17. Press release of the Ministry of the Interior and the Ministry of Education, March 10, 2022, https://www.interieur.gouv.fr/actualites/communiques/mise-en-place-dune-cellule-de-lutte-contre-lislamisme-radical-et-repli.
18. Rapport no. 595 (2019–2020), "Radicalisation islamiste: Faire face et lutter ensemble," July 7, 2020, p. 95, http://www.senat.fr/rap/r19-595-1/r19-595-1.html.
19. The General Secretariat of the Interministerial Committee for the Prevention of Delinquency and Radicalisation (SG-CIPDR), Twitter, July 27, 2021, https://twitter.com/SG_CIPDR/status/1420071675861819394.
20. Étude d'Impact: Projet de loi confortant le respect des principes de la République, December 8, 2020, p. 8, https://www.assemblee-nationale.fr/dyn/15/textes/l15b3649_etude-impact.pdf; my emphasis. The parliamentarians are relying on the definition of philosopher Christian Godin, from his *Dictionnaire de philosophie* (Paris: Fayard, 2004).
21. Étude d'Impact, p. 9.
22. *Le Figaro*, October 21, 2020, https://www.lefigaro.fr/politique/darmanin-se-dit-contre-les-rayons-de-cuisine-communautaire-dans-les-supermarches-ca-m-a-toujours-choque-20201021.
23. Sonia Mabrouk, "Interview with Jean-Michel Blanquer," October 22, 2020, https://www.vie-publique.fr/discours/276970-jean-michel-blanquer-22102020-lattaque-terroriste-contre-samuel-paty.
24. Saïd Bouamama, "Communautarisme: 'Un spectre hante la France,'" in *Racismes de France*, ed. Omar Slaouti and Olivier Le Cour Grandmaison (Paris: La Découverte, 2020), 252–53.
25. Bouamama, "Communautarisme," 254.
26. Mohammed and Talpin, *Communautarisme?*, 10.
27. Charles Taylor, *Multiculturalism* (Princeton, NJ: Princeton University Press, 1995).

28. Francesco Ragazzi, "Counter-Radicalisation, Islam, and Laïcité: Policed Multiculturalism in France's Banlieues," *Ethnic and Racial Studies* 46, no. 4 (2023): 707–27.
29. Francesco Ragazzi, "Policed Multiculturalism?," 163.
30. Mahmood Mamdani, *Good Muslim, Bad Muslim: America, the Cold War, and the Roots of Terror* (New York: Doubleday, 2004).
31. He further points out how the boundary between "trusted" and "suspect" Muslims is porous and ambivalent: "the 'trusted' Muslims of yesterday can become the 'suspects' of tomorrow and vice versa." Francesco Ragazzi, "Suspect Community or Suspect Category? The Impact of Counter-Terrorism as 'Policed Multiculturalism,'" *Journal of Ethnic and Migration Studies* 42, no. 5 (2016): 734.
32. Ragazzi, "Counter-Radicalisation, Islam, and Laïcité."
33. Luc Lenoir, "Loire: Un imam expulse vers les Comores," *Le Figaro*, May 3, 2022, https://www.lefigaro.fr/faits-divers/loire-un-imam-expulse-vers-les-comores-20220503. On the state's selection of imams through the titre de sejour process, see Solenne Jouanneau, "Régulariser ou non un imam étranger en France: Droit au séjour et définition du 'bon imam' en pays laïque," *Politix* 86, no. 2 (2009): 147–66. On the expulsion of imams for reasons of "public order" and Republican values, see chapter 5.
34. Salafism is a complex and diverse Sunni Islamic movement that pays particular attention to the practice of the earliest generation of Muslims, derives law directly from the Qur'an and Sunna rather than from the canonical legal schools, and takes up distinctive social practices. However, the term is generally used in French public discourse as an imprecise synonym for potentially violent "radicalization," by definition incompatible with Republican values. On Salafism as an international social movement, see Aaron Rock-Singer, *In the Shade of the Sunna: Salafi Piety in the Twentieth-Century Middle East* (Oakland: University of California Press, 2022), and Henri Lauzière, *The Making of Salafism: Islamic Reform in the Twentieth Century* (New York: Columbia University Press, 2015). On Salafism in France, see Samir Amghar, "Le salafisme en France: De la révolution islamique à la révolution conservatrice," *Critique internationale* 40, no. 3 (2008): 95–113, and Mohamed-Ali Adraoui, *Salafism Goes Global: From the Gulf to the French Banlieues* (New York: Oxford University Press, 2020).
35. "Christophe Castaner liste les signes de radicalisation?," *Europe1*, October 9, 2019, https://www.europe1.fr/politique/christophe-castaner-liste-les-signes-de-radicalisation-religieuse-vous-avez-une-barbe-vous-meme-lui-repond-un-depute-3924324. Ishaan Tharoor, "Are You a Jihadist? The French Government Made This Checklist," *Washington Post*, January 29, 2015, https://www.washingtonpost.com/news/worldviews/wp/2015/01/29/chart-are-you-a-jihadist-the-french-government-made-this-checklist/.
36. Ministre de l'Intérieur, "Forum de l'islam de France: Une étape nouvelle dans le dialogue entre les pouvoirs publics et le culte musulman," February 5, 2022, https://www.interieur.gouv.fr/actualites/communiques/forum-de-lislam-de-france-etape-nouvelle-dans-dialogue-entre-pouvoirs.
37. "Loi du 9 décembre 1905 concernant la séparation des Eglises et de l'Etat," article 2.
38. Solenne Jouanneau, "Faire émerger un 'islam français': Paradoxes d'une action publique sous contrainte," *Sociologie* 8, no. 3 (2017): 248.
39. Bernadette Sauvaget, "Islam de France: Le role attribué au CFCM jette le trouble,"

Libération, February 19, 2020, https://www.liberation.fr/france/2020/02/19/islam-de-france-le-role-attribue-au-cfcm-jette-le-trouble_1778899/.
40. Malika Zeghal, "La constitution du Conseil Français du Culte Musulman: Reconnaissance politique d'un Islam français?," *Archives de sciences sociales des religions* 129 (2005): 97–113.
41. "Communiqué du CCMTF, CIMG France, Foi et Pratique," February 7, 2021, https://cimgfrance.fr/index.php/2021/02/07/communique-du-ccmtf-cimg-france-foi-et-pratique-2/.
42. "L'installation d'un conseil national des imams du CFCM reporté en raison de la crise sanitaire," *Le Figaro*, January 3, 2022, https://www.lefigaro.fr/flash-actu/l-installation-d-un-conseil-national-des-imams-du-cfcm-reportee-en-raison-de-la-crise-sanitaire-20220103. It is worth noting that the CFCM continued to exist as an independent organization even after the state declared it "dead" and replaced it with FORIF. However, its purpose as the primary Muslim interlocutor of the state was hollowed out.
43. In his speech inaugurating FORIF, Interior Minister Gérald Darmanin stated that "secularism is not ignorance of religion; it is rather the organization of their coexistence." Gérald Darmanin, speech on February 5, 2022, p. 2, https://www.vie-publique.fr/discours/283686-gerald-darmanin-05022022-culte-musulman.
44. Solenne Jouanneau, "L'imam, clerc sans clergé ni église: Les répertoires d'une autorité dissimulée dans les cadres de l'interaction," *Genèses* 88, no. 3 (2012): 6–24.
45. This language of a "pact" may conceivably be an appeal to the discourse of *dar al-sulh* or *dar al-ahd*, classical Islamic terminology for a territory of "treaty," an alternative to both the "abode of Islam," and the "abode of conflict." For an analysis of this framework in the European context, see Tariq Ramadan, *Western Muslims and the Future of Islam* (New York: Oxford University Press, 2004), 66–69.
46. Charte des Principes pour l'Islam de France, January 17, 2021, article 1, https://www.cfcm-officiel.fr/presentation-de-la-charte-des-principes-pour-lislam-de-france-au-president-de-la-republique/.
47. Charte des Principes, article 5.
48. Charte des Principes, article 3.
49. Charte des Principes, article 5.
50. Charte des Principes, article 4.
51. Charte des Principes, article 4.
52. Charte des Principes, article 6.
53. Charte des Principes, article 6.
54. Charte des Principes, article 7.
55. Charte des Principes, article 9.
56. Omar Slaouti and Olivier Le Cour Grandmaison, eds. *Racismes de France* (Paris: La Découverte, 2020); Fabrice Dhume, et al, *Du racisme d'État en France?* (Paris: Bord de l'Eau, 2020).
57. Charte des Principes, article 9.
58. Charte des Principes, article 9.
59. Timothy Tackett, *Religion, Revolution, and Regional Culture in Eighteenth-Century France: The Ecclesiastical Oath of 1791* (Princeton, NJ: Princeton University Press, 1986), 19–20. The loyalty oath backfired spectacularly.

NOTES TO PAGES 136–141

60. Emmanuel Macron, "La République en actes," speech at Les Mureaux, October 2, 2020, https://www.elysee.fr/emmanuel-macron/2020/10/02/la-republique-en-actes-discours-du-president-de-la-republique-sur-le-theme-de-la-lutte-contre-les-separatismes.
61. Étude d'Impact: Projet de loi confortant le respect des principes de la République, p. 9.
62. Assemblée Nationale, "Projet de loi confortant le respect des principes de la République," December 9, 2020. https://www.assemblee-nationale.fr/dyn/15/textes/l15b3649_projet-loi.
63. "Décret n° 2021-1947 approuvant le contrat d'engagement républicain," December 31, 2021, https://www.legifrance.gouv.fr/jorf/id/JORFTEXT000044806609.
64. Despite the numerous parallels between anti-Semitism and Islamophobia, Samuel Everett explains the disjunct between these two concepts in the context of French institutions, in which anti-Semitism is regularly linked with racism but Islamophobia is ignored entirely. Samuel Sami Everett, "Interfaith Dialogue and Faith-Based Social Activism in a State of Emergency: Laïcité and the Crisis of Religion in France," *International Journal of Politics, Culture, and Society* 31 (2018): 437–54.
65. On religious hors contrat schools, including Muslim schools, see Carol Ferrara, "Breaking the Republican Mold: French Independent Schools and Agonistic Pluralism amidst Franco-Conformity," *French Cultural Studies* 35, no. 2 (2024): 129–47.
66. Radio France, September 8, 2020, https://www.radiofrance.fr/franceinter/certificats-de-virginite-une-pratique-peu-frequente-qui-divise-les-medecins-2731753.
67. Ismahane Chouder, Malika Latrèche, and Pierre Tevanian, *Les filles voilées parlent* (Paris: La Fabrique, 2008).
68. Lila Abu-Lughod, *Do Muslim Women Need Saving?* (Cambridge, MA: Harvard University Press, 2015), 25.
69. Kirsten Wesselhoeft, "Gendered Secularity: The Feminine Individual in the 2010 Gerin Report," *Journal of Muslim Minority Affairs* 31, no. 3 (2011): 399–411.
70. Ministry of the Interior, press release, October 14, 2022, https://www.interieur.gouv.fr/actualites/communiques/deux-ans-apres-lassassinat-de-samuel-paty-ministere-de-linterieur-poursuit. This case is discussed further in chapter 5.
71. Open letters include one from the Coalition for the Freedom of Association dated June 14, 2021, https://www.lacoalition.fr/IMG/pdf/courrier_des_associations_pour_saisine_du_cc_sur_pjl_principes_republicains_et_separatisme.pdf; others dated May 11, 2021, https://syndicat-asso.fr/wp-content/uploads/2021/05/lettre-ouverte-s%C3%A9paratisme.pdf, and May 12, 2021, https://snjcgt.fr/2021/05/12/9665/; and one on a European scale dated June 3, 2021, https://www.ldh-france.org/le-projet-de-loi-francaise-sur-le-separatisme-suscite-des-inquietudes-pour-les-droits-et-les-libertes-civiles-la-commission-europeenne-doit-interpeller-la-france/.
72. Open letter dated June 14, 2021, https://www.lacoalition.fr/IMG/pdf/courrier_des_associations_pour_saisine_du_cc_sur_pjl_principes_republicains_et_separatisme.pdf.
73. Open letter dated May 12, 2021, https://snjcgt.fr/2021/05/12/9665/.
74. *Mediapart*, September 20, 2022, https://www.mediapart.fr/journal/france/200922/contre-des-ateliers-de-desobeissance-civile-le-prefet-de-la-vienne-degaine-la-loi-separatisme.

75. SaphirNews, January 11, 2021, https://www.saphirnews.com/Separatisme-le-culte-musulman-auditionne-a-l-Assemblee-nationale-exprime-ses-inquietudes-et-voeux_a27741.html; SaphirNews, January 9, 2021 https://www.saphirnews.com/Separatisme-les-cultes-entre-malaise-et-inquietude-ce-qu-il-faut-retenir-des-auditions-a-l-Assemblee-nationale_a27739.html.
76. Open letter dated March 10, 2021, https://eglise.catholique.fr/sengager-dans-la-societe/laicite/513979-les-chretiens-inquiets-du-projet-de-loi-separatisme/.
77. *Le Figaro*, July 21, 2022, https://www.lefigaro.fr/actualite-france/les-trois-religions-chretiennes-unies-face-a-la-loi-separatisme-20220721.
78. Open letter dated March 10, 2021, https://eglise.catholique.fr/sengager-dans-la-societe/laicite/513979-les-chretiens-inquiets-du-projet-de-loi-separatisme/.
79. Open letter dated March 10, 2021, https://eglise.catholique.fr/sengager-dans-la-societe/laicite/513979-les-chretiens-inquiets-du-projet-de-loi-separatisme/.
80. Open letter dated March 19, 2021, https://www.saphirnews.com/Loi-separatisme-pretres-et-imams-de-Marseille-expriment-ensemble-leur-malaise_a27913.html.
81. "Etude d'Impact: Projet de loi confortant le respect des principes de la République," p. 8.

CHAPTER 5

1. On "narrative secularism," see Valérie Amiraux and David Koussens, "From Law to Narratives: Unveiling Contemporary French Secularism," RECODE Working Paper Series no. 19 (2013): 1–14.
2. As in English, "*immatériel*" in French has two senses, meaning both "abstract" and "not pertaining." "Immaterial public order" refers to the first sense of this term.
3. Jean Baubérot, *Les sept laïcités françaises* (Paris: Éditions de la maison des sciences de l'homme, 2015); Jean Baubérot, *La laïcité falsifiée* (Paris: La Découverte, 2012); David Koussens, *L'épreuve de la neutralité: La laïcité française entre droits et discours* (Brussels: Bruylant, 2015).
4. Hennette-Vauchez and Valentin, *L'affaire Baby Loup ou la Nouvelle Laïcité*; Hanane Karimi, "De l'application à l'extension de la nouvelle laïcité: Le cas des mères accompagnatrices," *Mouvements* 107, no. 3 (2021): 104–12.
5. Vincent Valentin, "L'effacement de la laïcité libérale en France," *Canadian Journal of Law and Society* 36, no. 2 (2021): 303–21.
6. The language of "public order" appears in the law of 1905 as well, as I discuss in more detail below.
7. Vincent Valentin, "Les nouvelles configurations de l'ordre public," *Philosophiques* 46, no. 1 (2019): 121; my emphasis.
8. Valentin, "L'effacement de la laïcité libérale en France," 308.
9. The notion of *vivre ensemble* was taken up by the European Court of Human Rights, as I discuss below.
10. Valentin, "L'effacement de la laïcité libérale en France," 317–18.

11. John Bowen, "How the French State Justifies Controlling Muslim Bodies: From Harm-Based to Values-Based Reasoning," *Social Research* 78, no. 2 (2011): 325–48.
12. Valentin, "L'effacement de la laïcité libérale en France."
13. Sylvain Mouillard and Bernadette Sauvaget, "Au Collectif contre l'islamophobie, de la suite dans les données," *Libération*, April 3, 2016.
14. CCIF, "Rapport CCIF 2018," 5.
15. CCIF, "Rapport CCIF 2018," 17. Macron expressed his "vigilance" toward the "radicalization of secularism" at a meeting with representatives of six major religions practiced in France, including Islam. "Macron 'vigilant' face au risque de 'radicalisation de la laïcité,'" *Le Point*, December 21, 2017.
16. CCIF, "Rapport CCIF 2019," 18.
17. Amélie Barras, *Refashioning Secularisms in France and Turkey: The Case of the Headscarf Ban* (New York: Routledge, 2014), 69.
18. Margot Dazey, "'On est devenus des experts de la laïcité': Le légitimisme républicain inaudible de représentants musulmans," *Cultures et Conflits*, no. 127/128 (2022): 19–38.
19. Alexandra Kassir and Jeffrey Reitz, "Protesting Headscarf Ban: A Path to Becoming More French?," *Ethnic and Racial Studies* 39, no. 15 (2016): 2683–700.
20. Kassir and Reitz, "Protesting Headscarf Ban," 2688.
21. Carol Ferrara, *Muslim and Catholic Experiences of National Belonging in France: Rethinking Boundaries, Inequities, and Faith in the Republic* (New York: Bloomsbury Academic, 2024), chapter 5. Ferrara shows how some Muslim educators argue that secularism is precisely what protects their schools, allowing them to receive state subsidies in the same vein as Catholic schools, which are much more culturally entrenched in France.
22. Jean Baubérot, *Histoire de la laïcité en France* (Paris: Presses Universitaires de France, 2000), 83.
23. "Loi du 9 décembre 1905 concernant la séparation des Eglises et de l' Etat," article 4. Baubérot notes that interestingly, the inspiration for article 4 came from the study of the US and Scottish contexts—"the transfer of an element of Anglo-saxon political culture that nuanced the Republican model." Baubérot, *Histoire de la laïcité en France*, 76–77.
24. Baubérot uses article 4 as the point of distinction between two historical models of laïcité, both present in the 1905 law. The first, represented by Ferdinand Buisson and the opposition to article 4, articulated an individualist view of separation, while the second, represented by Briand, joined by Jaurès, articulated a more supple view of separation that made room for religious collectivity and even authority. Baubérot, *Les sept laïcités françaises*, 65–69.
25. Baubérot, *Les sept laïcités françaises*.
26. Joan Wallach Scott, *Sex and Secularism*, 31.
27. Scott, *Sex and Secularism*, chapter 2.
28. Scott, *Sex and Secularism*, 109.
29. Karen Offen, *Debating the Woman Question in the French Third Republic, 1870–1920* (Cambridge: Cambridge University Press, 2018); Blanca Rodríguez-Ruiz and Ruth Rubio Marin, *The Struggle for Female Suffrage in Europe: Voting to Become Citizens* (Boston: Brill, 2012), 313.

30. Mohamad Amer Meziane, *Des empires sous la terre: Histoire écologique et raciale de la sécularisation* (Paris: La Découverte, 2021).
31. Abd al-Rahman Al-Jabarti, *Napoleon in Egypt: Al-Jabarti's Chronicle of the French Occupation, 1798*, trans. Shmuel Moreh (Princeton, NJ: Markus Weiner, 1993).
32. Gérald Darmanin, "Discours à FORIF," February 5, 2022, https://www.interieur.gouv.fr/actualites/communiques/forum-de-lislam-de-france-etape-nouvelle-dans-dialogue-entre-pouvoirs.
33. "Secular colonialism becomes here the instrument of the realization of the reign of Christ on Earth. The Empire of Christ is realized on Earth no longer in the form of an empire of Faith, but as an empire of civilization and of industry." Meziane, *Des empires sous la terre*, 92.
34. Baubérot, *Histoire de la laïcité en France*, 54.
35. Meziane, *Des empires sous la terre*, 93. On *catho-laïcité*, see Oliphant, *The Privilege of Being Banal*, 12–18.
36. Meziane, *Des empires sous la terre*, 102. Meziane continues: "The fact that the law of 1905 was not fully applied in the French colonies does not signify a sort of betrayal of secularism, but the maintenance of the Napoleonic system of religions for reasons of public security and the defense of the State. The law of separation of 1905 did not abolish the state regulation of religion. Laïcité did not consist in separating religion from politics but in 'liberalizing' an already-secularized administration of religions as '*cultes*.'" Meziane, *Des empires sous la terre*, 103.
37. Jean Baubérot, *La laïcité falsifiée* (Paris: La Découverte, 2012).
38. "Macron 'vigilant' face au risque de 'radicalisation de la laïcité,'" *Le Point*, December 21, 2017, https://www.lepoint.fr/politique/attendu-sur-la-laicite-macron-commence-par-rencontrer-les-cultes-21-12-2017-2181659_20.php.
39. Baubérot, *Les sept laïcités françaises*.
40. On neutrality and its expansion from state actors to private citizens, see Stéphanie Hennette-Vauchez, "Séparation, garantie, neutralité . . . Les multiples grammaires de la laïcité," *Les Nouveaux Cahiers du Conseil constitutionnel* 4, no. 53 (2016): 9–19; David Koussens, *L'épreuve de la neutralité*; Fatima Khemilat, "Excluding Veiled Women from French Public Space: The Emergence of a 'Respectable' Segregation?," *Journal of Gender Studies* 30, no. 2 (2021), 214–26.
41. "Charte de la laïcité dans les services publics," 2021. https://www.gouvernement.fr/sites/default/files/contenu/piece-jointe/2022/12/charte_de_la_laicite-.pdf.
42. Hennette-Vauchez and Valentin, *L'affaire Baby Loup ou la Nouvelle Laïcité*, 22.
43. Hennette-Vauchez and Valentin, *L'affaire Baby Loup ou la Nouvelle Laïcité*, 12.
44. Hennette-Vauchez and Valentin, *L'affaire Baby Loup ou la Nouvelle Laïcité*, 21.
45. Hennette-Vauchez and Valentin, *L'affaire Baby Loup ou la Nouvelle Laïcité*, 24.
46. Myriam Hunter-Henin, "Religion, Children, and Employment: The *Baby Loup* Case," *International and Comparative Law Quarterly* 64 (July 2015): 717–31.
47. Hunter-Henin, "Religion, Children, and Employment," 721–24.
48. Eoin Daly, "Laïcité in the Private Sphere? French Religious Liberty after the Baby Loup Affair," *Oxford Journal of Law and Religion* 5, no. 2 (2016): 211–29.
49. Indeed, the Grenoble pool policy came in response to a diverse movement of women,

led by Muslim women and organized by the Alliance Citoyenne de Grenoble, which for years had been demanding the right to swim in the attire of their choice.
50. For example, Myriam Hunter-Henin conceptualizes *vivre ensemble* as a "democratic" framework "based on reciprocity." Hunter-Henin, *Why Religious Freedom Matters for Democracy: Comparative Reflections from Britain and France for a Democratic Vivre Ensemble* (New York: Hart, 2020), 14.
51. Valentin, "L'effacement de la laïcité libérale en France," 316.
52. Some authors have argued that the ECHR took vivre ensemble out of the register of immaterial public order, and identified it as a subjective right of all citizens. Valentin Gazagne-Jammes, "Le vivre ensemble: Exigence supérieure ou droit subjectif?," *Révue des Droits et Libertés Fondamenteaux*, no. 30 (2019): 1–8. However, I follow Fredette and others in understanding *vivre ensemble* as a subtype of immaterial public order, which was fundamentally at stake in the *S.A.S. v. France* case.
53. On this law and the political debates leading up to it, see many of the contributions to Eva Brems, ed., *The Experiences of Face Veil Wearers in Europe and the Law* (Cambridge: Cambridge University Press, 2014); Jennifer Fredette, "Becoming a Threat: The Burqa and the Contestation over Public Morality Law in France," *Law and Social Inquiry* 40, no. 3 (2015): 585–610; Kirsten Wesselhoeft, "Gendered Secularity: The Feminine Individual in the 2010 Gerin Report," *Journal of Muslim Minority Affairs* 31, no. 3 (2011): 399–411.
54. Loi 2010-1192 du 11 octobre 2010 interdisant la dissimulation du visage dans l'espace public.
55. For a detailed overview of the complex legislative process of the ban on face coverings, see Fredette, "Becoming a Threat," 587–89.
56. Valentin, "L'effacement de la laïcité libérale en France," 316.
57. Christophe Bouriau, André Moine, and Marie Rota, eds., *Le vivre ensemble saisi par le droit* (Paris: A. Pedone, 2021).
58. S.A.S. are the initials of the plaintiff in this case.
59. Quoted in Hakeem Yusuf, "S.A.S. v. France: Supporting 'Living Together' or Forced Assimilation?," *International Human Rights Law Review* 3 (2014): 285.
60. Yusuf, "S.A.S. v. France," 282.
61. Megan Pearson, "What Happened to 'Vivre Ensemble'? Developments after SAS v. France," *Oxford Journal of Law and Religion* 10, no. 2 (2021): 185–205.
62. This was underscored by memes that circulated early in the COVID-19 pandemic, juxtaposing the fine for covering one's face with a niqab with the fine for appearing in public with one's face uncovered by a mask.
63. Judith Surkis, "Hymenal Politics: Marriage, Secularism, and French Sovereignty," *Public Culture* 22, no. 3 (2010): 531–56.
64. Gerald Darmanin, Twitter, July 28, 2022, https://twitter.com/GDarmanin/status/1552604961133023234.
65. In another recent case, Mmadi Ahamada, imam of the mosque of Saint-Chamond, was denied the renewal of his residency permit and deported to the Comoros with his wife and three young children, on the basis of his words in an Eid sermon, which were judged "discriminatory and contrary to male-female equality" and a "danger to public order."

Le Progrès, March 30, 2022, https://www.leprogres.fr/societe/2022/03/30/l-imam-de-saint-chamond-assigne-a-residence-jusqu-a-son-expulsion.

66. Frank Peter, "Islamic Sermons, Religious Authority, and the Individualization of Islam in France," in *Religiosität in der säkularisierten Welt*, ed. Manual Franzmann, Christel Gärtner, and Nicole Köck (Wiesbaden: VS Verlag für Sozialwissenschaften, 2006), 303–19; Shireen Hunter, *Reformist Voices of Islam* (New York: Routledge, 2009).

67. "Loi du 9 décembre 1905 concernant la séparation des Eglises et de l'Etat."

68. "Loi du 9 décembre 1905 concernant la séparation des Eglises et de l'Etat."

69. Valentin, "Les nouvelles configurations de l'ordre public."

70. Judith Surkis, *Sex, Law, and Sovereignty in French Algeria, 1803–1930* (Ithaca, NY: Cornell University Press, 2019).

71. Mona Oraby, "Law, the State, and Public Order: Regulating Religion in Contemporary Egypt," *Law & Society Review* 52, no. 3 (2018): 574–602.

72. Oraby, "Law, the State, and Public Order." On public order in Egypt, see also Hussein Agrama, *Questioning Secularism: Islam, Sovereignty, and the Rule of Law in Modern Egypt* (Chicago: University of Chicago Press, 2012).

73. Marie-Odile Peyroux-Sissoko, "Immaterial Public Order: Legal Response to Social Crisis?," *Hungarian Journal of Legal Studies* 58, no. 2 (2017): 224–32. Nadia Fadil makes a parallel argument about the function of the face veil ban in Belgium, showing how it served to unify state sovereignty at a moment of political weakness. Fadil, "Asserting State Sovereignty: The Face Veil Ban in Belgium," in Brems, *The Experiences of Face Veil Wearers in Europe and the Law*, 251–62.

74. For a comparison of Muslim and traditional Catholic spheres in contemporary France, see Ferrara, *Muslim and Catholic Experiences of National Belonging*.

75. Chantal Jouanno, "Rapport d'information sur la laïcité et l'égalité femmes-hommes," November 3, 2016, p. 49, https://www.senat.fr/rap/r16-101/r16-1011.pdf.

76. Jouanno, "Rapport d'information sur la laïcité et l'égalité femmes-hommes," 91.

77. Ministry of Education and Ministry of the Interior, press release, March 10, 2022. https://www.interieur.gouv.fr/actualites/communiques/mise-en-place-dune-cellule-de-lutte-contre-lislamisme-radical-et-repli.

78. Mohamad Amer Meziane, "On Police Violence and Systemic Islamophobia," *Political Theology* 22, no. 2 (2021): 125–29.

79. Fernando, *The Republic Unsettled*; see also Frank Peter, *Islam and the Governing of Muslims in France: Secularism without Religion* (London: Bloomsbury Academic, 2021).

80. Ragazzi, "Counter-Radicalisation, Islam, and Laïcité"; Meziane, "On Police Violence and Systemic Islamophobia."

CONCLUSION

1. Urbania_fr, Instagram, May 23, 2023. https://www.instagram.com/reel/Csjg9XPAaUl/?igshid=NjZiM2M3MzIxNA%3D%3D.

2. Marwan Muhammad, Facebook, February 27, 2023.
3. Marwan Muhammad, Facebook, March 3, 2023; my emphasis.
4. In chapter 1, Yassine differentiated between "engaged Muslims"—activists like himself—and *les musulmans lambda*, or "average Muslims," who were less invested in community activities. Here, Marwan Muhammad uses the same term to emphasize that the political machinations around Islam in France are not only targeting activists like those at the CCIF, but are shaping the conditions of collective life even for "average Muslims" who are not on the front lines of civil rights battles or agitating to transform their communities.
5. Amira Mittermaier, *Giving to God: Islamic Charity in Revolutionary Times* (Berkeley: University of California Press, 2019), 8.

BIBLIOGRAPHY

Abdul Khabeer, Su'ad. "Hip Hop Matters: Race, Space, and Islam in Chicago." *City and Society* 30, no. 2 (2018): 141–64.
Abu-Lughod, Lila. *Do Muslim Women Need Saving?* Cambridge, MA: Harvard University Press, 2015.
Adraoui, Mohamed-Ali. *Salafism Goes Global: From the Gulf to the French Banlieues*. New York: Oxford University Press, 2020.
Agrama, Hussein. *Questioning Secularism: Islam, Sovereignty, and the Rule of Law in Modern Egypt*. Chicago: University of Chicago Press, 2012.
Ahmad, Irfan. *Religion as Critique: Islamic Critical Thinking from Mecca to the Marketplace*. Chapel Hill: University of North Carolina Press, 2017.
Al-ʿAlwani, Taha al-Jabir. *The Ethics of Disagreement in Islam*. Translated by AbdulWahid Hamid. Herndon, VA: International Institute of Islamic Thought, 2011.
Al-Jabarti, Abd al-Rahman. *Napoleon in Egypt: Al-Jabarti's Chronicle of the French Occupation, 1798*. Translated by Shmuel Moreh. Princeton, NJ: Markus Weiner, 1993.
Allouch, Annabelle. *Les nouvelles portes des grandes écoles*. Paris: Presses Universitaires de France, 2022.
Amghar, Samir. "Le salafisme en France: De la révolution islamique à la révolution conservatrice." *Critique internationale* 40, no. 3 (2008): 95–113.
Amiraux, Valérie, and David Koussens. "From Law to Narratives: Unveiling Contemporary French Secularism." RECODE Working Paper Series, no. 19 (2013): 1–14.
Arnaut, Karel, Jean-Michel Lafleur, Nadia Fadil, Jérémy Mandin, and Jaafar Alloul. "Leaving Europe: New Crises, Entrenched Inequalities and Alternative Routes of Social Mobility." *Journal of Immigrant and Refugee Studies* 18, no. 3 (2020): 261–69.
Asad, Talal. *Genealogies of Religion: Discipline and Reasons of Power in Christianity and Islam*. Baltimore, MD: Johns Hopkins University Press, 1993.
Asad, Talal, Wendy Brown, Judith Butler, and Saba Mahmood. *Is Critique Secular? Blasphemy, Injury, and Free Speech*. Stanford, CA: Townsend Papers in the Humanities, 2009.
Assemblée Nationale. "Étude d'Impact, Projet de loi confortant le respect des principes de la République," December 8, 2020. https://www.assemblee-nationale.fr/dyn/15/textes/l15b3649_etude-impact.pdf.

———. "Projet de loi confortant le respect des principes de la République," December 9, 2020. https://www.assemblee-nationale.fr/dyn/15/textes/l15b3649_projet-loi.

Attar, Farid ud-Din. *Conference of the Birds*. Translated by Dick Davis. New York: Penguin, 1984.

Aydin, Cemil. *The Idea of the Muslim World: A Global Intellectual History*. Cambridge, MA: Harvard University Press, 2017.

Aziz, Sahar. *The Racial Muslim: When Racism Quashes Religious Freedom*. Berkeley: University of California Press, 2021.

Babès, Leila. *L'Islam positif: La religion des jeunes musulmans de France*. Paris: Éditions de l'Atelier, 1997.

Barras, Amélie. *Refashioning Secularisms in France and Turkey: The Case of the Headscarf Ban*. New York: Routledge, 2014.

Baubérot, Jean. *Histoire de la laïcité en France*. Paris: Presses Universitaires de France, 2000.

———. *La laïcité falsifiée*. Paris: La Découverte, 2012.

———. *Les sept laïcités françaises*. Paris: Éditions de la maison des sciences de l'homme, 2015.

Beaman, Jean. *Citizen Outsider: Children of North African Immigrants in France*. Berkeley: University of California Press, 2017.

———. "France's Ahmeds and Muslim Others: The Entanglement of Racism and Islamophobia." *French Cultural Studies* 32, no. 3 (2021): 269–79.

Beauchemin, Cris, Christelle Hamel, and Patrick Simon. *Trajétoires et origines: Enquête sur la diversité des populations en France*. Paris: Ined éditions, 2015.

Bechrouri, Ibrahim. "From 'Red and Green Decay' to 'Islamo-leftism': The Counterinsurgency Fantasies of the French Elite." *Contemporary French and Francophone Studies* 27, no. 2 (2023): 240–51.

———. "'L'esprit de défense': Separatism, Counterinsurgency, and the Dissolution of the Collective against Islamophobia in France." *Modern and Contemporary France* 31, no. 2 (2023): 199–218.

Ben Jelloun, Tahar. *Hospitalité française*. Paris: Seuil, 1984.

Benaissa, Hichem. "Islam et capitalisme: Les entrepreneurs musulmans en France," *Entreprises et Histoire*, no. 81 (2015): 111–25.

———. "Depuis quand l'islam est un problème en France?" Interview by Jalal Kahliouli. *Bondy Blog*. February 18, 2021.

Bidar, Abdennour. *Plaidoyer pour la fraternité*. Paris: Albin Michel, 2015.

Bonneau, Cécile, Pauline Charousset, Julien Grenet, Georgia Thebault. "Grandes écoles: Des politiques 'd'ouverture sociale' en echec," *Éducation et formations* (2022): 156–74.

Bouamama, Saïd. "Communautarisme: 'Un spectre hante la France.'" In *Racismes de France*, ed. Omar Slaouti and Olivier Le Cour Grandmaison, 251–62. Paris: La Découverte, 2020.

Boubeker, Ahmed. "Les mondes de l'immigration des héritiers." *Multitudes* 49, no. 2 (2012): 100–110.

Boubekeur, Amel. "Post-Islamist Culture: A New Form of Mobilization?" *History of Religions* 47, no. 1 (2007): 75–94.

Boudhiba, Abdelwahab. "Le Message de l'islam." *Diogène* 205, no. 1 (2004): 128–35.
Bourdieu, Pierre, and Jean-Claude Passeron. *The Inheritors: French Students and Their Relation to Culture*. Translated by Richard Nice. Chicago: University of Chicago Press, 1979.
Bouriau, Christophe, André Moine, and Marie Rota, eds. *Le vivre ensemble saisi par le droit*. Paris: A. Pedone, 2021.
Bouteldja, Houria, and Sadri Khiari, eds. *Nous sommes les indigènes de la République*. Paris: Éditions Amsterdam, 2012.
Bowen, John. *Why the French Don't Like Headscarves: Islam, the State, and Public Space*. Princeton, NJ: Princeton University Press, 2006.
———. *Can Islam Be French? Pluralism and Pragmatism in a Secularist State*. Princeton, NJ: Princeton University Press, 2009.
———. "How the French State Justifies Controlling Muslim Bodies: From Harm-Based to Values-Based Reasoning." *Social Research* 78, no. 2 (2011): 325–48.
Brems, Eva, ed. *Experiences of Face Veil Wearers in Europe and the Law*. Cambridge: Cambridge University Press, 2014.
Brinbaum, Yaël, and Jean-Luc Primon. "Parcours scolaires et sentiment d'injustice et de discrimination chez les descendants d'immigrés." *Économie et Statistique* 464, no. 1 (2013): 215–43.
Brouard, Sylvain, and Vincent Tiberj. *As French as Everyone Else? A Survey of French Citizens of Maghrebin, African, and Turkish Origin*. Philadelphia, PA: Temple University Press, 2011.
Brunie, Juliette. "Affaire Baby Loup, l'admission du principe de neutralité dans les entreprises privées 'ordinaires.'" *Revue juridique de l'Ouest* (2015): 75–84.
Cadieu, Morgane. *On Both Sides of the Tracks: Social Mobility in Contemporary French Literature*. Chicago: University of Chicago Press, 2024.
Camus, Renaud. *Le Grand Remplacement*. Plieux: Chez l'auteur, 2010.
Cesaire, Aimé. *Discourse on Colonialism*. Translated by Joan Pinkham. New York: Monthly Review Press, 2000 [1950].
Chan-Malik, Sylvia. *Being Muslim: A Cultural History of Women of Color in American Islam*. New York: New York University Press, 2018.
Chouder, Ismahane, Malika Latrèche, and Pierre Tevanian. *Les filles voilées parlent*. Paris: La Fabrique, 2008.
Cohen, Mathilde, and Sarah Mazouz. "A White Republic? Whites and Whiteness in France." *French Politics, Culture, and Society* 39, no. 2 (2021): 1–25.
Daly, Eoin. "Laïcité in the Private Sphere? French Religious Liberty after the Baby Loup Affair." *Oxford Journal of Law and Religion* 5 no. 2 (2016): 211–29.
Darmanin, Gérald. "Discours à FORIF," February 5, 2022. https://www.vie-publique.fr /discours/283686-gerald-darmanin-05022022-culte-musulman.
Davidson, Naomi. *Only Muslim: Embodying Islam in Twentieth-Century France*. Ithaca, NY: Cornell University Press, 2012.
Davis, Muriam Haleh. "Racial Capitalism and the Campaign Against 'Islamo-gauchisme' in France." *Jadaliyya*, August 14, 2018. https://www.jadaliyya.com/Details/37858.

———. *Markets of Civilization: Islam and Racial Capitalism in Algeria*. Durham, NC: Duke University Press, 2022.

Dazey, Margot. "'On est devenus des experts de la laïcité': Le légitimisme républicain inaudible de représentants musulmans," *Cultures et Conflits*, no. 127/128 (2022): 19–38.

———. "Polite Responses to Stigmatization: Ethics of Exemplarity among French Muslim Elites." *Ethnic and Racial Studies* 46, no. 4 (2023): 686–706.

Deeb, Lara. *An Enchanted Modern: Gender and Public Piety in Shi'i Lebanon*. Princeton, NJ: Princeton University Press, 2004.

———. "Thinking Piety and the Everyday Together: A Response to Fadil and Fernando." *Hau: Journal of Ethnographic Theory* 5, no. 2 (2015): 93–96.

Deeb, Lara, and Mona Harb. *Leisurely Islam: Negotiating Geography and Morality in Shi'ite South Beirut*. Princeton, NJ: Princeton University Press, 2013.

Delaume, Chloé, ed. *Sororité*. Paris: Points, 2012.

Della Porta, Donatella, Pietro Castelli Gattinara, Konstantinos Eleftheriadis, and Andrea Felicetti. *Discursive Turns and Critical Junctures: Debating Citizenship after the Charlie Hebdo Attacks*. Oxford: Oxford University Press, 2020.

Delphy, Christine. *Un universalisme si particulier: Féminisme et exception française (1980–2010)*. Paris: Syllepse, 2010.

———. "La Non-Mixité: Une nécessité politique." *Les Mots Sont Importants* (blog). 2014. http://lmsi.net/La-non-mixite-une-necessite.

Dhume, Fabrice. "L'émergence d'une figure obsessionnelle: Comment le 'communautarisme' a envahi les discours médiatico-politiques français," *Revue Asylon(s)* 8 (2010). http://reseau-terra.eu/article945.html.

Dhume, Fabrice, Xavier Dunezat, Camille Gourdeau, and Aude Rabaud. *Du racisme d'État en France?* Paris: Bord de l'Eau, 2020.

Dikeç, Mustafa. *Badlands of the Republic: Space, Politics, and Urban Policy*. Malden, MA: Blackwell, 2007.

Domenach, Jean-Marie. *Regarder la France: Essai sur le malaise français*. Paris: FeniXX, 1997.

Duthu, Françoise. *Le maire et la mosquée: Islam et laïcité en Île-de-France*. Paris: Harmattan, 2009.

Éditions du Grand Remplacement. 2016. *Téléramadan*. Issue 1. Paris.

Eickelman, Dale, and James Piscatori. *Muslim Politics*. Princeton, NJ: Princeton University Press, 2004 [1996].

Eid, Ahmed. *Unmosqued: The Movie*. Eid Films, 2014.

El-Tayeb, Fatima. *European Others: Queering Ethnicity in Postnational Europe*. Minneapolis: University of Minnesota Press.

Elewa, Ahmed, and Laury Silvers. "'I *Am* One of the People': A Survey and Analysis of Legal Arguments on Women-Led Prayer in Islam." *Journal of Law and Religion* 26, no. 1 (2016): 141–71.

Ennasri, Nabil. *Les 7 défis capitaux: Essai à destination de la communauté musulmane*. Self-published, 2014.

Enright, Theresa. *The Making of Grand Paris: Metropolitan Urbanism in the Twenty-First Century*. Cambridge, MA: MIT Press, 2016.

Escafré-Dublet, Angéline, Virginie Guiraudon, and Julien Talpin. "Fighting Discrimination in a Hostile Political Environment: The Case of 'Colour-Blind' France." *Ethnic and Racial Studies* 46, no. 4 (2023): 667–85.

Esteves, Olivier. "France, You Love It but Leave It: The Silent Flight of French Muslims." *Modern and Contemporary France* 31, no. 2 (2023): 243–57.

Everett, Samuel Sami. "Interfaith Dialogue and Faith-Based Social Activism in a State of Emergency: *Laïcité* and the Crisis of Religion in France." *International Journal of Politics, Culture, and Society* 31 (2018): 437–54.

Fadil, Nadia. "Performing the Salat [Islamic Prayers] at Work: Secular and Pious Muslims Negotiating the Contours of the Public in Belgium." *Ethnicities* 13, no. 6 (2013): 729–50.

———. "Recalling the 'Islam of the Parents': Liberal and Secular Muslims Redefining the Contours of Religious Authenticity." *Identities* 24, no. 1 (2017): 82–99.

———. "Asserting State Sovereignty: The Face Veil Ban in Belgium." In *The Experiences of Face Veil Wearers in Europe and the Law*, ed. Eva Brems, 251–62. Cambridge: Cambridge University Press, 2014.

Fassin, Éric. "La démocratie sexuelle et le conflit des civilisations." *Multitudes* 26, no. 3 (2006): 123–31.

Fernando, Mayanthi. *The Republic Unsettled: Muslim French and the Contradictions of Secularism*. Durham, NC: Duke University Press, 2014.

———. "State Sovereignty and the Politics of Indifference." *Public Culture* 31, no. 2 (2019): 261–73.

Ferrara, Carol. "Breaking the Republican Mold: French Independent Schools and Agonistic Pluralism amidst Franco-Conformity." *French Cultural Studies* 35, no. 2 (2024): 129–47.

———. *Muslim and Catholic Experiences of National Belonging in France: Rethinking Boundaries, Inequities, and Faith in the Republic*. New York: Bloomsbury Academic, 2024.

Fredette, Jennifer. "Becoming a Threat: The *Burqa* and the Contestation over Public Morality Law in France." *Law and Social Inquiry* 40, no. 3 (2015): 585–610.

———. "Social Movements and the State's Construction of Identity: The Case of Muslims in France." *Studies in Law, Politics and Society* 54 (2011): 45–76.

Fregosi, Franck. "De quoi le gouvernement de l'islam en France est-il le nom?" *Confluences Méditerannée* 106, no. 3 (2018): 35–51.

Galonnier, Juliette. "Discrimination religieuse ou discrimination raciale?" *Hommes & migrations* 1324 (2019): 29–37.

Gauchet, Marcel. *Comprendre le malheur français*. Paris: Stock, 2016.

Gazagne-Jammes, Valentin. "Le vivre ensemble: Exigence supérieure ou droit subjectif?" *Révue des droits et libertés fondamenteaux*, no. 30 (2019): 1–8.

Grewal, Zareena. *Islam Is a Foreign Country: American Muslims and the Global Crisis of Authority*. New York: New York University Press, 2014.

———. "Destabilizing Orthodoxy, De-territorializing the Anthropology of Islam." *Journal of the American Academy of Religion* 84, no. 1 (2016): 44–59.

Godin, Christian. *Dictionnaire de philosophie*. Paris: Fayard, 2004.

Guénif-Souilamas, Nacira. "The Other French Exception: Virtuous Racism and the War of the Sexes in Postcolonial France." *French Politics, Culture, and Society* 24, no. 3 (2006), 23–41.

Guénif-Souilamas, Nacira, and Éric Macé. *Les féministes et le garçon arabe*. Paris: Éditions de l'Aube, 2004.

Hajjat, Abdellali. *The Wretched of France: The 1983 March for Equality and against Racism*. Translated by Andrew Brown. Bloomington: Indiana University Press, 2022.

Hajjat, Abdellali, and Marwan Muhammad. *Islamophobie: Comment les élites françaises fabriquent le "problème musulman."* Paris: La Découverte, 2013.

Hammer, Juliane. *More than a Prayer: American Muslim Women, Religious Authority, and Activism*. Austin: University of Texas Press, 2012.

Harchi, Kaoutar. *Comme nous existons*. Paris: Actes Sud, 2021.

———. "Le concept de transfuge est un concept blanc." Interview by Joseph Andras. *Frustration*, February 28, 2023. https://www.frustrationmagazine.fr/entretien-harchi-andras-i/.

Harrison, Olivia C. *Natives against Nativism: Antiracism and Indigenous Critique in Postcolonial France*. Minneapolis: University of Minnesota Press, 2023.

Hazan, Éric. *Paris sous tension*. Paris: La Fabrique, 2011.

Hefner, Robert, ed. *Shari'a Law and Modern Muslim Ethics*. Bloomington: Indiana University Press, 2016.

Hennette-Vauchez, Stéphanie. "Séparation, garantie, neutralité . . . Les multiples grammaires de la laïcité," *Les Nouveaux Cahiers du Conseil constitutionnel* 4 no. 53 (2016): 9–19.

———. "The State of Emergency in France: Days without End?" *European Constitutional Law Review* 14, no. 4 (2018): 700–720.

Hennette-Vauchez, Stéphanie, and Vincent Valentin. *L'affaire Baby Loup ou la nouvelle laïcité*. Paris: Lextenso, 2014.

Houllebecq, Michel. *Soumission*. Paris: J'ai Lu, 2015.

Howe, Justine. *Suburban Islam*. New York: Oxford University Press, 2018.

Hunter, Shireen. *Reformist Voices of Islam*. New York: Routledge, 2009.

Hunter-Henin, Myriam. "Religion, Children, and Employment: The *Baby Loup* Case." *International and Comparative Law Quarterly* 64 (July 2015): 717–731.

———. *Why Religious Freedom Matters for Democracy: Comparative Reflections from Britain and France for a Democratic Vivre Ensemble*. New York: Hart, 2020.

Ibrahim, Ahmed Fekry. *Pragmatism in Islamic Law: A Social and Intellectual History*. Syracuse, NY: Syracuse University Press, 2015.

Ingram, Brannon. *Revival from Below: The Deoband Movement and Global Islam*. Berkeley: University of California Press, 2018.

Institut Français d'Opinion Publique. "Le Pessimisme des Français en Question." *IFOP Focus*, no. 101, January 2014.

Institut nationale de la statistique et des études économiques (INSEE). "Populations légales 2020." December 2022. https://www.insee.fr/fr/statistiques/6683037.

———. "Mobilité sociale." March 2020. https://www.insee.fr/fr/statistiques/4797592.

Jahangeer, Roshan A. "Good Islam, Bad Islam? France's Republican Principles, Anti-

Veiling, and the 'New Secularism.'" In *Islamophobia and/in Post-Secular States*, ed. Sharmin Sadequee. Edmonton: University of Alberta Press, forthcoming.

Jamal, Amina. *Jamaat-e-Islami Women in Pakistan: Vanguard of a New Modernity?* Syracuse, NY: Syracuse University Press, 2013.

Jouanneau, Solenne. "Régulariser ou non un imam étranger en France: Droit au séjour et définition du bon imam en pays laïque." *Politix* 86, no. 2 (2009): 147–66.

———. "L'imam, clerc sans clergé ni église: Les répertoires d'une autorité dissimulée dans les cadres de l'interaction." *Genèses* 88, no. 3 (2012): 6–24.

———. "Faire émerger un 'islam français': Paradoxes d'une action publique sous contrainte." *Sociologie* 8, no. 3 (2017): 247–64.

Jouanno, Chantal. "Rapport d'information sur la laïcité et l'égalité femmes-hommes." November 3, 2016.

Jouili, Jeanette. "Rapping the Republic: Utopia, Critique, and Muslim Role Models in Secular France." *French Politics, Culture, and Society* 31, no. 2 (2013): 58–80.

———. "Refining the Umma in the Shadow of the Republic: Performing Arts and New Islamic Audio-Visual Landscapes in France." *Anthropological Quarterly* 87, no. 4 (2014): 1079–1104.

———. *Pious Practice and Secular Constraints: Women in the Islamic Revival in Europe*. Stanford, CA: Stanford University Press, 2015.

Kahf, Mohja. *Hagar Poems*. Fayetteville: University of Arkansas Press, 2016.

Kamali, Mohammed. "The Scope of Diversity and 'Ikhtilaf' (Juristic Disagreement) in the Shari'ah." *Islamic Studies* 37, no. 3 (1998): 315–37.

Karimi, Hanane. "The Hijab and Work: Female Entrepreneurship in Response to Islamophobia." *International Journal of Politics, Culture, and Society* 31, no. 4 (2018): 421–35.

———. "De l'application à l'extension de la nouvelle laïcité: Le cas des mères accompagnatrices." *Mouvements* 107, no. 3 (2021): 104–12.

Kashani, Maryam. *Medina by the Bay: Scenes of Muslim Study and Survival*. Durham, NC: Duke University Press, 2023.

Kassir, Alexandra, and Jeffrey Reitz, "Protesting Headscarf Ban: A Path to Becoming More French?" *Ethnic and Racial Studies* 39, no. 15 (2016): 2683–700.

Keaton, Trica Danielle. *You Know You're Black in France When . . . : The Fact of Everyday Antiblackness*. Cambridge, MA: MIT Press, 2023.

Kepel, Gilles. *Les banlieues de l'Islam: Naissance d'une religion en France*. Paris: Éditions du Seuil, 1987.

———. *Quatre-vingt-treize*. Paris: Gallimard, 2012.

———. *Terreur dans l'Hexagone*. Paris: Gallimard, 2017.

Khemilat, Fatima. "Excluding Veiled Women from French Public Space: The Emergence of a 'Respectable' Segregation?" *Journal of Gender Studies* 30, no. 2 (2021), 214–26.

Khiari, Sadri. *La contre-révolution coloniale en France: De de Gaulle à Sarkozy*. Paris: La Fabrique, 2009.

Khoja-Moolji, Shenila. *Rebuilding Community: Displaced Women and the Making of a Shia Ismaili Muslim Sociality*. New York: Oxford University Press, 2023.

Khosrokhavar, Farhad. *L'Islam des jeunes*. Paris: Flammarion, 1997.

Kleinman, Julie. *Adventure Capital: Migration and the Making of an African Hub in Paris.* Berkeley: University of California Press, 2019.

Koussens, David. *L'épreuve de la neutralité: La laïcité française entre droits et discours.* Brussels: Bruylant, 2015.

Laurence, Jonathan, and Justin Vaisse. *Integrating Islam: Political and Religious Challenges in Contemporary France.* Washington, DC: Brookings Institution Press, 2006.

Lauzière, Henri. *The Making of Salafism: Islamic Reform in the Twentieth Century.* New York: Columbia University Press, 2015.

Le Bras, Hervé. *Se sentir mal dans un France qui va bien: La société paradoxale.* Paris: Éditions de l'Aube, 2009.

Les Femmes Dans la Mosquée, "Lettre ouverte au Recteur de la Mosquée de Paris," Oumma.com. November 28, 2013. https://oumma.com/lettre-ouverte-au-recteur-de-la-mosquee-de-paris/.

Lhomme, Fabrice, and Gérard Davet. *Un président ne devrait pas dire ça . . .* Paris: Stock, 2016.

Macron, Emmanuel. 2018. Interview with Jean-Jacques Bourdin and Edwy Plenel. http://www.bfmtv.com/mediaplayer/video/retrouvez-l-integralite-de-l-interview-d-emmanuel-macron-sur-bfmtv-rmc-mediapart-1060153.html.

——. "Protéger les libertés en luttant contre le séparatisme islamiste," Press conference in Mulhouse, February 18, 2020. https://www.elysee.fr/emmanuel-macron/2020/02/18/proteger-les-libertes-en-luttant-contre-le-separatisme-islamiste-conference-de-presse-du-president-emmanuel-macron-a-mulhouse.

——. "La République en actes," Speech in Les Mureaux, October 2, 2020. https://www.elysee.fr/emmanuel-macron/2020/10/02/la-republique-en-actes-discours-du-president-de-la-republique-sur-le-theme-de-la-lutte-contre-les-separatismes.

Mahmood, Saba. *Politics of Piety: The Islamic Revival and the Feminist Subject.* Princeton, NJ: Princeton University Press, 2005.

——. "Can Secularism Be Other-wise?" In *Varieties of Secularism in a Secular Age,* ed. Michael Warner, Jonathan VanAntwerpen, and Craig J. Calhoun, 282–99. Cambridge, MA: Harvard University Press, 2010.

——. *Religious Difference in a Secular Age: A Minority Report.* Princeton, NJ: Princeton University Press, 2016.

Mamdani, Mahmood. *Good Muslim, Bad Muslim: America, the Cold War, and the Roots of Terror.* New York: Doubleday, 2004.

Marlière, Éric. *La fabrique sociale de la radicalisation: Une contre-enquête sociologique.* Boulogne-Billancourt: Berger-Levrault, 2021.

Marzouki, Nadia. *Islam: An American Religion.* New York: Columbia University Press, 2017.

Mas, Ruth. "Why Critique?" *Method & Theory in the Study of Religion* 24, no. 4/5 (2012): 389–407.

Masquelier, Adeline. *Women and Islamic Revival in a West African Town.* Bloomington: Indiana University Press, 2009.

Maurin Eric. *Le ghetto français: Enquête sur le séparatisme social.* Paris: Seuil, 2004.

Mazouz, Sarah. *Race.* Paris: Anamosa, 2020.

Médine. "Grand Paris." 2017.
Meziane, Mohamad Amer. *Des empires sous la terre: Histoire écologique et raciale de la sécularisation*. Paris: La Découverte, 2021.
———. "On Police Violence and Systemic Islamophobia." *Political Theology* 22, no. 2 (2021): 125–29.
Mittermaier, Amira. *Giving to God: Islamic Charity in Revolutionary Times*. Berkeley: University of California Press, 2019.
Mohanty, Chandra. *Feminism without Borders: Decolonizing Theory, Practicing Solidarity*. Durham, NC: Duke University Press, 2003.
Moll, Yasmin. "Subtitling Islam: Translation, Mediation, Critique." *Public Culture* 29, no. 2. (2017): 333–61.
Morin, Edgar. *La fraternité, pourquoi?* Paris: Actes Sud, 2019.
Mouffe, Chantal. *The Return of the Political*. New York: Verso, 1993.
Mouvement des Indigènes. "Nous sommes les indigènes de la République." January 2005. https://indigenes-republique.fr/le-p-i-r/appel-des-indigenes-de-la-republique/.
Muhammad, Marwan. *Foul Express*. [Mérignac]: Éditions Sentinelles, 2014.
———. *Nous (Aussi) Sommes la Nation: Pourquoi il faut lutter contre l'islamophobie*. Paris: La Découverte, 2017.
Muhammed, Marwan, and Julien Talpin. *Communautarisme?* Paris: Presses Universitaires de France, 2018.
Mwasi. 2018. *AfroFem*. Paris: Syllepse.
Ndiaye, Pap. *La condition noire: Essai sur une minorité française*. Paris: Calmann-Levy, 2008.
Niane, Seydi Diamil. *Moi, musulman, je n'ai pas à me justifier*. Paris: Groupe Eyrolles, 2017.
Niang, Mame-Fatou. "Des particularités françaises de la négrophobie." In *Racismes de France*, ed. Omar Slaouti and Olivier Le Cour Grandmaison, 190–213. Paris: La Découverte, 2020.
Niang, Mame-Fatou and Julien Suaudeau. "21st-Century Universalism Will Be Anti-Racist, or It Won't Be at All." October 2020. https://www.rosalux.eu/en/article/1812.21st-century-universalism-will-be-anti-racist-or-it-won-t-be-at-all.html.
Nirenberg, David. *Anti-Judaism: The Western Tradition*. New York: Norton, 2013.
Norton, Anne. *On the Muslim Question*. Princeton, NJ: Princeton University Press, 2013.
Offen, Karen. *Debating the Woman Question in the French Third Republic, 1870–1920*. Cambridge: Cambridge University Press, 2018.
Oliphant, Elayne. *The Privilege of Being Banal: Art, Secularism, and Catholicism in Paris*. Chicago: University of Chicago Press, 2021.
Oraby, Mona. "Law, the State, and Public Order: Regulating Religion in Contemporary Egypt." *Law & Society Review* 52, no. 3 (2018): 574–602.
Ouassak, Fatima. "Protégeons nos enfants, ensemble!" In *Sororité*, ed. Chloé Delaume, 149–56. Paris: Syllepse, 2021.
Oubrou, Tareq. "Le musulman ne doit pas s'exposer." *Le Point*. June 13, 2019.
Pearson, Megan. "What Happened to 'Vivre Ensemble'? Developments after *S.A.S. v. France*." *Oxford Journal of Law and Religion* 10, no. 2 (2021): 185–205.

Peter, Frank. "Islamic Sermons, Religious Authority, and the Individualization of Islam in France," in *Religiosität in der säkularisierten Welt*, ed. Manual Franzmann, Christel Gärtner, and Nicole Köck, 303–19. Wiesbaden: VS Verlag für Sozialwissenschaften, 2006.

———. *Islam and the Governing of Muslims in France: Secularism without Religion*. London: Bloomsbury Academic, 2021.

Peyroux-Sissoko, Marie-Odile. "Immaterial Public Order: Legal Response to Social Crisis?" *Hungarian Journal of Legal Studies* 58, no. 2 (2017): 224–32.

Ragazzi, Francesco. "Policed Multiculturalism? The Impact of Counter-Terrorism and Counter-Radicalisation and the 'End' of Multiculturalism." In *Counter-Radicalisation: Critical Perspectives*, ed. Christopher Baker-Beall, Charlotte Heath-Kelly, and Lee Jarvis, 156–74. New York: Routledge, 2014.

———. "Suspect Community or Suspect Category? The Impact of Counter-Terrorism as 'Policed Multiculturalism.'" *Journal of Ethnic and Migration Studies* 42, no. 5 (2016): 724–41.

———. "Counter-radicalisation, Islam, and Laïcité: Policed Multiculturalism in France's Banlieues." *Ethnic and Racial Studies* 46, no. 4 (2023): 707–27.

Ramadan, Tariq. *Western Muslims and the Future of Islam*. New York: Oxford University Press, 2004.

Rock-Singer, Aaron. "The Sunni Islamic Revival." In *The Oxford Handbook of the Sociology of the Middle East*, ed. Armando Salvatore, Sari Hanafi, and Kieko Obuse, 395–409. Oxford: Oxford University Press, 2020.

———. *In the Shade of the Sunna: Salafi Piety in the Twentieth-Century Middle East*. Oakland: University of California Press, 2022.

Rodríguez-Ruiz, Blanca, and Ruth Rubio Marin. *The Struggle for Female Suffrage in Europe: Voting to Become Citizens*. Boston: Brill, 2012.

Roy, Olivier. "La peur d'une communauté qui n'existe pas." *Le Monde*, January 9, 2015.

Rosanvallon, Pierre, Jean-Pierre Le Goff, Éric Maurin, and Emmanuel Todd. "Tribune: Quelle crise des banlieues?" *Libération*, November 21, 2005.

Salomon, Noah. *For Love of the Prophet: An Ethnography of Sudan's Islamic State*. Princeton, NJ: Princeton University Press, 2016.

Salomon, Noah, and Jeremy Walton. "Religious Criticism, Secular Critique, and the 'Critical Study of Religion': Lessons from the Study of Islam." In *The Cambridge Companion to Religious Studies*, ed. Robert Orsi, 403–20. Cambridge: Cambridge University Press, 2011.

Sarkozy, Nicolas. Speech given at Mosquée Tariq Ibn Zyad, Les Mureaux, France, on March 29, 2003.

Sayad, Abdelmalek. *The Suffering of the Immigrant*. Translated by David Macey. Malden, MA: Polity Press, 2004.

———. *L'immigration ou les paradoxes de l'altérité*. Vol. 3, *La fabrication des identités culturelles*. Paris: Raisons d'Agir, 2014.

Schielke, Samuli. "Second Thoughts about the Anthropology of Islam, or How to Make Sense of Grand Schemes in Everyday Life." *Zentrum Moderner Orient Research Papers*, no. 2. 2010.

Scott, Joan Wallach. *Politics of the Veil*. Princeton, NJ: Princeton University Press, 2007.
———. *Sex and Secularism*. Princeton, NJ: Princeton University Press, 2018.
Sharify-Funk, Meena, and Munira Kassam Haddad. "Where Do Women 'Stand' in Islam? Negotiating Contemporary Muslim Prayer Leadership in North America." *Feminist Review* 102, no. 1 (2012): 41–61.
Shahrokni, Shirin. *Higher Education and Social Mobility in France: Challenges and Possibilities*. New York: Routledge, 2021.
Shehabuddin, Elora. *Sisters in the Mirror: A History of Muslim Women and the Global Politics of Feminism*. Berkeley: University of California Press, 2021.
Sidi Moussa, Nedjib. *La fabrique du musulman*. Paris: Libertalia, 2017.
Sifaoui, Mohamed. *Taqiyya! Comment les frères musulmans veulent infiltrer la France*. Paris: Éditions de l'Observatoire, 2019.
Silverstein, Paul. *Postcolonial France: Race, Islam, and the Future of the Republic*. London: Pluto Press, 2018.
Simon, Patrick. "Le tigre de papier communautaire." In *Communautarisme?*, ed. Marwan Muhammad and Julien Talpin, 41–54. Paris: Presses Universitaires de France, 2018.
Slaouti, Omar, and Olivier Le Cour Grandmaison, eds. *Racismes de France*. Paris: La Découverte, 2020.
Soufi, Youcef. *The Rise of Critical Islam: 10th–13th Century Legal Debate*. New York: Oxford University Press, 2023.
Stovall, Tyler. "From Red Belt to Black Belt: Race, Class, and Urban Marginality in Twentieth-Century Paris." In *The Color of Liberty: Histories of Race in France*, ed. Tyler Stovall and Sue Peabody, 351–70. Durham, NC: Duke University Press: 2001.
Surkis, Judith. "Hymenal Politics: Marriage, Secularism, and French Sovereignty." *Public Culture* 22, no. 3 (2010): 531–56.
———. *Sex, Law, and Sovereignty in French Algeria, 1803–1930*. Ithaca, NY: Cornell University Press, 2019.
Taylor, Charles. *Multiculturalism*. Princeton, NJ: Princeton University Press, 1995.
———. *A Secular Age*. Cambridge, MA: Harvard University Press, 2007.
Tackett, Timothy. *Religion, Revolution, and Regional Culture in Eighteenth-Century France: The Ecclesiastical Oath of 1791*. Princeton, NJ: Princeton University Press, 1986.
Tribalat, Michèle. *Voyage au coeur du malaise français*. Paris: La Découverte, 1999.
Valfort, Marie-Anne. "La religion, facteur de discrimination à l'embauche en France." *Revue Économique* 68, no. 5 (2017): 895–907.
Valentin, Vincent. "Les nouvelles configurations de l'ordre public." *Philosophiques* 46, no. 1 (2019): 119–36.
———. "L'effacement de la laïcité libérale en France." *Canadian Journal of Law and Society* 36, no. 2 (2021): 303–21.
Vergès, Françoise. *The Wombs of Women: Race, Capital, and Feminism*. Translated by Kaiama L. Glover. Durham, NC: Duke University Press, 2020.
Viellard-Baron, Hervé. "L'Islam en France: Dynamiques, fragmentation et perspectives." *L'Information géographique* 80, no. 1 (2016): 22–53.
Wacquant, Loïc. "A Janus-Faced Institution of Ethnoracial Closure: A Sociological

Specification of the Ghetto." In *The Ghetto: Contemporary Global Issues and Controversies*, ed. Ray Hutchison and Bruce D. Haynes, 1–32. Boulder, CO: Westview Press, 2012.

Wadud, Amina. *Inside the Gender Jihad: Women's Reform in Islam*. Oxford: Oneworld, 2006.

Warikoo, Natasha. *The Diversity Bargain, and Other Dilemmas of Race, Admissions, and Meritocracy at Elite Universities*. Chicago: University of Chicago Press, 2016.

Wesselhoeft, Kirsten. "Gendered Secularity: The Feminine Individual in the 2010 Gerin Report," *Journal of Muslim Minority Affairs* 31, no. 3 (2011): 399–411.

———. "On the 'Front Lines' of the Classroom: Moral Education and Muslim Students in French State Schools." *Oxford Review of Education* 43, no. 5 (2017): 626–41.

———. "Mixité, Gender Difference and the Politics of Islam in France after the Headscarf Ban." In *The Routledge Handbook of Islam and Gender*, ed. Justine Howe, 146–60. New York: Routledge, 2021.

———. "Muslim Ethics and the Ethnographic Imagination." *Journal of Religious Ethics* 51, no. 1 (2023): 108–20.

Wihtol de Wenden, Catherine, and Rémy Leveau. *La beurgeoisie: Les trois âges de la vie associative issue de l'immigration*. Paris: CNRS, 2001.

Wolfreys, Jim. *Republic of Islamophobia: The Rise of Respectable Racism in France*. New York: Oxford University Press, 2018.

Woodly, Deva. *Reckoning: Black Lives Matter and the Democratic Necessity of Social Movements*. New York: Oxford University Press, 2022.

Yilmaz, Ferruh. *How the Workers Became Muslims: Immigration, Culture, and Hegemonic Transformation in Europe*. Ann Arbor: University of Michigan Press, 2016.

Yonnet, Paul. *Voyage au centre du malaise français: L'antiracisme et le roman national*. Paris: Éditions Gallimard, 1993.

Yusuf, Hakeem. "*S.A.S. v. France*: Supporting 'Living Together' or Forced Assimilation?" *International Human Rights Law Review* 3 (2014): 277–302.

Zeghal, Malika. "La constitution du Conseil Français du Culte Musulman: Reconnaissance politique d'un Islam français?" *Archives de sciences sociales des religions* 129 (2005): 97–113.

———. "Competing Ways of Life: Islamism, Secularism, and Public Order in the Tunisian Transition." *Constellations* 20, no. 2 (2013): 254–74.

Zenati, Moncef. *La fraternité humaine en Islam*. Aubervilliers: Maison d'Ennour, 2008.

Zemmour, Eric. *Le suicide français: Ces quarante années qui ont défait la France*. Paris: Albin Michel, 2014.

Zuber, Valentine. "La laïcité française, une exception historique, des principes partagés." *Revue du droit des religions* 7 (2019): 193–205.

Zwilling, Anne-Laure. "A Century of Mosques in France: Building Religious Pluralism." *International Review of Sociology* 25, no. 2 (2015): 333–40.

INDEX

activism, 11, 18, 20, 27, 44, 52, 56–57, 76, 89–90, 92, 108, 122; and activist organizations, 10, 15; anti-racist, 47, 70, 163; and culture, 21; and education, 89–90; and feminism, 30, 93, 97; gender-based, 11; moral, 59; Muslim, 71, 75, 81, 97, 143, 146–48, 161–65, 199n4; pious, 62
adab al-ikhtilaf. See *ikhtilaf*
anti-racism, 17, 30, 69–70, 99, 120, 135, 163
Arabic (language), 1, 12–13, 36, 38, 114; musicals, 91
Arabness, 13
Arabs, 14, 19, 25

Baby Loup legal case, 9, 153–54, 178n28
banlieues, 1, 19, 22–25, 27, 35, 37, 60, 73, 180n54; streetscapes of, 58; working-class, 4, 23, 35, 59, 71; and young people, 71, 78
BarakaCity, 17, 122
Blanquer, Jean-Michel, 18, 127
Bonapartism, 21, 150
Boubeker, Ahmed, 15, 69
Bowen, John, 15, 38, 146
brotherhood. See *fraternité*

capitalism, 66–67, 75, 82, 84, 175n3; racial, 184n3
Centers of Combat against Radical Islamism and Communalist Withdrawal (CLIR), 126, 161
Chan-Malik, Sylvia, 98, 180n65

Charter of Principles for French Islam (2021), 5, 17, 30, 120–21, 130–32, 136–38, 142, 165
choice, 95–96, 110–15
civil rights, 2, 59, 81, 93, 199n4; activism, 46, 151; organizations, 2, 8, 127
class, 23, 26, 29; citizenship, 156; defectors, 75; and French Muslims, 51, 70; hierarchy, 25, 66; inequality, 72; and migration, 177n17; mobility, 39, 70–71, 76–77; and race, 180n54; solidarity, 25. *See also* middle class; working class
Collective against Islamophobia in France (CCIF), 17, 47, 70, 120, 122, 127, 146–49, 184n31, 188n2, 199n4
colonization, 26, 66, 67–69, 99, 149, 159, 180n63; and governance, 131, 152; legacy of, 16; and racism, 67; and schools, 151; subjects of, 59; and territories, 24, 150; and violence, 20
communalism (*communautarisme*): accusations of, 119, 123–24, 128, 144–45; and communitarianism, 188n1; definition of, 126; discourse of, 122, 130; and economic development, 72–73; and fear, 19–21, 120, 127, 132, 145; and French politicians, 16, 143; and identity politics, 119; and Islamophobia, 30; logic of, 125; and Macron, 126; "Muslim," 4, 119–20; and public order, 5; and Republic, 11; rhetoric of, 30, 122, 124–28; and secularism, 9, 129; and separatism, 19, 120, 124, 142; and state surveillance, 8, 30; and urban planning, 72

community, 1, 14, 36, 42, 49–50, 75–76, 106, 173, 181n65, 199n4; activists, 3, 56, 175n4; associations, 3; building, 5–6, 8, 71, 82; French Muslim, 19–20, 41, 47, 74, 86; as governance, 128; life, 157; local, 38, 47; Maghrebi, 54; moral, 9–11, 16, 63, 144–46, 152, 162, 165, 167; and mosques, 38, 77–78, 105; multifunctional, 53; Muslim, 2–3, 5–6, 9–11, 16, 18–22, 26, 28–30, 38–39, 41, 44, 48, 56–59, 62, 65, 70, 73, 77, 79–80, 83, 85, 87, 90, 95, 109, 119–21, 125, 128–29, 142–44, 162, 164, 179n50; national, 19, 124–25, 127–28, 133; nonprofits, 43, 53; norms, 95, 112; organizations, 5, 8, 18, 24, 26, 44, 54, 56, 64, 66, 121, 126, 136–42, 158, 161, 167, 184n31; organizers, 40; practice of, 31; religious, 52, 54, 62, 77, 83–84, 98, 108, 177n26; and umma, 133–34; universal, 124; and women, 96, 104, 107
counterterrorism, 122–23, 129, 161–62
critical race theory, 17
critique, 15, 29, 42, 50, 61, 63, 92, 101, 185n21; double, 95, 103–4, 110; forms of, 30; fraternal, 6–8, 16, 31, 41, 52, 66, 75, 77, 90, 93–94, 120, 163–66, 168, 176n14, 177n20; of imperialism, 26; Islamic moral, 47; leftist, 190n14; and Muslims, 20, 70, 163; political, 47, 59; of racial discrimination, 17; social, 3, 6, 95, 98, 109; sororal, 166

Darmanin, Gérald, 18, 127, 132, 150–51, 157–58, 182n13, 192n43
decolonial thought, 59, 69, 107–109

education, 14, 44, 55, 77, 90, 140, 142; advanced, 3; children's, 46, 138; elementary, 43; elite, 66; higher, 3, 25, 36, 69, 71, 79–80, 175n3; Islamic, 3, 38, 43, 54, 89; moral, 85, 87; Muslim, 75; postsecondary, 78; religious, 54–55, 66, 106, 166; secondary, 43; secular, 66, 78; spiritual, 47
employment, 23, 25, 44, 83, 85, 154
English (language), 12, 74, 85, 93, 188n1
ethics, 11, 82, 84, 89, 132–33, 167; of disagreement, 42, 44, 48–50, 52; of discontent, 177n20; and law, 51; Muslim, 29, 66, 172; religious, 119, 170, 173; secular, 16; and sisterhood, 94–95, 107; social, 8, 20, 29, 66, 93–94, 166–68
ethnicity, 25, 43–44, 51, 126
Europe, 122; and the far right, 29; and Islam, 27, 56, 96; and populism, 44; and race, 4, 26; and religious discrimination, 4; and women, 96
European Court of Human Rights (ECHR), 156, 194n9

far right, 4, 29, 44–45, 164
feminism, 30, 94–96, 99, 103, 108, 112–13, 119, 188n42; and activism, 93, 97; and antiracism, 99; and collectives, 112; decolonial, 108–9, 112; French, 11, 30, 163; and groups, 95; and iftars, 8, 107–9; liberal, 112; Muslim, 14, 97, 103, 163; and sisterhood, 8, 96–99
Forum of French Islam (FORIF), 132, 150, 164, 182n13, 192nn42–43
Foundation of French Islam, 5
fraternité, 7–8, 27, 60, 93, 96, 165
freedom, 95–96, 109–12, 115; of association, 30, 120, 141–43; of conscience, 153–54, 159; individual, 145; and Muslims, 58; religious, 139, 148–49, 151–52, 157, 159, 178n27; space of, 107; of speech, 18; of thought, 133; true, 98; and women, 94, 140. *See also* choice
French Council for the Muslim Religion (CFCM), 17, 45, 131–32, 141, 182n13, 192n42
French Republic, 13, 125–26, 189n6; and communalism, 11; and education, 77; failures of, 25; and *fraternité*, 165; freedom of association, 143; freedom of conscience, 159; and "individual," 45; and Islam, 65, 71, 124, 134, 175n5; and Muslims, 46, 59, 78, 133–34, 142; pillars of, 137; and public life, 59; and public opinion, 110; and public sphere, 111, 123, 141–42; and secularism, 130, 138, 147, 152; and self-image, 17; threats to, 134

gender, 3–4, 15, 28, 30, 107–8, 139, 159–60; and activism, 11, 93, 109, 112; and difference,

94, 150; and environments, 29; equality, 133, 156; inequality, 139; and justice, 57; mixed-gender prayers, 51, 183n27; and mixing, 94, 130; and mosque space, 104; parity, 10, 145, 160; and race, 97; and sexuality, 19

gentrification, 23, 72–73, 91

hadith, 49–50, 52, 89, 104, 183n26
Hamidullah, Muhammad, 12
headscarf affairs, 4, 9, 14, 21, 35, 41, 61, 76, 83, 110, 115, 124, 137, 139, 147, 153–54
Hollande, François, 111–12
housing, 36, 44, 46, 85

iftars, 8, 107–9
ikhtilaf, 44, 48–51, 79, 183n21, 183n26
imams, 27, 29, 100–101, 130, 132–33, 142, 165, 197n65; expulsion of, 5, 191n33; in Paris, 55; training of, 37, 131
immigration, 2, 25, 35, 51, 68, 76, 81; and ethnicity, 43; Muslim "inheritors of," 29–30, 46–47, 52, 69–70; and national myth, 45; postcolonial, 10, 52; precolonial, 2; waves of, 24
Iquioussen, Hassan, 38, 157–60, 164–65
Islam, 10, 15, 26, 46, 57, 59, 73–74, 78, 81–82, 134, 143, 147, 180n65, 184n5; associations, 52; bookstores, 12; and brotherhood, 7; and charity, 40; "choosing," 114; conservative, 95; and culture, 3, 21, 64, 71, 121; and culture wars, 154; and education, 3, 38, 44, 54, 85, 89; Enlightenment, 132, 137, 167; and ethics, 20, 44, 47, 55, 84; and feminists, 103, 108; in France, 42, 55–56, 65, 92, 99, 104, 135, 146, 161, 199n4; and French news media, 4, 15; governance of, 122, 158, 164; institutions, 29, 37, 41, 45, 52, 55, 60, 72, 78, 91; and intellectual culture, 8, 64; and jurisprudence, 22, 48, 65, 139; and knowledge, 37, 54; and law, 49, 51, 183n23; and leftists, 18, 60, 124, 189n14; moral community, 11, 111–12; and parenting, 54; and piety, 11, 80, 185n5; political, 133–34, 136; and political discourse, 4, 130; political instrumentalization of, 44; practice of, 5, 130, 146; and prayers, 96; and public space, 145; radical, 136; and Ramadan, 61; and reformism, 22; representations of, 5; and Republicanism, 58, 132; revival, 20, 37, 43, 52, 62, 68–69, 92, 113; and rituals, 56; and schools, 8, 24, 27, 37, 41–42, 53, 56, 71, 83, 86, 88; and sciences, 2, 12, 14, 49, 54, 88–89, 166; and secularism, 11, 16, 22, 95, 112, 146; and secular knowledge, 67, 95; and separatism, 17, 128; traditions, 9, 43, 48–49, 67–69; in United States, 28; and values, 2–3, 7, 78, 159, 186n1; and women, 4, 98

Islamic State (ISIS), 122
Islamism, 123–24, 126, 179n50
Islamo-leftism, 124, 189n14
Islamophobia, 3, 8, 29, 47, 57, 70, 97, 103, 127, 163–64, 179n50, 180n62, 193n64; and discrimination, 8; gendered, 8, 107; and graffiti, 102; political, 30, 120

kinship, 7–8, 66, 93, 163, 165–66, 173

laïcité, 9, 137–38, 147–48, 177nn27–28, 195n24, 196n36; juridical, 146; *nouvelle*, 144; *référents laïcité* (secularism specialists), 140, 155. *See also* secularism

language, 126; and autonomy, 110–11, 115; of choice, 95, 109–11; of communalism, 125–26; of feminism, 113; of *fraternité*, 165; moral, 95, 112, 115, 162; of public order, 144–45, 157; of radicalization, 147; of security, 129; of separatism, 125

Law to Strengthen Respect of the Principles of the Republic (2021), 121, 126, 136
Le Bourget, France, 37, 67, 87
LGBTQ: organizing, 30, 120; rights, 4

Macron, Emmanuel, 110–11, 123, 125–26, 131–32, 136–37, 152, 182n13, 195n15
Mahmood, Saba, 61, 109–10, 112–13, 115, 172
middle class, 2, 23–24, 36, 45, 66, 71, 186n1; Muslim, 3, 10, 17, 24, 59
Ministry of Education, 4, 18, 127

mixité, 93–94, 186n3; and *non-mixité*, 97–98, 110
Mosquée de Paris, 24, 99–102, 104, 107, 109, 163
mosques, 27, 35–38, 100, 105, 110; and administrations, 101; attacks against, 124–25; and attendance, 86; Cairene mosque movement, 113, 115; construction of, 39, 69, 81, 106; and culture, 40, 62, 107; and events, 78; "feeling of the mosque," 68; and France, 51, 53; and Friday prayers, 57; fundraising for, 50, 53, 86; governance of, 98; and imams, 65, 197n65; and Islamic schools, 42; leadership of, 110; local, 41, 54, 76; male-dominated, 98; moral challenges to, 66; and Muslim communities, 87; in Paris, 104; "right to the mosque," 98; and schooling, 55; and social initiatives, 42; and study groups, 61, 67; and women, 67, 93, 96, 106–7, 112
Muhammad, Marwan, 46–47, 164–65
multiculturalism, 19, 120, 124, 128–29, 131, 153
Muslim publics, 20, 53, 84
Muslims of France (MF). *See* Union of Islamic Organizations of France (UOIF)
Muslim Students of France (EMF), 69, 78, 80, 85

National Council of Imams, 131, 133, 136, 137
nationality, 16, 25, 28
non-Muslims, 19, 43, 80, 84, 108, 110–11, 133
North Africans, 24, 68–69, 131

Oubrou, Tareq, 5

Paris: and activists, 10; *arrondissements*, 22; cultural institutions, 25, 66; "Grand Paris," 72–73; and imams, 55, 64; and Islamic culture, 38, 44, 46, 67, 93; and metropolitanization, 23–24; and mosques, 65, 104; and Muslims, 5, 9, 24, 29, 37–38, 41, 44, 49, 62, 71–72, 90–92, 107; and social actors, 8; and universities, 76; and urban zones, 19; and women, 53–54; and Young Muslims of France (JMF), 57–58, 78

Parti des Indigènes de la République (PIR), 59, 184n34
piety, 56, 67, 90, 101, 108, 113, 115; expression of, 57; filial, 68; forms of, 26, 36, 112; individual, 37; Islamic (Muslim), 62, 80, 95, 158, 173, 185n5; personal, 20, 47, 57, 69; weight of, 61
political activists, 3, 45–47, 77–78, 80, 87
prayer, 50, 86, 134; *'asr*, 49; midday, 99; rooms, 36, 38–39, 100–105, 113, 120
public discourse, 3, 95, 119–20, 165; and France, 19, 21–22, 61, 125; and Islam, 5, 19, 22, 122
"public order," 133, 137, 139, 142, 145–46, 168; articulation of, 26; and French law, 160–61; immaterial, 9–10, 30, 156–60, 162; and Islam, 5, 17, 167; language of, 30, 144, 157; loyalty to, 136; maintenance of, 96, 159; material, 159–60; and national cohesion, 135; and Republican identity, 165; rhetoric of, 122; and secularism, 141, 152, 156; threats to, 123, 138, 158–60
public schools, 4, 78, 87, 90, 97, 111, 115, 148
public services, 153–54

Qur'an, 1, 14, 48, 79, 91, 104, 135, 150, 188n43, 191n34; and Arabic, 114; and equality, 102, 133; French-language, 12–13, 36; recitation of, 43, 78; schools, 81, 100

race, 23, 25–26, 28, 44, 70, 180n54, 181n65, 181n67; and discrimination, 44; and gender, 97; and Islam, 15, 43; and national origin, 51; negation of, 4
racial-religious forms, 23, 26, 67, 69, 129, 152, 180n65
religion, 36, 38, 43–44, 61, 88–89, 114–15, 125–26, 155, 178n27; alienation from, 57; and authority, 64, 119, 121, 134; classes, 54; and collectivity, 68–69, 119, 195n24; and discrimination, 4, 17–18, 25–26, 70, 85; and education, 53–55, 66, 76, 78, 96, 106, 113, 166; and engagement, 3, 7, 16, 20, 40, 59, 61–62, 90, 142, 178n28; ethnographies of, 166; freedom of, 141–42, 159; and French

approach, 136, 150–51; French civil, 149; governance of, 122, 130; institutionalized, 40; and Islam, 133–34, 164, 179n39; and neutrality, 9, 144, 153–54, 161; and North Africans, 131; and observance, 86–87, 114; organized, 67, 148; and politics, 132; privatized, 96; and public powers, 153; and public space, 130; and race, 23, 25–26, 28, 44, 67, 70; recognition of, 121; and secularism, 192n43, 196n36; and social life, 175n4; and speech, 140; state regulation of, 196n36; study of, 6; symbolic use of, 112; and women, 149, 152

religious communities, 41, 52, 54, 62, 66, 77, 81, 83–84, 98, 108, 121, 124–25, 143, 177n26

religious freedom, 139, 149, 151–52, 157

religious institutions, 6, 130, 132, 138–42, 148, 158

religious obligations, 50, 79–80, 97

religious practices, 37, 57, 86, 89, 94, 100–101, 109, 111–14, 130–31, 133, 145, 155, 157, 159

religious study, 8, 36, 74–75, 151

Republicanism, 5, 13, 15–16, 58; and belonging, 42; and cultural nationalism, 15; and *égalité*, 60; and emancipation, 112; and *fraternité*, 7, 60, 93; and identity, 165; and identity politics, 11, 16; and Islam, 7, 15, 65, 71, 132; and law, 130; and *liberté*, 60; and loyalty, 142; and moral imperatives, 5; and Muslims, 58; and nationalism, 28; and patriotism, 137; and political culture, 30, 120; and political mythology, 19; reawakening, 136; "Republican Contract," 137–38, 141; and schools, 114–15; and secularism, 62; and values, 59, 93, 119–20, 143, 151, 160

rights, 95, 110–12, 115, 137, 150; framework of, 30; individual, 96

Salafism, 123, 130, 136, 191n34

Sarkozy, Nicolas, 38, 72, 131, 182n13

Scott, Joan Wallach, 94, 149–51, 177n27

secularism, 10, 13, 88, 90, 115, 129–30, 138, 141–42, 147–48, 179n39, 192n43, 195n21, 196n36; and colonialism, 16, 196n33; combative, 137, 144; critique of, 70; defense of, 9; discourse of, 94, 110; and education, 66, 78; and equality, 111; evolution of, 11, 156; and feminism, 113; French, 9, 15, 30, 70, 95–96, 112, 115, 130, 147, 149–50, 152, 158–62, 177n27; and gender, 150; and governance, 122, 132, 161; identitarian, 137, 140, 144–46, 149; and Islam, 11, 16, 22, 58–59, 151, 154, 161–62; juridical, 144, 159; and knowledge, 67; and law, 121; and legal principles, 30, 94, 154–55, 162; liberal, 95–96, 112; and liberty, 114; and Muslim identity, 56, 90, 112; and Muslim piety, 62; narrative, 144, 194n1; and national identity, 16; and neutrality, 137–38, 152–55; patriarchal, 96; political, 16, 21, 95, 110, 144, 150; privatization of, 9, 137, 152–53; radicalization of, 152, 195n15; and religiosity, 112; and religious freedom, 139; and secular ethics, 16, 25; and secular norms, 15; and secular pact, 151; secular sensibilities, 110; and society, 111; state, 16, 130, 136; and universalism, 150; and women, 149

secularism law of 1905, 141, 144–45, 148–49, 151–52, 159, 196n36. *See also* secularism

separatism, 17–19, 122, 126–27, 142; and anti-separatism, 5; and communalism, 120, 124; language of, 125; rhetoric of, 120; and separatism law, 30, 121, 132, 136–43, 153–55, 160, 163, 165

sexuality, 3, 19, 94; and democracy, 94; and equality, 4; and liberty, 21; and norms, 94; and violence, 138

shaykh, 42–43, 51, 64, 89

sisterhood. See *soeurénité*

social activists, 3–4, 81, 85–86, 162, 167

soeurénité, 8, 92–99, 104–7, 109–10, 112, 119

solidarity, 3, 6, 66, 72; axes of, 165–66; bonds of, 68, 163; class, 25; collective, 128; and community, 18; and disagreement, 8; forms of, 84, 109, 120, 163, 168; and friendship, 43; and kinship, 7–8, 163; Muslim, 9, 98, 108, 180n50; and politics, 93; repression of, 128; and sisterhood, 94, 102, 106–7, 109; spaces of, 98; spiritual, 93

Special Committee to Fight Radical Islamism and Communalist Withdrawal (CLIR), 161
state racism, 135, 192n56

terrorism, 4, 28–29, 61, 122–23, 127, 137, 175n5

umma, 30, 49, 120, 133–34, 142, 179n50
Union of Islamic Organizations of France (UOIF), 37, 57, 59, 69, 147, 158
United States, perceptions of Islam in, 28, 56

vivre ensemble, le (coexistence), 145, 155–57, 162

white nationalism, 4, 60
Women in the Mosque, 100, 102–4, 108, 163
women's rights, 4, 21, 94, 151, 156, 160
working class, 2, 4, 25, 45, 47, 66, 81; families, 74; households, 175n3; immigrants, 68; and inheritance, 30; mothers, 97; Muslim, 80; suburbs, 23, 35, 59, 71

Young Muslims of France (JMF), 57–60, 62, 78, 80, 85, 158

www.ingramcontent.com/pod-product-compliance
Lightning Source LLC
Chambersburg PA
CBHW032337300426
44109CB00041B/1081